Children and Social

Also available from Bloomsbury

Childhood and the Philosophy of Education, Andrew Stables
State and Education Policy, Helen M. Gunter

Children and Social Change

Memories of Diverse Childhoods

Dorothy Moss

B L O O M S B U R Y
LONDON · NEW DELHI · NEW YORK · SYDNEY

Bloomsbury Academic

An imprint of Bloomsbury Publishing Plc

50 Bedford Square	175 Fifth Avenue
London	New York
WC1B 3DP	NY 10010
UK	USA

www.bloomsbury.com

First published by Continuum International Publishing Group 2011
Paperback edition first published 2013

British Library Cataloguing-in-Publication Data
A catalogue record for this book is available from the British Library.

ISBN: HB: 978-0-8264-3531-6
PB: 978-0-5674-7333-2

Library of Congress Cataloging-in-Publication Data
Moss, Dorothy, 1952-
Children and social change: memories of diverse childhoods/Dorothy Moss.
p. cm.
Includes bibliographical references.
ISBN 978-0-8264-3531-6
1. Children-Social conditions. 2. Children-Economic conditions. 3. Social
change. 4. Children-Social conditions-Case studies. 5. Children-Economic
conditions-Case studies. 6. Social change-Case studies. I. Title.

HQ767.9.M677 2011
305.230941'09045–dc22

2010052873

Typeset by Newgen Imaging Systems Pvt Ltd, Chennai, India

Contents

Acknowledgements

With special thanks to all the respondents who participated in this research, sharing their time and their memories of childhood with such openness and commitment to the project. I am also very grateful to the two academics who reviewed the manuscript and provided very constructive feedback. Thanks to Caroline Hancock who transcribed the interviews. Ingrid Richter was my academic mentor throughout the research; a special thanks to her. Many others also advised me about particular aspects of the research as it progressed and I am grateful to all of them. Thanks also to the Carnegie Research Institute at Leeds Metropolitan University who funded the initial research and to the staff at Continuum for enabling and supporting publication. Thanks to my family, and especially my grandchildren for repeatedly reminding me of the importance of listening to children's views and opinions.

Chapter 1

Introduction

Background to the Research

Research into children's everyday experience tends to focus on particular settings and concerns, for example, the home and family, community and state regulated provision related to protection, health, education and day care. There is important research into other issues considering, for example, the impact of poverty, employment and unemployment, war, crime and justice, migration and homelessness. This generally (not always) focuses on children directly caught up in events. As children become older, greater attention is given to their complex transitions to adult status and adult spheres.

The field of childhood studies tends to focus on the spaces in society where children are most visible, positioned there through family, wider social relations and social events. This focus is valid and appropriate, but some aspects of some children's everyday experience are in danger of being overlooked. The assumption underpinning the research in this book is that, whether or not children are directly caught up in certain events (such as war and migration), all children's lives are touched in important ways. The 'Pathways through Childhood' research on which this book is based (Moss, 2006a) examines experiences not commonly associated with everyday childhood, shifting attention to wider social change and considering direct, indirect; close and distant threads of influence. It is a qualitative study that draws on adult memories to examine everyday childhood in relation to arenas such as parental employment, religion, policing, war, technological change and migration. It explores children's understanding and practice taking into account common and diverse experiences.

The methodology is informed by concepts of space, time and memory, developed from the work of different scholars (see Chapter 2). These include Maurice Halbwachs (1925/1992) and Barbara Misztal (2003), who have researched social memory; Barbara Adam (2006) who focuses on the sociology and politics of time and Henri Lefebvre (1991) and Doreen Massey (2005), both of whom explore the social production of space. Academic studies of childhood have increased in recent years, reflecting developments in workforce and state intervention strategies as well as the international movement for children's rights (Welch, 2008a; Moss and Richter, 2011). Bourdieu (1968/1991) argues that forms of knowledge and system arrangements shape the conceptualization of research objects. As childhood is associated in the main with some and not other processes (such as schooling), then only some experiences get attention. In the case of the research discussed in this book, the concern is to add to academic scholarship that broadens the frameworks for understanding childhood by considering how children engage with wider social institutions and events in their everyday lives.

The attempt to broaden the canvas for examining childhood, which is one of the key concerns of this book, is central to the movement for children's rights and the recognition that children are full social participants rather than adjuncts to the family. In recent years, important research and scholarship have pursued this aim. Aitken (2001, p. 6), for example, draws attention to the wide influences on children's experience that may be overlooked if the research focus is too narrow. Other research approaches in relation to childhood are becoming richer and more varied. Concerns about social mobility and social class are re-emerging as important foci, supported by quantitative evidence (Blanden et al., 2005). Concern with social justice is also renewed (Goldson and Muncie, 2006; Moss, 2008; Muncie, 2009). Social studies of childhood give more attention to differences related to spatial context and influence (Aitken, 2001; Holloway and Valentine, 2000; Matthews, 2003; Mayall, 2006; Moss, 2006b):

> On the one hand, I am concerned with the endless carving up and claiming of space by different individuals and constituencies and how that process disenfranchises young people. On the other hand, I am concerned about the connectedness of all spaces, and all cultures, even those at the other side of the world. (Aitken, 2001, p. 11)

Attention is also being given to the complex time frames shaping children's lives and related qualitative approaches are being strengthened; their scope and range extended (Neale and Flowerdew, 2003; Morrow, 2003; Brannen, 2004; James and James, 2004; Henderson et al., 2007). Neale et al. (2007–2012) longitudinal qualitative research into 'Young Lives and Times' is a good example. There is increased recognition of children from different social backgrounds and the potential of children themselves to be researchers (Kellett, 2005; Jones, 2009). Hence, the research discussed in this book, is part of a wider academic and social movement concerned with deepening understanding of the wide influences on children's lives, their rights and their engagement in social change. This is reminiscent of earlier struggles concerned with furthering women's rights through problematizing their everyday experiences (Smith, 1987).

Children can exercise power from a relatively powerless position (Moss, 2006a). They are not a homogeneous group (Welch, 2008a). Research approaches are developing that focus on the relationship between macro, meso and micro events in children's lives and the way they negotiate the social world. These are all constructive moves, drawing on combined and eclectic research approaches concerned to further children's interests and perspectives. Adam points out that research approaches that give visibility to space and time avoid researchers needing to make, ' . . . unacceptable choices between biological and social determinants . . . between realism and relativism . . . between meta-narratives and particularism' (1998, p. 6). This is echoed by Neale and Flowerdew in relation to children's lives, 'The temporal aspects of childhood no longer have to be seen exclusively in terms of children's innate biology, nor ties to institutional forms of socialization and control but can be explored through the textures of their day-to-day lives' (2003, p. 195).

Research Aims and Questions

The 'Pathways through Childhood' research (Moss, 2006a) was developed at a university in the north of England on a small internal grant. The aims of the research are:

1. to examine everyday childhood in relation to arenas more commonly associated with the world of adults;
2. within this context, to explore children's understanding and experience of the spaces around them and their agency in the production of space and time;
3. to explore how children interpret and respond to dominant spatial and temporal systems, institutions and critical events;
4. to examine the strengths and limitations of drawing on adult reminiscences of the spaces and times of childhood as research data or 'pockets of history' (Brannen, 2004, p. 425);
5. to consider memory as social, familial and personal;
6. to consider patterns of inequality, diversity and commonality related to pathways through childhood.

The research involves a qualitative study drawing on personal memories of childhood. It examines social arrangements and social change, considering the ways these influence children, whether or not they are directly caught up in events. The central research questions are, 'How do wider social, cultural, economic and political events, systems and arrangements influence children's everyday lives? How do children practice childhood in relation to these influences?'

The research draws on different, sometimes competing, schools of thought to give visibility to the ways that children's everyday experiences connect to wider social arrangements. It considers the effects of social position, social division, the influence of family, state, community and nation and the ways children carve out space and time for themselves. The canvas of the research is broad and the sample relatively small (see below). Space, time and social memory are drawn on as sensitizing concepts (see above and Chapter 2). Clearly no simplistic causative historical links between past and present can be drawn because social contexts differ over time and processes of social change are too complex, ' . . . these causal theories have a notable limitation. They may bear little relationship to the actuality or dynamics of real lives' (Neale and Flowerdew, 2003, p. 191).

The 'Pathways' research explores personal memories of childhood. All the participants were asked to recall memories of major social changes whether or not they had experienced events directly or were recalling family or other social stories. In addition, respondents were asked to recall different spaces, including those outside the normal boundaries of their everyday lives. The research approach is discussed more fully in Chapter 2.

Introduction to the Research Participants

The decision to base the research on memories of childhood was practical and ethical. Direct work with children in matters concerned with war, migration, policing and religion might have taken respondents to places they were not ready to revisit or created changes for them that the researcher was not in a position to support them through, because of limited resources. Some of the adult participants found aspects of the research challenging (two withdrew from the second interview) and, in retrospect, the decision not to work directly with children was appropriate in the circumstances.

The sample involved 17 adult respondents, selected for two reasons. The first was their professional and academic commitment to children's rights and their willingness to give up their time to research that is intended to deepen understanding of children's lives. Their academic and other work experiences with children span psychology, sociology, social work, teaching, youth and community work, leisure and sport, equality and advocacy and the creative therapies. These experiences in their adult lives were clearly highly influential in the sort of memories of their own childhood they selected to share with the researcher and the ways in which they analysed and framed the memories. However, for reasons of confidentiality, it is not appropriate to share their current academic and professional roles.

The second reason for their selection was the diversity of their experiences as children. They come from different social class backgrounds, ethnicities, generations, faith communities, colour, gender, sexual orientation and disability. One went to boarding school, two experienced lengthy hospitalization as children, one began to face long-term mobility difficulties as a young person and two had to cope with the death of their mother. The research is based in England, but a significant number experienced part of their childhood outside England, some through residence, others through extended and repeated visits to kin, including in Northern Ireland, Scotland, Germany, Pakistan, India, Italy, St Kitts, Nigeria and South Africa.

This choice of participants made it possible to draw on a wide canvas of childhood experience, to explore different times and places, and to consider different children's engagement, with children's interests in mind. The span of childhood remembered was from 1950 to 1996. From concerns that the sample might be too narrow, a rich and diverse range of experiences and pathways through childhood was shared by these participants. This was a group that in adulthood would certainly not be termed 'vulnerable' and now live relatively privileged lives. Here they shared a range of experiences that enrich understanding of the complexity of social change, the impact of inequality, children's resilience and the very wide range of social experience in childhood. Fuller cameos of each participant as a child are introduced below. These provide snapshots of the children to assist the reader as the data unfolds. Other important aspects of the lives of these children become clearer later in the book. The span of each childhood is included next to their names and names have been changed.

Kate (1950–1968)

Kate lived in a small town in northern England. Her father was a 'White British lapsed Catholic', who worked as an architect and came from a working-class family. Kate's mother had faced poverty during her childhood. Kate had two older brothers. When she was a young child, the family lived in a big house with a very big garden. Later they moved to a semi-detached house. Kate was very religious during part of her childhood, although her parents did not share her beliefs.

Martin (1951–1969)

Martin lived in northern England on the outskirts of quite a big town. His father was a consultant bacteriologist and his mother, a 'housewife' and later a part-time teacher. They lived in a semi-detached house and then a detached four-bed house. The family heritage was Scottish. Grandparents had worked in textiles, animal health and farming. Martin visited Scotland regularly. When he was 9 years old, he went to a private boarding school.

Julie (1952–1970)

Julie lived in a city in northern England. Her mother's parents were Welsh and her father's, English. She had older brothers. Her father was a manager who lost his job and then bought a shop where both parents worked. The family lived above the shop in an area of 'back-to-back' houses. They also took in lodgers. Julie had some extended illness as a child. Her mother died when she was a young teenager. Julie had her own first child at 16 and lived with her husband in a rented property.

Sylvia (1952–1970)

Sylvia lived in a large terraced house in a north English city. Her father's parents were German and Slovakian Jews and he came to England as a refugee in 1939. Her mother's (Christian) parents were comfortably off. Religious heritage, 'race' and the aftermath of war were a source of deep tension. Sylvia's mother had long-term mental health problems and her parents separated when she was 11. Her mother then took in lodgers.

Claudia (1954–1972)

Claudia's father was Romanian and her mother German. They came to England as a result of the Second World War (1939–1945). Claudia was born in a rural part of south-east England and had a younger sister. Her sister sadly died as a young adult. Claudia's father worked as a farm hand, a labourer and later at an airport. There were short periods of unemployment.

Her mother worked as a maid, a shop assistant and in agricultural work. They lived in a rented farm cottage and then managed to buy a house.

Pamela (1955–1973)

Pamela's father came from a middle-class and her mother from a working-class background. There was some disapproval of father 'marrying down'. He was born in Canada and was brought to England as a baby. Pamela had a younger brother. Both children were affected by mobility difficulties and spent periods in hospital. Both parents became school science technicians. The family lived in London throughout Pamela's childhood, in a large three-bed semi-detached house which they owned and then an older detached property.

Paulina (1956–1974)

Paulina was born in St Kitts and moved to a city in northern England when she was 5. Her mother was a seamstress and her father a police guard in the Caribbean and a factory worker in England. She had brothers. In St Kitts she remembered living near the coast in a house built on stilts. In England she lived in a terraced house, where they took in lodgers for a while. Her parents separated. Christianity was important to Paulina as a child.

George (1958–1976)

George's father was a clerk and his mother did various part-time jobs including cleaning, clerical work and catering. His father's heritage was Welsh and his mother's Irish. The family lived in an industrial town in north-west England. His parents both had health difficulties and had experienced the loss of babies before George was born. They lived in a terraced house with a yard throughout his childhood which they came to own through rental purchase. There was a close sense of community where he lived.

Rehana (1960–1978)

Rehana was born in a small town in Pakistan. She comes from a Muslim community. Her grandparents on her father's side were landowners. Her mother's mother made and sold crafts and was widowed young. Rehana's mother worked with an international, non- governmental organization, but sadly she died when Rehana was 4. Her father worked as a soldier and after migrating to England, in a bakery and carpet mill in England. They lived in a courtyard house in Pakistan, then a terraced house in England.

Richard (1961–1979)

Richard's family emigrated from north-west England to South Africa when he was 3, during apartheid. The family returned to England when he was 16. His parents were 'very working class' before emigration, which they decided to do because of debt. While in South Africa, they lived in two modern apartments in different high-rise blocks at a port. Richard's father worked as a welder, mainly in shipping. As the children got older, his mother worked part-time in a shop

James (1961–1979)

James had one sister and a very close extended family. He was born in an industrial town in Northern Ireland and grew up during the conflict there, sometimes known as 'The Troubles'. His family was Protestant. Although the place he lived was some distance from the greatest conflict, many frightening events took place and the tense atmosphere influenced his childhood. His mother worked in administrative posts. His father was a skilled engineer.

Cathy (1962–1980)

Cathy was born in a city in north-west England and lived with her sister and parents in a small terraced house. Her father worked in haulage and her mother was a cleaner. Cathy and her sister took a lot of responsibility for cleaning the home. Grandparents had also worked in manual occupations and were from the local area. The girls and their father were committed football fans.

Lara (1964–1982)

Lara had three siblings. Her mother was Italian and worked in nursing, and driving disabled children to and from school. Her father came from St Lucia and worked in a factory. They lived in a city in northern England, first at her grandma's, then a council flat and then a council house on a very White* council estate. Money was 'tight' and it was 'hard hiding

---

* The terms 'White' and 'Black' are capitalized w hen used as labels related to ethnicity.

from the rent man' in her early childhood. In her early teens her parents separated. Lara began to be affected by a long-term condition limiting her mobility at 16.

Rachel (1964–1982)

Rachel's family were middle class, both of skilled working-class heritage. She had two sisters. Her father had some Canadian heritage. He became a director and her mother, after being a 'housewife', got part-time work in the fashion industry. Rachel loved sports and physical activity. The family lived on the outskirts of London. When she was 8 they moved to a large detached rambling house which was 'swopped' with an elderly friend who couldn't manage it any longer.

Apara (1968–1986)

Apara was born in Nigeria. Her father was from a royal Yoruba family and they lived in a very comfortable home. Her parents separated and she went to north-east England when she was 5 years old. She had siblings. First she lived with her mother's parents in a flat, and then moved to a semi-detached house on a council estate. Apara's mother's family were committed to the labour movement. Her mother worked in the administrative posts.

Tessa (1969–1987)

Tessa and her sister lived in a village in northern England. Her mother was from a working-class background and her father more middle class. Her father's parents had some Scottish links and her mother's father, Welsh. Father worked in farming and mother ran her own playgroup and then worked with horses. The family first lived in a bungalow, then a rented cottage, a detached house and a lodge. In Tessa's later teens her father was made redundant and he worked in temporary less secure manual jobs.

Madhi (1978–1996)

Madhi was of Indian heritage and her family were originally from a village in Gujarat. Her family caste, Kutchi, had been farmers. There were strong links to Kenya as her parents settled there before migrating to London, where Madhi was born. Her father worked as a laboratory technician in

London. Her mother worked in a sandwich factory and as a cleaner. Madhi loved sports and physical activity throughout her childhood. She lived in a large three-bed semi-detached house. They took in lodgers when she was very young. She had memorable visits to India.

Introduction to the Chapters

Chapter 2 discusses the research approach more fully, focusing particularly on the way that the sensitizing concepts of memory, space and time have been drawn on to access and analyze these childhood experiences. It is argued that a research approach that is sensitive to the influence of social memory, space and time, deepens understanding of children's lives by giving visibility to a wide range of social influences that might otherwise be overlooked. The chapter reviews literature related to the key concepts drawn on in the methodology and then discusses the research methods, drawing on examples of data to illuminate this.

Chapter 3, 'Children and Migration', commences the data analysis with a broad sweep, both spatial and temporal. It considers the way that all the children were touched by migration. Their family networks extended to different regions. They were told stories of relatives who have gone to different, distant places. Their lives were influenced by continuing communications with kin at a distance. Communications involved visits and the sending and receiving of gifts and financial support. This chapter repositions important understanding of migration in childhood. Migration is not just a subject about groups of children who have recently arrived in a new place, perhaps considered 'other' to those born there. Migration is formative in the lives of all the children in important and meaningful ways.

Chapter 4 continues the analysis by drawing attention to the micro-macro relations of the home, drawing on participants' experiences of the places where they lived at different times. Different areas of home life are explored, for example, bathing, eating and sleeping. The focus is on the routine domestic practices and normative uses of space that children experience. Referring back to issues raised in Chapter 3, home is analyzed in relation to wider spatial and temporal influences. It provides shelter from the unpredictable environment and is informed by wider social expectations of family life. In this chapter home is not considered a fixed place, but an outcome of a series of changing material and social relationships, expectations and events linked to the wider society.

Chapter 5 explores the ways other people's work informs everyday childhood as well as the impact of children's own first jobs. It is argued that the 'public' sphere of employment influences children's lives in ways that are under-researched. The paid work of parents is experienced at a visceral level by children from a very early age, for example, the smell of work that parents bring with them when they return from work. In childhood, public and private worlds merge in complex ways. The influences of social class background, ethnicity and gender are very apparent. Children experience anxiety at times of parental unemployment and job transition. Employment is not just something that happens outside the home. It generates a field of intense human relations and energy that enters the child's world, shaping expectations, involving feelings of pleasure, anxiety, uncertainty and pride.

A further aspect of social experience that is under-researched relates to religious beliefs and practices (in the broadest sense). In Chapter 6, diverse religious belief systems, practices, institutions and people are considered in relation to children's everyday lives. Religion is conceptualized as a part of everyday childhood. This is whether the children involved came from families that actively practiced a particular belief system or not. A particular theme in this chapter is the way long spans of collective memory continue to shape children's everyday lives and the way they engage with this.

Chapter 7 looks more explicitly at the influence of aspects of the state and civil society in children's lives. It considers children's early experiences of state regulation in school, where they found themselves positioned in particular ways and learned the power of state functionaries such as teachers. It moves on to consider the different faces of policing in childhood, protective and punitive, fearful and amusing. It considers children's relationship to particular communities of identity, including conflict between the police and Black young people, the policing of sexual identity and family relations, and the policing of racist attacks. It considers children's growing understanding of different social and labour movements, industrial conflict and party politics. Children navigate complex state and civil society relations. They accept, resist and try to change their position and expectations of them.

Chapter 8 explores the complex ways that children's everyday lives are shaped by war and conflict including children directly caught up in events and children not. It includes direct and indirect memories and threads from the past, stories communicated to the respondents as children. Such communications were oral, archival (photographs, relics) and involved threads of familial and cultural memory. They included the dark secrets, hushed

voices and things children heard 'under the table' as well as repeated anecdotes of war. The argument of this chapter is that both past and present
wars are very influential and formative in childhood.

Chapter 9 considers children as consumers including the advent of
labour-saving devices, changing media and communications. It also discusses shifts in popular culture and children's engagement with this, considering fashion and music. The everyday lives of children are shaped by
complex temporal influences related to the past and present and involving dreams for future time. Consumer artefacts are socially created and
marketed with particular groups in mind, including families and children. The social concept of childhood at a given time, the age of the child
and their location in space are significant. Children's capacity to exercise
their own control and employ particular cultural resources differs in relation to all these influences. There are differences in the degree of freedom, their current desires, the choices available and the nature of their
imagined future.

Chapter 10 considers children and play, including their involvement in
wider family, community and national play through such things as parties
and parades that mark social transition. The children played in a wide
range of settings which involved them in deep emotional, physical and
mental creativity as they wove, connected and juxtaposed different threads
of social memory. They played alone and with siblings, friends, family
members and wider communities. Their play was in one sense continuous
and expansive and in another, restricted and regulated. Through play and
related events there was the possibility that they could exercise more social
control and create a social place for themselves.

The chapter concludes the data analysis and revisits earlier discussion
related to the connections between wider social change and everyday
childhood. It highlights the resilience of children and their deep social
engagement.

Chapter 11 returns to the key research concepts and questions considering how memory, space and time shape children's wider social engagement.
The chapter also revisits the methodology, considering how the selectivity
of memory shaped the research at a number of levels and the strengths
and limitations of this. It also considers the implications of the research in
relation to the present and future times of children.

There is no separate chapter on children's school experiences as these
inform all of the chapters in different ways. The ways that a child compares
schools after migration is discussed in Chapter 3; some of the domestic routines of school in Chapter 4. Selection for school is considered in Chapter 5

and in Chapter 6, school experience in relation to the power of religious functionaries. Chapter 7 explores children's experiences of school as part of wider state and civil society relations; Chapter 8, disruptions related to war. Chapters 9 and 10 include consideration of school as a site of leisure and play.

Those researching children's experiences have revealed the narrow and varied conceptions of childhood that have shaped adult understanding in the past. Children have been viewed as, for example, mini-adults, as less than fully human, or as merely investments in the future (Mills, 2000). Childhood has been viewed as a time for learning, a time to labour and, more recently, a time to play. Childhood has been viewed partially, as a subtraction from or transition to adulthood (Holloway and Valentine, 2000; Neale and Flowerdew, 2003; James and James, 2004). The study of childhood has focused on places and institutions concerned with certain aspects of children's experience, less so others. Hence, many children have been viewed through a fairly narrow lens, either through the places they are expected to occupy or through the traumatic events particular groups experience. The fact that children move through the same societies as adults sometimes escapes us.

The versions of childhood available in the social memory are limited. They are being opened up through new research which emphasizes children's rights, social justice, the importance of including the perspective of the child and considerations related to space and time. Hopefully the research discussed in this book makes a contribution to that movement. If we accept Halbwachs' (1925/1992) perspective, limited social versions of childhood also limit our personal remembering of childhood. Attention to the wider social landscape and children's engagement should enrich understanding of their everyday lives.

Chapter 2

Memory, Space, Time and Childhood: The Research Approach

Introduction

This chapter discusses the research approach, focusing particularly on the way that the sensitizing concepts of memory, space and time have been drawn on to access and analyze children's experiences. As discussed in Chapter 1, the research explores how wider social, cultural, economic and political events, systems and arrangements, influence children's everyday lives and how children practice childhood in relation to this. It is argued in this chapter that a research approach that is sensitive to the influence of social memory, space and time, deepens understanding of children's lives by giving visibility to a wide range of social influences that might otherwise be overlooked. The chapter includes three elements. First, running through the chapter is a review of literature related to the key concepts drawn on in the methodology. Secondly, the research methods and tools are discussed and thirdly, the analytic approach. In relation to the latter, some research findings are included. The participants in the research were introduced in Chapter 1. This chapter introduces some of their perspectives and experiences for the first time. It is well established that sensitivity to space and time in research helps generate rich data and contextualize, ground and analyse this because giving these concepts attention enables a research approach which relates personal experience directly to a wider set of social, economic and political relationships (Urry, 1996). Space and time are complex concepts with different interpretations, both quantitative and qualitative. Sociological understanding of memory, space and time enriches research by facilitating lines of research enquiry from children's lives to significant 'behind the scenes' influences (Layder, 1993, p. 249). These three key concepts are now discussed in turn.

Review of Key Concepts

Social Memory and Childhood

The first key concept drawn on in the research is 'social memory'. Halbwachs (1925/1992), writing in the first half of the twentieth century, distinguishes between different forms of memory, drawing attention to the ways in which personal memories are channelled through familial and other collective memories. These collective (or social) memories provide 'social frameworks' for engaging with everyday life. Current social arrangements develop from past human practices. Each social encounter is therefore also an encounter with the past. The 'Pathways' research explores the relationship between children's everyday experience and the social memories they engage with related to family, community and nation. Social memory is considered an important part of the 'present' time of childhood. Social memories are encountered through family and household arrangements, meetings with state functionaries, places of religious worship, games, leisure, school, work and popular culture. Children move through arrangements for living that have emerged from the past, for example, long spans of collective memory inform children's daily experience of religion and shadows from wars long past inform everyday encounters years later. Children must continuously encounter and adapt complex shared ideas, experiences and practices from the past, 'So it is when people are alone, face to face with themselves, other people appear and with them the groups of which they are members' (Halbwachs, 1925/1992, p. 182). It is through these rich and complex influences from the past that children understand their present time:

> It is in this sense that there exists a collective memory and social frameworks of memory; it is to the degree that our individual thought places itself in these frameworks and participates in this memory that it is capable of the act of recollection. (ibid., p. 38)

Clearly children are not passive recipients of the influences from the past, but they have to work through what is handed down to them by the wider society.

Misztal (2003) reviews four stages of theoretical development in the understanding of social memory. The first key scholar she discusses is Halbwachs (above). His work on collective memory aimed to increase the visibility of continuities between past and present for the purpose of understanding social change. Although children have limited visibility in his work, his approach is of immense value for understanding the relationship between personal, familial and social influences in children's lives. Misztal discusses his work on the 'collective nature of social consciousness' (2003, p. 50). A student of Durkheim, Halbwachs explores the social functions of collective memory, particularly in providing social anchors and temporal continuity for families, communities and nations. He explores different aspects of collective memory, including memories related to religion, the state and social class. Childhood receives some attention, but mainly in relation to familial memory.

Following this, the second area Misztal (ibid.) considers concerns theorists such as Hobsbawm and Ranger (1983), who examine in more depth the power relations involved in the production of social memory. In *The Invention of Tradition*, Hobsbawm points out the way that ' . . . the past is moulded to suit the present dominant interests' (1983, p. 1), arguing that, 'Traditions which appear or claim to be old are often quite recent . . . In fact, where possible, they normally attempt to establish continuity with a suitable historic past'. The reservoir of social memories available at any given time and place, will relate to the interests and influence of powerful social groups. This has particular implications for our understanding of children and social change. At the time of writing, 'oath taking' and loyalty ceremonies are being promoted, in relation both to the acquisition of British citizenship and to the transition from childhood to adulthood (Goldsmith, 2007). Such ceremonies involve the engineering of social memory, creating traditions based on romanticized versions of quite bloody social histories. Writing of 'heroes and myths' Misztal (2003) , ' . . . as nations need to establish their representations in the past, their memories are created in tandem with forgetting [and] . . . not only is the past forgotten, but also there is a parallel forgetting of the present' (pp. 17–18 quotes Billig (1995)).

Awareness of the power involved in the production of social memories is one inspiration for the oral history movement and the focus on the memories of marginalized groups whose experiences have been hidden or distorted. The 'popular memory approach' is the third stage considered by Misztal (2003, p. 61). This involves opening up the social memory archives and generating new analysis of past events. Histories are enriched and distortions revealed in the 'traditional' archives. The experiences of children and young people continue to form an important part of the oral history movement.

Following this, the fourth stage (ibid.) involves post-structuralist and other inter-actionist approaches that were developed in order to explore the complexity of social memory making, the focus of attention being the intersection between different accounts of similar events related to social class, ethnicity, gender, age, disability and geographical heritage. The ways that knowledge and understanding are produced from interaction between dominant, different and marginal perspectives become more visible (ibid., p. 64). As memories of the past are socially produced, the relativity of that process becomes clearer and the way the past is interpreted through the present, ' . . . the forms memory will take are invariably contingent and subject to change' (Huyssen, 1995, p. 2). The awareness that recollections of the past are mediated through present time also informed the work of Halbwach's in the 1920s, 'To sum up: social beliefs, whatever their origin, have a double character. They are collective traditions or recollections, but they are also ideas or conventions that result from knowledge of the present' (1925/1992, p. 188). Atwood challenges those who argue that there is little to be learned from examining the past because the past is always viewed through the present, ' "The past is another country" ', begins the English novel *The Go-Between*; "they do things differently there". Yes, they do . . . but they also do quite a few things the same' (2005, p. 220). She asks whether memory provides less legitimate versions of the past than some history just because events are constructed from experience rather than being a direct account of experience. Even if memory could be considered 'fictitious', 'Fiction is where individual memory and experience and collective memory and experience come together in greater or lesser proportions' (ibid., p. 209) and fiction may well intensify our understanding of the social world, 'History may intend to provide us with grand patterns and overall schemes, but without its brick-by-brick, life-by-life, day-by-day foundations it would collapse' (ibid., p. 211).

As histories have not traditionally been written by children, the social frameworks for remembering childhood are quite narrow. Some researchers now focus on developing children as researchers, working directly with them to generate their own accounts of experience (Kellett, 2005; Neale et al. 2005; Jones, 2009). The research discussed here however, is based on adult memories, but the parameters of memory are deliberately widened from traditional expectations of childhood, the aim being to add to the understanding of children and wider social change.

The Social Production of the Spaces of Childhood

Lefebvre (1991) argues that places are historically produced from interaction. There are significant messages about children and society contained in the places children occupy and the routes and networks through daily life available to them:

> Space is divided up into designated (signified, specialized) areas and into areas that are prohibited (to one group or another). It is further subdivided into spaces for work and spaces for leisure and into daytime and night time spaces. (ibid., pp. 319–20)

Space has a threefold dialectical character (ibid.). The first dimension of space to be considered is space as 'practice'. There are everyday routes through space that people are required to follow. Consider, for example, the way children's movement between public and private spheres has changed over time:

> Then gradually space becomes specified and functional . . . The working class family is to be fixed, by assigning it a living space with a room that serves as a living space, with a room that serves as a kitchen and dining room, a room for the parents which is the place of procreation and a room for the children, one prescribes a form of morality for the family. (Foucault, 1980a, p. 149)

With the advance of industrialization and urbanization 'home' became a more private rather than work related space, and children's movement through home took a new form. Children's movement into the public sphere also takes particular forms at different times and places, for example, the transition from home to school may be different in different societies for girls and boys.

The second dimension of 'space' is the idea that space is 'representation' (Lefebvre, 1991). Complex meanings are communicated by different places. For a child, for example, the place where he or she sleeps in the home may convey many messages. It may be comforting and warm when they are tired and cold. It may be a place where they must conform to adult demands, 'Go to bed'. It may be a place associated in the dark, with tales from the past of monsters, goblins and things under the bed. Lefebvre uses the term 'landscape' to explore space as representation (ibid.). Space is not fixed or static but dynamic, conveying strong social messages and signals. These messages are contained as residues in the stories, symbols and celebrations of past practices, 'Here what we might have called representation is no longer a process of fixing, but an element in a continuous production; a part of it all, and itself constantly becoming' (Massey, 2005, p. 28). Ardener uses the concepts of ground rules and social maps to explore similar ideas about space:

> Societies have generated their own rules, culturally determined, for making boundaries on the ground, and have divided the social into spheres, levels and territories with invisible fences and platforms to be scaled by abstract ladders and crossed by intangible bridges with as much

trepidation or exultation as on a plank over a raging torrent. (1993, pp. 11–12)

Children cross boundaries laid out for them with uncertainty and excitement including the boundary between sleep and waking.

The third dimension of space (Lefebvre, 1991, p. 42) is 'representational'. This is the idea that space is both living and lived. Children actively engage with the landscapes they occupy. As Massey puts it, 'Space does not exist prior to identities/entities and their relations. More generally . . . identities/entities, the relations "between" them, and the spatiality which is part of them, are all co-constitutive' (2005, p. 10). Children carve out space and time for themselves from the landscapes they occupy. In relation to the places intended for sleeping, children will negotiate and fight with adults in order to delay going to bed; they will imagine their own night-time stories and they will sleep and dream their own dreams.

Combining Halbwachs' (1925/1992) and other theories of understanding of social memory with this understanding of the social production of space enables lines of research enquiry to be drawn from the personal experiences of children to the landscapes they engage with. The power relations contained there and the way children negotiate 'boundaries on the ground' become more visible.

Temporality and Childhood

Of equal significance to this research is the third concept, 'temporality'. Three aspects of this concept are discussed here in relation to childhood. The first relates to the complexity of temporal influences in childhood, the second to transition and the third to the power relations involved with time. These three aspects are closely connected.

First, temporal influences in childhood are complex and interwoven (Adam, 1995). They involve time in different ways: the stages of physical growth; the time schedules of the household, the clock led and seasonal times of school, the times of employment, of industry and the times of the wider environment, community and faith, including agriculture and the environment. Children are engaged in carving out space and time for themselves from these complex multiple and overlapping temporal influences. Children live through complex rhythms and have to weave complex influences (Adam, 1990; Davies, 1990). The concept 'centres of action' reveals the concrete ways children adapt within changing times and settings. Hence children are 'symphonies in rhythm' (Adam, 1990, p. 74) and ' . . . live structures of temporality' (Huyssen, 1995, p. 4).

The second but connected aspect of temporality to consider relates to time and transition, both the complex and fragmented transition from child to adult status (Morrow, 2003) and wider social transition and change. Childhood is a time of complex personal transition. This involves past, present and future time. The passing of time involves, ' . . . memories in the present of the past, expectations and desires in the present of the future' (Jaques, 1982/1990, p. 22). Pathways to adulthood relate to social expectations. Children may be conceptualized as 'investments in the future' (Welch, 2008a) and their future time may be 'colonized' in particular ways (Adam, 2003). Wider social change and transition also involve past, present and future times. The past is experienced through the recurring effects of past events on the present. The children of Bhopal in India (Dinham with Sarangi, 2002) continue to suffer the consequences of chemical poisoning by Union Carbide 25 years after the event and the campaign for justice still continues at the time of writing. Future times are also contested in the present. At the time of writing, campaigns against carbon emissions related to global warming have the future of children at their heart (United Nations Climate Change Conference, 2009).

The third aspect of temporality, closely connected with the above and relevant to understanding children and social change, concerns power. Time is not simply something to be measured by the clock. In fact, clock time is something historically imposed. Davies (1990) discusses the ways that linear conceptualizations of time are associated in particular with the male priesthood and the development of Judeo-Christian religion. The idea that the world could be controlled through prayer led to the development of mechanisms to measure time and regulate prayer, regardless of local time systems. The awareness of the social regulation of time as a vehicle to extract profit has informed both Marxist and feminist theories. Thompson (1967) points out that a dominant orientation to *clock* time is a feature of industrial capitalism, ' . . . not the task, but the value of time when reduced to money, is dominant. Time is now currency, it is not passed but spent' (quoted in Davies, 1990, p. 26). Struggles over time and its value shape the economy and struggles over time also inform childhood. The times of education are led by the times of industry and sometimes sit uneasily with the biological clock of children, who may wish to sleep rather than go to school and to play rather than learn punctuality and the related social order. Adam demonstrates that time (as well as space) is created to 'human design', 'When the invariable time of the clock is imposed on living systems, it tends to be the living systems that are required to adapt to the machine-time rather than the other way round' (2006, p. 123). Hence, children's everyday lives are complex temporal engagements that involve the exercise of power to carve out space and time for themselves (Davies, 1990). Children live in present time, imagine future time and draw on past times (Jaques, 1982/1990). The social arrangements they encounter may be designed with their future in mind but children's time may be colonized in different ways (Adam, 2003) and their lives crafted in ways that relate to wider socio-political interests.

From Halbwachs (1925/1992) and others, we learn the present power of social memories in children's lives and the way these are transmitted in childhood through family, community and nation. From Lefebvre (1991) and Massey (2005), we learn the dynamic influences of space and the complexity of the landscapes children engage with. From Adam (1990; 1995; 2002; 2003; 2006), we learn about the complexity of temporal influences shaping childhood and the power involved there. The next step is to consider how these concepts were applied in the research.

Research Methods and Tools

The concepts of memory, space and time overlap, yet are different. They facilitate consideration of many different social influences in childhood. The dangers of seeing children's lives as overly determined by social structures and adult worlds or as restricted to particular arenas such as home and school may be avoided. The coming together of theoretical work on time, space and memory is particularly important for research into childhood. The 'long time' of environmental pollution may be as significant to the child as the 'short time' of a fall in the playground. The child's day is driven by the clock time of adult paid work; a calendar and schedule which is replicated in education time. There are significant messages about children and society contained in the places children occupy and the routes and networks through daily life available and not available to them. Social memory, spatiality and temporality cannot easily be separated although each draws attention to different dimensions of children's social experience and when applied in research, help to broaden the frameworks for understanding childhood. I now move on to consider how some of these issues and questions informed the research methods and tools. The aim was to draw on adult memories of childhood (see Chapter 1) but the selectivity of memory and the complexity of personal, familial and other social memories meant that there were particular difficulties in this.

In each time period, different expectations shape children's sense of themselves. Childhood experience may be traditionally associated with school and home, less associated with the wider social sphere that is considered to be the realm of adults. Adults who are asked to remember childhood may automatically turn to those spheres conventionally associated with childhood rather than look elsewhere. When adults remember their own childhood, contemporary ideas influence their selection and evaluation of memories because the articulation of memory involves a dialogue between past and present and the social frameworks for remembering childhood may be quite narrow. Working in retrospect with adults remembering childhood, involves the complexity of drawing on adult reminiscences as research data or 'pockets of history' (Brannen, 2004, p. 425).

When the process of remembering is considered at a personal level, memories are clearly drawn from clusters of events including absences and presences, smells, tastes and journeys. There is some pleasure in memories. There may be aspects that are not always factually correct. Events associated with strong emotion may be recalled easily – or may be buried. Memory involves direct and indirect experience that is sometimes hard to distinguish (Misztal, 2003). Familial memory involves the selective development of archives, including photographs, film, letters, stories and memorabilia (ibid.). Collective memory involves the selective development of public symbols, 'traditions', rituals, institutional practices (ibid.) and the social production of spatial arrangements (Lefebvre, 1991). The power of social memory relates to this selectivity, 'Interpersonal rehearsal plays an important role in maintaining and consolidating . . . memories' (Misztal, 2003, p. 81 quoting Finkenauer et al. 1997). Social memories become anchored in social arrangements through dissemination and repetition, influencing the 'present time' of childhood.

Adult personal memories of childhood are often accessed through family memory, which is a way in which narratives from the past continue into the present. Halbwachs discusses familial memories as particular threads of shared memories based around kinship:

> Family recollections in fact develop as in so many different soils . . . Despite the distances among them that are created by opposition of temperaments and the variety of circumstances, they all shared the same daily life . . . Beyond and dominating all this there operates a feeling, both obscure and precise of kinship. (1925/1992, p. 56)

Halbwachs recognizes families as complex and potentially divided groups. He argues that familial memory consists, ' . . . not only of a series of individual images of the past. They are at the same time models, examples, and elements of teaching' (ibid., 59). Hence, familial memory is selective, particularly in relation to accounts of the past that families choose to share with their children. Families construct their history not only to share the past but to educate their children. As Misztal (2003) puts it, ' . . . family traditions, secrets and particular sentiments . . . objectified in old letters, photographs and family lore, are sustained through family conversations, as past events are jointly recalled and co-memorised' (p. 19 quoting Billig, 1995). Through this building of family tradition, some actors will be more influential than others. It is important to understand the way that power operates within, as well as external to families. Adult memories of childhood have been filled with familial narratives, and families choose to channel past experiences to children in particular ways and with particular emphases. The very process of remembering is not unitary, 'Many of our earliest memories are actually recollections of stories we heard from adults about our childhood . . . a collection of overlapping testimonies from our narrative environment' (ibid.).

In the case of the research discussed in this book which draws on adult memories of childhood, it was therefore important to be sensitive to the selectivity of memory and to deliberately 'stretch' the parameters for remembering childhood. The research tools were designed with this in mind. Rather than relying on free flows of memory, memories were explicitly invited, relating to spheres of social experience less traditionally associated with childhood, such as civil unrest, national celebrations and political events. The intention was to create a wide social lens on childhood, one that was not restricted by current ideas about children's natural place in society. Bearing in mind also the complex relationship between personal, familial and social memory, it was decided not to restrict memory selection by trying to distinguish between personal experience and familial and other stories. One of the problems encountered in memory work involved the difficulty of distinguishing 'real' experience from that which is socially constructed through the process of memory making, and to distinguish direct from indirect experience. In this research, personal experience, familial stories, communal experiences and contemporary reflection on the past all came to have a legitimate place and rather than this presenting a limitation; this approach ultimately helped to deepen understanding of children and social change, for example, it allows us to trace the threads from the Second World War that emerge in children's later encounters (see below).

In addition to the complexities of memory work, developing spatial and temporal concepts as research tools is also complex. Too rigid an approach restricts the visibility of important processes, for example, attempts to log events in relation to the clock and map uses of space overlook both simultaneity and the meanings attached to space and time (Urry, 1991; Rose, 1993; Saraswathi, 1994). On the other hand, space–time concepts may be too generic to be useful. It is important to draw on concepts that make particular spatial and temporal relations visible. In the case of this research, the concepts of space and time were separately associated with different research tools. This accorded with meanings of space and time as respondents understood them and meant their childhood experience was viewed through the lenses of space and time separately. This material could then be triangulated in relation to the research questions. However, in relation to the research analysis the concepts of space and time were used in more overlapping ways (see below).

The research tools were threefold. The first was a guided semi-structured interview. Respondents were invited to share memories of particular social experience related to war, migration, employment, policing, religion, civil unrest, national celebrations, and so forth. They were told these memories could be direct experience, familial stories or other indirect experience. This created legitimate space to share other people's memories and provided one means of accessing social memories. Ideas about time, social change and memory shaped the design. The second tool also involved a guided interview. Here the focus was the influences of place and the social production of space. Respondents were asked for recollections of the places of childhood in relation to aspects of living such as play, learning, working, domestic routines, travelling and other significant events and relationships. The diversity of their experience involved different living arrangements and geographical connections. The focus was on the child moving through the setting, and ideas about memory, space and childhood informed the design. Interviews were used for both these aspects because they allowed some probing as well as free-flowing narrative. Some of the questions were quite difficult to respond to at first, as they were not typical of the sorts of questions asked about children's experiences. The third research tool was a structured questionnaire designed to gather concrete data related to social and familial position and transitions across space–time, such as geographic and social mobility. Data elicited related to the child, parents (or carers), grandparents and some extended family. It concerned occupations, ethnicity and geographical heritage. Respondents were also asked to track changes in their own childhoods including transitions related to changing household arrangements, housing, employment, child care, income, health and illness. Ideas about family, mobility and social divisions informed the design and the questionnaire format ensured coverage of the areas. I now move on to discuss how the research analysis developed and introduce some of the perspectives and experiences of children.

The Research Analysis: Understanding Children's Social Involvement

The first stage of the research analysis involved organizing the data in relation to the main themes, for example, clustering data related to children's experiences of migration, employment, consumption, and so forth. The second phase involved analysing how social memory, space and time were influential across these themes. Five overlapping questions began to emerge across the different thematic areas and these inform the discussion in the subsequent chapters of this book. These questions are, first, as social arrangements are constructed and conceptualized through selective social memory, how does this shape children's experience? Secondly, as memory takes different forms (personal and social), how do these interrelate in children's lives? Thirdly, what are the effects of movement through space and time, including encounters with new places and communities? Fourthly, the selectivity of social memory leads to silences in the social memory. What are the implications of this? Fifthly, in light of complex space–time relations, how do children carve out space–time for themselves? These questions are now considered in turn and in each case some children's experiences are introduced and discussed in order to illustrate the analytic framework that informs the rest of the book.

Selective Memory and Childhood

Some aspects of family experience were shared repeatedly with the children; others were hidden. In the research for this book, Apara repeated the story of her grandmother, recounted to her in childhood. Apara was born in Nigeria and moved to England when 5, in the 1970s. Her mother was from an English working-class heritage and her father, upper-class Nigerian. The story emerged from the economic depression in England, 30 years before Apara was born. Her grandmother worked in a meat factory during the 1930s,

> my grandmother . . . basically kept the family going . . . also her sister's family . . . she worked in a factory . . . that made meat products. She used

to look after the pigs . . . For years, she kept [the two families] fed, by wearing [wellingtons] to work and stuffing pounds of sausages down [them] by winding them round her legs . . . So when you think of the weight of them, and having to . . . walk.

This was a story of a 'heroine' committed to her family's welfare. The memory shared with the child celebrated this, containing education about the potential of women to overcome adversity. The undercurrent was hunger associated with the depression, the struggles against the owners of capital and the legitimacy of lawbreaking in this situation. The politics informing the story was from working-class struggle (Apara's mother's family were socialists). In this way, Apara's experiences as a child were informed by a familial and collective past. The memory belonged to the family archive and was formative in her childhood, transmitting past events, a political position, a sense of pride and amusement.

National memories are selectively enacted in the celebrations that children engage with (or not), designed in particular interests. Children are positioned differently to each other in relation to these. Madhi remembers watching the royal celebrations on the TV in the early 1980s. This could have related to the wedding of Charles and Diana in 1981 or the Queen Mother's eightieth birthday celebrations a year earlier. She would have been 2 or 3 years old, of Indian heritage living in England. Her family were relatively low paid, having moved from a higher social status in India, then Kenya, before she was born:

There were these images of people . . . on the streets. . . . all white, all working class/middle class, eating food, with balloons . . . I remember thinking, 'I don't know what this is all about, but we're not doing anything'. Nobody where we lived [was] doing it, so it was just something on the TV. You just remember these mass produced teacups with the Queen's face on them.

Hobsbawm and Ranger (1983) argue that events such as this perpetuate stories about the social respect to be accorded certain people over others. They are a selective version of a remembered past. For relative newcomers, the national memories being celebrated related to a royal family who ruled the British Empire. Madhi's family had different memories that cast a different light on empire and royalty, stories related to oppression by the British in India:

I . . . got this lovely story from my . . . family. My grandfather used to get really pissed off . . . with the British coming in and try and improve their rules, their laws, their culture, their lifestyle, when my grandfather thought we had our own one that was very dear to him . . . So during times of curfew at night, my grandfather would go and stand on the rooftops. If there were any helicopters or anything going up in the sky, he would basically say in Gujarathi, 'Tell them to Fuck Off!'

British royalty was probably not celebrated at that time in Madhi's family, and she felt an outsider, watching not participating. It would have been difficult to reconcile conflicting social memories transmitted through her family and the wider society. This positioned her at a distance, attempting to understand events through competing social frameworks (Halbwachs, 1925/1992). Combinations of social memories are transmitted through family, community and nation. These create complex landscapes of social memory that children need to navigate.

Navigating Landscapes of Memory

Personal and social memories interrelate and are hard to disentangle. The social landscapes children navigate are informed by social memories based around kin, community and nation. Different forms of memory are visible at a turning point for Madhi, while she was visiting India. She was told by her father to hand out food to long lines of poor people. Aged 12 or 13, she struggled to cope; shocked by the condition in which these very poor people lived. She somehow knew she should not display emotion:

My dad decided that we were going to do some voluntary work . . . it was on the river Ganges . . . I was a really spoilt, young teenager . . . who couldn't stop fighting with my . . . brother . . . and acting like a right old pest . . . we had to feed the poor . . . my Dad was putting food on the plate and I was giving them the plates . . . This queue of hundreds of people . . . I was gonna burst into tears . . . I was like . . . 'Don't you dare cry, because these people are homeless, hungry, have got nowhere to live, and you've been moaning endlessly' . . . I had this knot in my throat . . . It was just horrible seeing that poverty . . . my Dad and I never really talked about why we did it.

This memory involved strong emotion at a personal level. In addition, it revealed the relationship with father, who encouraged her participation; the passing on of familial memory related to this aspect of her Indian heritage.

The tradition of giving to poor people was, in Halbwachs' (1925/1992) term, a collective memory of those better off assisting the poor in this society and religion (Hinduism). The requirement to bury personal feelings was a strong part of the religious tradition involving sublimation of self and personal desire. This was a response to poverty in an unequal society with little organized welfare. The place was highly significant; along the Ganges, a sacred place, where the tradition was enacted. Madhi experienced shame at her 'selfishness' and attempted to sublimate emotion to navigate this landscape.

Powerful social memories may be experienced with no intervening human agent. Richard was 11 in South Africa in the 1970s. His family had moved from poverty and low-paid employment in England. They were White, hence more privileged under apartheid. On his way from school, he regularly crossed a foot bridge. White people were allowed to cross on one side, Black people on another and there was a metal fence in the middle. Everyday he jumped this barrier and walked on the side meant for Black people. He was not necessarily seen but the potential was always there. He was a bit scared each time, but far less so than a Black child would have been in similar circumstances where the consequences would have been worse:

> there was a footbridge . . . literally divided in half by a metal fence . . . there was one side for the whites and one side for the blacks. You know they weren't even allowed to walk on the same bit of concrete across the footbridge. But what I remember doing . . . I used to hop across and deliberately walk on the black side as my way of saying this was ridiculous – I always remember that, sort of deliberately hopping over the fence.

The design of the bridge contained a template for cruel behaviour. The memories of those that designed apartheid dominated the social landscape the child was experiencing. His route was prescribed and he transgressed these rules. However, his experience was not just informed by memories of the designers of apartheid in the landscape. He had a counter-narrative from his family about the evils of apartheid:

> We were aware of things . . . like the murder of Biko . . . as a family . . . we used to read the newspapers with the official police descriptions of what

happened to people like Biko . . . and there were others as well, you know they 'slipped on a piece of soap'.

This also underpinned his feeling of disgust and informed this small act of resistance (jumping over also gave some physical pleasure).

Inequalities position children differently in the social landscape. The education they experience (the form of social memory they encounter) influences their powers to navigate and the direction taken. Particular pathways open or opportunities close. George lived in England in the 1960s, of English working-class heritage. He talked of his parent's work:

> My first experience of work . . . was . . . my Dad's absence . . . he would come in later, smelling of Brylcreem and sweat . . . My second . . . was going with . . . Mum when she was doing this cleaning to this posh house. So I associated work with, it was a bit exotic, going to a semi-detached house, with a back garden, rather than a yard, and they had a pet . . . and reading Woman's Realm and posh biscuits, it's all kind of connected.

The class and gender pathways involved in the landscape were visible. George's father was often absent at work. His mother moved from a working- to a middle-class neighbourhood to provide domestic service. George, for whom she was primary carer, sometimes went with her. Many similar women have to leave their own children behind. The routes to work are laid out for women of her class. These are the 'spatial practices' informing the landscape, containing memories further back, of many poorer women's journeys to work for better off families (Gregson and Lowe, 1994). George enjoyed the garden, the women's magazines, the posh biscuits and the pet. As well as current pleasure, these were 'signs' of other possibilities he had not experienced, relating to social class, gender and sexuality. In Lefebvre's (1991) terms, they were 'spatial representations' signalling the terms of entry to this space. George's mother was providing domestic service and was permitted time-limited access to this more privileged home. George was curious and took pleasure in the exotic experiences associated with his mother's paid work. The space was lived by the boy and was 'representational space' (ibid.).

Although children navigate the landscape and the social memories conveyed there, through prescribed routes, they are able to transgress boundaries they encounter, through, for example, small resistances, inquisitiveness and play. Resources from the family inform the nature and direction of these journeys and the capacity to detour. Encounters on the way are formative for future times.

Movement through Space and Time

One memory may be part of several chains of memory leading to and from other people (Misztal, 2003 citing Shils, 1981). The theme 'chains of memory' has a social dimension. It is a means of exploring connections in everyday childhood between present and past, individual and group and different places. 'Chains' imply something binding and metallic so the concept has been replaced here by 'threads' of memory. These are woven in different ways, numerous strands may be threaded together and they may strong or fragile or malleable (Davies, 1990).

When considering what is 'resonant' in childhood (sound, texture, smell, feeling) it is important to consider where this leads; the events connected and their significance for the child. When asked to remember war, Claudia, who had no direct experience, talked of darkness, silences and depressed feelings in the family and uncertainty and fear at school. Her parents, German and Romanian, moved to a village in England after the Second World War. It was the early 1960s. She was 5, and working class:

> I don't think I was conscious of war per se . . . but I remember being at primary school . . . being conscious of being different . . . people calling me names and perhaps not understanding things very well . . . thinking that there was something not quite right . . . I've got memories of talking to two boys about something, and I think that I was talking to them in German rather than English, or using words that were German, and them looking at me, as if I was weird . . . that's a very powerful memory.
>
> I'm also aware of anxieties at home . . . there . . . was a group of people . . . that were all in POW camps over here . . . they formed this sort of social club . . . You know, with children, your conversations are like under the table . . . it's hidden by the table cloth.

These events were informed by threads of social memories from the past and different places, transmitted to her from her parents and school peers. Different social memories of war underpinned the playground encounter creating uncertainty. Where did Claudia fit in the Second World War games? Traumatic past events related to war, imprisonment and migration informed family life. The attempt to shelter the child from this had limited success, '[My parents would] be speaking German . . . I was probably quite fluent . . . could understand a lot . . . You'd know, if they definitely started talking German among themselves . . . you shouldn't be listening'. Claudia's parents' anxiety and lack of confidence arose from their lives having been disrupted by war and being involved on the German side. Although the brutalities of the Second World War were past (15 years), they shaped everyday events. Claudia was part of the 'post-war generation' but the residues of war were powerful and highly formative. Here everyday engagement involved weaving threads of memory from war. She learned not to ask her parents questions, 'I don't want to know what they think really', took pleasure in the lighter atmosphere in another child's house, ' . . . I used to just love going round there . . . it was quite different, slightly chaotic, but very friendly and open and warm, which my parents house wasn't really . . . ' Her mother would not let her join the Brownies (a quasi militaristic church based girl's organization):

> My mum absolutely forbad me to go, because she thought it would cost money, and was really uncertain about it. Now whether it was anything else, whether she was reflecting back on her own youth and the Hitler youth, I don't know.

Threads of social memory are passed through networks of kin, artefacts, institutions, ceremonies and other social arrangements. So there are strong effects over long periods of time. There are also powerful effects when children or their families move between places (see Chapter 3). A person's position in family, group, community and nation will influence how the past is remembered (Misztal, 2003). Social memories will vary in relation to these influences. Political and personal change, war and migration may all rupture social memory. Coser (1992) points out that at the end of the Cold War (1940s–1990s), Soviets had to, 'shed their own collective memory like a skin' (in Halbwachs, 1925/1992, p. 21). The migrant does not merely enter another country. She or he encounters a new field of social memories and leaves the old one behind, which may lead to a feeling of hollowness on transition (see Chapter 3), 'Arriving in a new place means joining up with, somehow linking into, the collection of interwoven stories of which that place is made' (Massey, 2005, p. 119). Such stories relate to environmental as well as social change. Apara and Richard migrated at a similar age (Richard was 3 and Apara, 5) but in different directions. They conveyed the physical as well as social experience of arrival. Apara came from Nigeria to a city in north-east England:

> it was real fog, and I'd never seen fog like that and it was . . . standing on one side of the road . . . you couldn't see the little green man when it was time to cross the road . . . it was only the sound.

Richard arrived in South Africa from a city in north-west England:

> It was boiling hot . . . standing in this place . . . the shimmering heat . . . when you look across .and the horizon is sort of moving and shimmering with the heat . . . and the cattle with the long horns.

The pathways these children followed after arrival were different. Richard gained some economic and social privileges as a White child under apartheid. Apara faced racial violence in the White working-class neighbourhood where her family moved. Both societies were informed by racial and class hierarchies that positioned children differently according to colour. Some of the wide social arrangements these children experienced may have appeared to them fixed and unchangeable, the processes giving rise to such arrangements are only visible to children when they are told about them.

The Implications of Silence in the Social Memory

Understandings from second wave feminism related to gender, sexuality and power occurred as outcomes of group remembering (Grewal et al., 1988; Haug, 1992). Feminist consciousness raising groups began to name experiences which had previously been unnamed because there had not been a language to articulate those experiences or relevant social frameworks to recall them. In the process of group remembering these personal memories became social memories and related social practices developed (e.g., refuges, incest survivor groups and changes in the law). For decades there had been social silence related to sexual abuse and domestic violence. The silence related to this abuse was not necessarily a forgetting, although, ' . . . forgetting can be just as convenient as remembering' (Atwood, 2005, p. 212) and 'the division of the past into "memorable" and "forgettable" is a social convention' (Misztal, 2003, p. 11). In relation to childhood therefore, it is also important to consider, ' . . . how we erase and re-write ourselves over time . . . ' (Atwood, 2005, pp. 214–15), 'The past no longer belongs only to those who lived it; the past belongs to those who claim it, and are willing to explore it, and to infuse it with meaning for those alive today' (ibid., p. 229).

Nawal El Saadawi in her autobiography discusses the extreme violence she experienced as a child, which was carried out by adults and condoned by other adults. She conveys her personal frustration with the frameworks and language available to her to give an account of her experiences:

> Perhaps the whole of my life has been this search for the real hidden behind what is false. When I was a child I could not tell from where came deception, from where came the lies. Was it my eyes that could not see, or was it the people around me describing things in a way which was unreal, including that self which was me? (2007, p. 53)

Aspects of children's experience become socially forgotten, remain unnamed and remain buried for years. These socially forgotten aspects of childhood therefore fail to inform current understanding of child-hood and practices in relation to children (until they are unearthed). Children's experience may remain silent, insufficiently informing social memory. First, since children have little power to be heard, important experiences remain unarticulated. Secondly, experiences may be trivial-ized in ways that suit particular interests. Thirdly, there may be insufficient social frameworks for them to understand and describe what is happen-ing (Halbwachs, 1925/1992). Fourthly, social arrangements may be taken for granted, a naturalized part of childhood (ideas about biological and therefore social differences between boys and girls are an example) (Haug, 1992). Some institutions and ideas become so imbued with authority that many aspects of the trajectories that gave rise to them remain invisible. These are 'fossils' in the social memory (Halbwachs, 1925/1992). Unless events are democratically interpreted in the interests of and involving chil-dren, they form part of the social landscape that is hard for children to navigate.

Julie and Lara were both attacked in their early teens. Julie was standing at a bus stop in the mid-1960s:

> I remember being flashed . . . in a bus queue . . . I was 14 or 15 maybe. Allowed to go to town on my own on the bus and I think I'd got to the

stage where every Saturday morning I'd go and do a little bit of wandering round town . . . I was stood . . . in the middle of a bus queue, and there's this guy with a Mac behind me, playing with himself when I turned round, and you just think you're imagining things, or you think it's your fault. It was probably years before I told anyone.

Lara remembers standing at a bus stop in the 1970s, aged 13:

I was just waiting for the bus . . . just stood, like everyone else, waiting for the bus, and National Front rally going on, at city square, as they did in those days, and a few of them must have come down . . . I was totally oblivious . . . the next minute, I'd been kicked and punched on the floor by these grown men . . . I was only a tiny, little, skinny girl . . . if it wasn't for the police, I don't know what would have happened. [The police took her to hospital; the men were arrested and prosecuted]

Both these children were targets because of their lack of physical and social power. The sexual attack remained unarticulated for many years. The racial attack had to be acted on because of Lara's physical injuries. Julie was very confused and had no framework to understand the sexual attack. She may have been relating it to her own sexuality, ' . . . or you think it's your fault'. Lara was more prepared but still deeply shocked, 'My mum used to always say to us, "Don't ever walk with your head down. Always walk with your head straight up, and look somebody straight in the eye. 'Cause the minute you drop your head, you're vulnerable."' Both attacks were minimized through the social frameworks available to understand and challenge events at the time. The terms 'flashed' and 'playing with himself' are social clichés that minimize the sexual abuse Julie experienced (Haug, 1992). The National Front 'rally' provides a context for the attack on Lara where members of this fascist group gathered and clearly incited each other to racial violence. The policemen supported Lara but the weekly 'rally' remained un-policed. The term 'rally' reduces social understanding of the purpose of this gathering. The fossils (Halbwachs, 1925/1992) in social memory at the time of both these attacks were the social hierarchies related to gender, 'race' and childhood. Both attacks aimed to keep particular children in their place. For Julie and Lara, their capacity to deal with these attacks emotionally related to the social frameworks available from the family and wider society. These enabled them to articulate the experience (or not) defend themselves and be socially protected. Silences and distortions that arise in the social memory prevented this.

There are aspects of experience that we might consider inanimate, static, merely contextual or timeless. From the perspective of daily life, memories of childhood reveal some fixed, immoveable features that may be barely recognized as influencing daily experience, although profoundly influential. This would include the 'long time' of environmental change (Adam, 1998), which from the point of view of daily life may not be observable, yet if intervention does not occur there could be catastrophic effects for children, for example, through the effects of global warming. From Haug's (1992) perspective, the 'timeless' in memory work would include 'sentimental clichés' (p. 64) or 'conformist abstractions (p. 23)' and 'norms of behaviour' (p. 23). She argues that these facets of everyday life lead to inarticulateness and silences around very important aspects of experience. An example might be when the gendering of the consumer market in toys is taken for granted as 'natural' and seen as a response to biological, rather than social, differences. Social memories of past practices are not just contained in social ideas and beliefs, but in the very fabric of routine social arrangements (Lefebvre, 1991). For those remembering childhood, therefore, aspects of experience may be considered to have little significance and be poorly remembered. The routine tasks of care are examples. These are hard to remember but highly significant for children's well-being (see Chapter 4). Hence, from all these perspectives on space, time and memory, we learn that parts of childhood may be remembered as 'fossilized relationships' (Haug, 1992, p. 26) and that there will be significant silences which are important to analyse:

> The frameworks of memory exist both within the passage of time and outside it . . . these frameworks are in part captivated by the course of time. They are like those wood floats that descend along a waterway so slowly that one can easily move from one to the other, but which nevertheless are not immobile and go forward. (Halbwachs, 1925/1992, p. 50)

Different people populate memories of childhood, including those that police, teach, sell goods and those who parent. Each role involves a tradition and social memories of what the role should involve. That events, people and things located in time are perceived as timeless is nowhere more apparent than in relation to religion. Of 'religious collective memory', Halbwachs argues:

> we can also say of every religion that it reproduces in more or less symbolic forms, the history of migrations and fusions of races and tribes, of

great events, wars, establishments, discoveries and reforms that we can find at the origin of societies that practice them. (ibid., p. 84)

When adults remember childhood, some of the things remembered they perceive as 'timeless'. This may include the houses they occupied, the roles of the adults that populated their worlds, the habits and conventions they encountered. However, being children, many of the conventions of social life are not yet learned. Children may be less habituated to cliché (Haug, 1992) but adults remembering childhood may remember through cliché, or research questions may be structured through cliché. The researcher and participant must give attention to these matters in order to gain clearer insight and reveal silences in the social memory related to children.

Carving out Space and Time

Two children's experiences are now discussed to demonstrate that despite the barriers and silences so far discussed, children are creatively engaged in carving out space and time for themselves. Rachel was of mixed work-ing- and middle-class heritage, growing up in the 1970s–80s. She gave two examples of negotiating clothing in relation to her emerging social iden-tity. First, aged 11:

> We had a leaving do at the end of primary school . . . all the parents got written to say we're having this disco . . . this is the dress code. Girls will be wearing skirts and dresses, boys must wear smart trousers . . . I just said, 'I'm not going.' The thought, by that point in my life, of having to wear a skirt or a dress, was so traumatic for me . . . My mother had battled with me prior to that, to send me to children's parties, in the party frocks, The last one of which I came home with it rolled up under my arm, I'd been up a tree the whole time . . . with frilly knickers! And all the lace was hanging off, and I was covered in dirt.

This was a time of transition, to mark the end of one stage of schooling where the clock times of school were relaxed and the school admitted pupils in the evening. The dress code regulated how these children would behave, even in this freed up space–time. 'Clichés' of respectability and gender came to these children from the wider society. They were expected to wear clothes that were 'fossils', representing ideas of what children should wear that were generated in past times (in another higher social class). Rachel fiercely rejected this apparel alongside the associated 'girly' identity. Later, her clothing choice was freer:

> I became a bit of a 'New Romantic' once that all kicked off, with all the scarves and the pirate look, that was an identity. That was quite fluid gender wise, that was something I became quite aware of, so you had Boy George and Alison Moyet and you didn't know whether they were male or female, and that was like, wow, that's really interesting, I like that.

The choice of gender fluidity in fashion reflected Rachel's sexuality at 15 (she was beginning to know she was lesbian) together with her thoughtfulness in dressing. To some beholders her sexuality would be blurred (to others not) and the fashion was captivating. She selected this clothing with reference to her own feelings, peers and cultural signals. Clothing previously prescribed in relation to class and gender respectability was now chosen in relation to a desire for gender and class fluidity. Clothing is intensely negotiated (both individually and in groups) because it involves a presentation of self to others. Her negotiation of clothing intersected with social ideas about respectability from interconnected systems related to gender, class, race and religion. The global popular culture industries presented some fashion options. Out of this, Rachel carved space and time for herself and avoided forms of social labelling (Lees, 1993)

Cathy talked of her engagement with religious practices as a child. She was of working-class heritage, growing up in the 1960s–70s. Her parents both worked long hours for low pay, hence she and her sister were relatively unsupervised and carved their own routes through the local community. This brought them in touch with different religious practices. This was a time of conflict in Northern Ireland and there were powerful associations in north-west England. Cathy's family was (technically) Protestant. She remembers being taken to Orange Lodge celebrations in the park:

> I do think of orange, this vivid colour, and I guess, in my memory, it was like a church fete, that kind of atmosphere . . . I remember the kind of bands. The music associated with it and how it was very enjoyable, it was a good sing. It was like, 'Oh the Orange Lodge are here'. I had no notion of, of course, of what it was about at that age.

She also regularly visited a convent because of her links with an Irish Catholic neighbour:

> She'd come over . . . after the Dublin Uprising [in 1917]. We became almost honorary Catholics . . . We lived in the terraced houses . . . but there was this huge convent at the top of the road . . . These little girls of 9 and 7, there'd be a secret knock and this door would open . . . these huge high walls . . . we would be stood there, and a nun, in full regalia would be stood, 'Ah sure . . . come on in girls', and you'd come in, . . . you'd see the door close behind you . . . it was always as if there was nothing outside, you'd come into this completely different world.

Then away from the convent and back in the terrace houses:

> Sometimes the nuns would come to Aunty [Mary's] house . . . and draw the curtains . . . then we'd be sat, in this little Séance environment . . . clearly frightened, 'What's going to happen now?' But actually, all it was about was that the nuns wanted to have a swill of sherry . . . they didn't want anyone to see!! So this image of the two or three nuns crowded in this tiny terrace house, knocking back the sherry.

Cathy sat outside the sectarianism of religious practices that surrounded her. Had she been living in Northern Ireland at this time, she would have been more locked into one religious community, her movement more limited. James talked about growing up there during the conflict, known through the euphemism the 'Troubles', in the 1960s–1970s:

> predominantly Protestant community, my family were very . . . religious. My dad was . . . also very pro the Orange Order . . . So I learned from that and was very pro that, and . . . very aware . . . there is no back out clause. You're in or you're not in and that's it.

As a children both Cathy and James were involved in religious practices grounded in times past, including forms of worship, celebration and the re-enactment of conquest. Their later adult knowledge about the conflict in Northern Ireland cast a shadow over the memories. These religious practices sustained conflict into the future, celebrating, for example, William of Orange's victory over the Catholic King James in 1690. The children carved space and time for themselves in different ways. For Cathy religious practices provided pleasure, mystery, fear, confusion and a sense of awe. For James, in addition, there was a deep sense of belonging that pulled him into conflict, 'Proud to be part of that . . . it's more than civic pride, it's more a national pride . . . Very, very proud of your identity and your culture and defended that, physically, on many occasions as well'.

Conclusion

Children's navigation of the social landscape involves a range of complex engagement and the carving of space–time for self. Neale and Flowerdew (2003, p. 192) argue that complex relations of time form the textures of children's everyday lives and 'the interplay of time and texture' is an important route of research analysis to give visibility to their engagement in adult worlds. Social arrangements (fashion or religion) are understood and shaped by the past, are lived in the present and the way they are lived has implications for the future. Children are involved in those processes. Their circumstances place them in a particular relation to these arrangements and they carve out space–time accordingly. According to Giddens, there are different planes of temporality: *duree* – daily experience; *dasein* – the life course and *longue duree* – the time of social institutions (1991). Children's everyday action involves the turns and twists of time including events directly experienced and the longer times (ibid.) of institutions and the environment. They are not separated from these processes but actively involved.

> On the one hand, children's participation in the production of social space always takes place through unequal relations of power, and therefore through power struggles. On the other hand, the ways in which spaces mould and produce children are both responsible for and beholden to their agency as human subjects. (Gallagher, 2006, p. 165)

This chapter has discussed the research approach in the research project that informs this book, a project concerned to illuminate children's experience of social change. It has been argued that research methodology that gives attention to children's part and place in the landscape, involving complex relations of space, time and social memory, uncovers important (sometimes distant) social influences, different routes and pathways, and different sorts of engagement related to their position and circumstances.

Children are directly involved in wide social experience. Social arrangements and events are constructed and interpreted through familial and collective memory. Giving attention to the temporal and spatial complexity of childhood reveals some less visible formative connections in their everyday lives. These include connections between past and present time, between children, families, communities and nations, and between different places. Children carve out space and time for themselves from this complex social landscape. The following chapters focus on different aspects of their engagement.

Chapter 3

Children and Migration

Introduction

When constructing the order of chapters in this book, it felt important to begin the discussion of children's experiences of social change by focusing on migration rather than 'home'. This is because 'home' is an outcome of movement and change in family life. One aim of this chapter is to reposition understanding of migration and childhood. All children's lives involve experiences related to migration. Family networks extend to different regions. Stories of relatives going to different places are passed down and inform the family archive (Halbwachs, 1925/1992). Children's lives are influenced by continuing communications with kin in other places, involving visits and the sending and receiving of gifts and financial support. The focus of migration studies in childhood tends to be on the lives of those coming to new places, considering their reception by the state, in communities and schools, the learning of new languages and the hostility and welcome they might face (Cunningham and Tomlinson, 2005). Migration is not just a subject about groups of children who have recently arrived in a new place, perhaps considered 'other' to those born there. Migration touches the lives of all children, although experienced differently. All the children in the research experienced the impact of migration, some directly, some indirectly; some related to international and some, to internal movements of people. They experienced encounters with new people and different cultural arrangements. Their family histories involved complex connections across countries and continents, for example, Apara's English mother married a Nigerian. Apara was born in Nigeria and moved back to England when 5, but this was not the only migration shaping her life:

We weren't the first people in our family to migrate . . . my grandfather's grandmother had migrated from Ireland, after the potato famine . . . and my grandmother, her father was Scottish. So we had this idea we were this mix and we had this heritage.

This chapter is in four parts. It first, considers the different migrations that influenced children's lives including whether these directly involved the children themselves, their parents, or more distant relatives. Some of the 'pull and push' factors are discussed including the need for employment, the flight from persecution and war and some of the economic exploitation involved. The second aspect the chapter considers is international journeys and arrivals. Here the focus is on four children who themselves went on long journeys to settle in new countries. This part also considers some of the bonds built with other newcomers. The third aspect considered is the importance of continuing ties with other places. These ties between children and different countries and regions could be economic or social and included visits and stories told down the generations. Finally, responses to incomers are considered including the welcome and hostility afforded to new arrivals and to those considered 'outsiders'. It is through consideration of all these dimensions that the ways in which migration touches all children's lives becomes more visible.

Different Migrations and Childhood

Several migrations influenced the lives of children in the research. These included: the movement of people from the former British colonies to the United Kingdom from the 1950s to the 1970s; the movement of people from southern to northern Europe in the post-Second World War period; migration between the 'New World' and 'Old World' which continued through the twentieth century but began much earlier; migration of refugees and others related to the Second World War as well as more local regional migration, for example, between Scotland, Wales, Ireland and England, between the countries of the Caribbean and from rural to urban areas in general (Hayter, 2000).

The social forces underpinning migration are sometimes known as the 'pull and push' factors. These influences are complex. Economic migration, for example, involves the needs of those moving for better paying employment and the need of the destination for a workforce. Migration may also relate to war and persecution. Such influences may intertwine (ibid.). Workers from the former British Empire were recruited and came to the United Kingdom in the 1950s and 1960s. London Transport recruited people from Trinidad and Jamaica; Woolf's rubber factory in Southall recruited in the Punjab and the northern textile industries recruited in India and Pakistan (ibid.). Rehana and Paulina came to England as children from Pakistan and St Kitts respectively, as part of this movement. Lara and Madhi, although born in England, had parents who were also part of this and slightly later movements. Lara's father moved from St Lucia, and her mother came with her mother as a child from Italy. As a result, Lara, who was English born, experienced strong ties to Italy throughout her childhood, as well as links to the Caribbean. Madhi's parents moved from Kenya:

> I remember my dad said to me once that they couldn't make ends meet and 'cause his sister was living in [England], she'd said to him, 'Come over here', because with his qualifications, he could get a job . . . Within a week of moving to England, he did get a job, and he's done that job for his entire life, until he retired. (Madhi)

The 'push' factors in the case of Madhi's family, was the growing discrimination they faced in Kenya at the time, which in turn related to the colonial era and the ways that workers from the Asian subcontinent were positioned in some African countries, including Kenya and Uganda. As a consequence of these patterns of migration in her family, Madhi had ties to India, Kenya and other countries in Africa where family had settled. Her education and beliefs were deeply informed by these connections.

The migration of people from Europe to the Americas, Australia and other parts of the world from the eighteenth century onwards, continued through the twentieth century (Hayter, 2000). This informed the experiences of children in the research, particularly in the post-Second World War period, when, for example, White workers were actively recruited from the United Kingdom to South Africa and Australia (ibid.). In South Africa, there was recruitment of a skilled White British workforce rather than the employment of the black indigenous majority population whose skills were ignored, denied the vote and racially segregated:

> My mum and dad met on a huge sprawling housing estate in [England] . . . and had us three children, very young and . . . got in a financial mess . . . My dad was a welder . . . saw this advert, for an opportunity to go to South Africa, where they'd just found oil in the middle of the desert. Part of the deal, they would pay passage and board for so long, and basically because they were in a mess here and getting things repossessed, they decided to make a clean break. (Richard)

Such migration meant upward social mobility for Richard and his family, but was also part of a process that entrenched the Black population in poverty and away from centres of power and influence.

The impact of immigration on the country of arrival varies. The indigenous population may gain, as was the case with immigration from the former colonies to Western Europe in the latter part of the twentieth century (Castles and Kosack, 1973), or may lose, as was the case in South Africa. Migration influences the economic and social well-being of whole classes of people and their children. White working-class families in South Africa experienced economic progress where Black families and children became more marginalized and excluded. In the United Kingdom, migrants from the former colonies benefited the indigenous population, stimulating economic growth and filling gaps in the labour market (Harris, 2000). However they and their descendents came to be viewed as expendable when their labour was no longer required (Solomos et al., 1982).

The British state began to maintain connections with white émigrés who travelled to places like Canada, Australia and South Africa, through building concepts of 'patriality' into British citizenship and nationality laws (Hayter, 2000). This protected their rights of return and sustained the family ties of these groups of principally White migrants. This meant that Richard and his family were able to return to England more easily when the conflict related to apartheid grew in the 1970s. Richard was by then 16 and in danger of being forced into the South African army.

More distantly, movement to the 'New World' in earlier times also influenced children in the research, 'My grandfather's parents, emigrated to Canada, in the 1920s' (Rachel). 'My paternal grandfather, emigrated to Canada' (Pamela). As children they were told about these distant places and people. There were continuing ties with descendents of earlier migrants. The children developed understanding of different regions from family stories and continuing communications with kin:

> Very aware of connections to the family, distant relatives in . . . the usual venues for Irish immigrants . . . Canada, Australia, and the States . . . One Uncle, he went off to . . . Australia, and became . . . a bit of a real sort of macho, pioneering spirit. (James)

These earlier migrations were also shaped by unemployment and conflict. Famine and oppression in Ireland and Scotland led many to emigrate. But for those who talked about these connections, the emphasis was on the individual courage of particular ancestors and their overcoming of hardship, as narrated in the familial archive (see also the section under Continuing Ties, below).

Hence, migration was a formative influence for many of the children in the research and touched their everyday lives in different ways, whether

Children and Migration

45

they had migrated themselves or not. Lara learned, for example, about the vulnerability and risk associated with arrival in a new place from her mother's accounts of experience:

> [Mum] was born Italian and my father's St Lucian . . . obviously a mixed race couple in the 1960s didn't go down very well . . . My mum had her first child when she was 16, to an unknown father . . . She was quite a vulnerable young lady, and obviously very naïve as well, so she was taken advantage of. (Lara)

Regional migration was also significant. The processes that shape internal migration within the United Kingdom between the countries of Wales, Northern Ireland, Scotland and England are not dissimilar to those shaping wider international migration. They relate to persecution, the need for work, marriage and the interplay of other influences. They involved children in, visits to and ties with geographically closer places. Sometimes the original migration was many years before they were born, sometimes more recent, nevertheless, ongoing ties informed their everyday experiences:

> My mother's mother died in childbirth and she was a Jones, so her father must have been from Wales . . . My mother must have come to live in the Manchester/Salford area with her grandparents. (Julie)

> My mother moving from Scotland to England . . . after she was married . . . then my mother's brothers inherited the farm and they then sold the original farm. (Martin)

Children in the research were also deeply affected by migration consequent on the dislocations of war and conflict, even when these were before they were born. Claudia's and Sylvia's families were exiles and refugees from the Second World War and their everyday childhood was informed by these events long after that war had finished (see Chapter 8). Families who lived in the United Kingdom during that war, experienced the Blitz and the movement of city children to safer areas. The abuse her father experienced at this time when he and his sister moved to the countryside without their parents shocked Rachel when she found out about it:

> Child abuse . . . He had a younger sister that he really had to look after, 'cause she'd be crying herself to sleep at night. He'd have to be the brave boy . . . seven or eight. They had to get taken away from some people,' cause they weren't being fed properly.

In addition to migration informing their own family movement and history, all the children encountered 'newcomers' in their communities of residence. All learned from their family and the wider society what the appropriate judgment of 'foreigners' and 'outsiders' should be.

International Journeys and Arrivals

This section focuses on those children with direct experience of moving to a new country. The focus is on the experiences of Rehana, who moved from Pakistan to England when 11, Apara, who moved from Nigeria to England, when 5, Paulina, who moved from St Kitts to England when 5, and Richard, who moved from England to South Africa when 3. Both Paulina's and Rehana's families came to England in 'bits and pieces', involving separation from close family members as children:

> My dad came over first. So that's what I remember, losing my dad.
>
> So it seemed like he was a long time away, but it was only about a year it was, before we were then brought to England. (Paulina)
>
> My dad brought us in bits and pieces . . . my eldest brother had come the earliest . . . with my dad, and then my mum and two youngest brothers followed a few months after . . . and then one of my middle brothers. We were left behind . . . I was the last one to come over. (Rehana)

The stages of journeying and arrival were vividly recollected by Rehana (she was older than the others when she moved):

> I remember sitting on this horse cart and then onto the rickshaw and then sitting on a taxi and going onto the airport in another town, and getting on the plane with my dad . . . It was just a very strange experience.

Even though Apara was much younger when she left Nigeria, she remembered, 'The planes . . . 'cause it was a very long journey . . . it was from Lagos to Heathrow, and then another plane up to [the north of England]'. Both remembered turning points on the journey, intense emotions and self-awareness that they were travellers:

> In my excitement, or in my bewilderness, I lost the tickets, the next leg of the journey tickets . . . My dad had given them to me, to put them in my little bag. (Rehana)

We had to take a train, and it was me and my mother and brother, huddled together on the platform. (Apara)

Threads of collective memory may be jeopardized through migration as children lose touch with particular people, communities and ways of living (Coser, 1992 in Halbwachs, 1925/992). Rehana had lived in Pakistan in quite a privileged household as a child. It was the 1960s and her father was on the plane with her. Many parties had been held in Pakistan to mark her leaving. She sat on the plane:

I felt very hollow inside as if something had been removed from my guts. I had that feeling of emptiness, something hollow in me, as if one chapter of my life, I'm leaving behind. So many happy, sad memories . . . when would I be able to go back and see them and what would it be like? It's a very strange feeling, thinking that . . . I was very quiet . . . I kept going to the aeroplane toilet and reading my friends' letters, saying all nice things to me, 'Don't forget us', 'Write to us' . . . little poems in them for me . . . it was a night flight so the plane was dark . . . just reading all these letters to keep myself moved, to keep as if I was still in touch, not letting go of the memories.

Rehana attempted to anchor memories of the people she was leaving behind. Although looking forward to joining her siblings, she feared a trailing away of social memories of friends and community in another place and time.

The arrival in a new place involved a new series of encounters that needed to be assimilated (Massey, 2005). There was a 'strangeness on arrival', which was conveyed by both Rehana and Richard:

It was like the evening time . . . it got really dark on the motorway, and I just still remember the feeling . . . . very mysterious . . . These little 'cats eyes' in the road . . . and there's a bit of the motorway where there's some lights, so you could see the lights, and every time, even after all those years, every time I drive through that bit, I get the same feelings . . . I still get that feeling of strangeness on arrival. (Rehana)

arriving at Capetown and there was a statue . . . I was looking up . . . I remember that clearly with the mountain . . . in the background. (Richard)

Arrival was strong multi-sensory experience of difference (see Chapter 2). Compared with Pakistan, England was, 'Very cold and it was very dull. . . . very misty . . . really depressing . . . Having come from such a bright, colourful place' (Rehana). As well as the outside space, the houses starkly contrasted to the children's former homes. The new houses related to patterns of living that had evolved over generations in very different climates and physical environments: 'It felt like "I'm walking into nothingness again!" This small closed up house with dim lights . . . it just felt really, really strange. It's narrow corridor and then going into the back room . . . all very strange' (Rehana). The different environment also involved different patterns of agriculture and food production and therefore different food:

> I remember my grandmother giving me toast and me sucking the butter off and asking for more butter, 'cause I just thought it was a fantastically wonderful taste, and doing it about twice before she said, 'No, you actually have to eat the bread!' (Apara)

Migrant children needed to understand the changes in relation to past places and experiences. Halbwachs (1925/1992) argues that we understand our selves in relation to a past that has been constructed by others. Misztal (2003, citing Schwartz, 2000) refers to Goffman's work on 'Keying'. Activities are understood in relation to one event through comparison. Apara's memories of the new experiences on arrival in England were woven and starkly juxtaposed with memories of Nigeria:

> I was taken into reception class [in England] . . . I had been going to school in Nigeria . . . a private school . . . state of the art and I loved my school . . . we had things like Chocolate Milk and we had this fantastic playground in the compound, including this fantastic house, that was built to child size, that you could go in and play . . . I don't remember focusing or being aware of the colour of the children [in England]. They were all white . . . when I was in living in Nigeria I did have lots of friends that were black but I had friends that were white, that were like me, mixed race . . . I asked to go to the toilet [in England] . . . We walked across the playground, which was cold and windy, and we went to this horrible looking shed really . . . It was the same at my grandparents' house, cause I mean I'd come from proper plumbing and all the rest of it in Nigeria, and my grandmother and grandfather still had an outside toilet . . . I don't remember being aware of it straight away, but I know that quite soon I became aware that my colour was an issue for lots of the children and some of the adults.

Comparison of schools, food, play, plumbing and attitudes to skin colour, informed these clustered memories. When considering the power of social memory, Halbwachs (1925/1992) discusses the ways that social movement from one group to another involves the interplay of modes of thinking and behaviour. The process of migration involved some forgetting and some selective remembering in order to draw on the past to understand the present. The transition for children may have enabled some critical distance to develop in relation to the everyday arrangements they encountered. When coupled with a hostile response from the community where they arrived, this critical distance was vital for survival.

Journeys involved expectations. These varied according to destination – the images and traditions originating from the centre of the former British Empire were impressive for children unless they were presented with a counter narrative (Hobsbawm, 1983). For example, Rehana and Paulina remembered being very excited about going to England:

> because we used to study English . . . Big Ben and Madame Tussauds . . . Houses of Parliament and London Bridge. We had images of all those in our books . . . People thought I was very privileged. (Rehana)

> some of the stories . . . 'Your dad has gone to prepare, 'cause there's gold on the streets'. (Paulina)

Such expectations were disappointed, 'When we came, it was snowing, and picking up snow and thinking it was gold, and when it was melting and disappearing in my hand, crying about it' (Paulina). With a growing hostile climate related to Black immigration in the United Kingdom from the 1960s onwards, fuelled by politicians and the media (Solomos et al., 1982) and targeted at anyone who appeared darker skinned, some of the children and their families experienced racial attacks and abuse:

> So when I was born, my mum used to have lots of problems in the street . . . with racism. People used to call her, you know, she was dirty 'cause she had a black child . . . 'cause she was Italian, they used to be really insulting as well. We used to get spit on . . . they used to set things alight through the letterbox. It used to be dreadful. (Lara)

In the late 1950s, Claudia also faced discrimination (see Chapter 2). Although light skinned, her mother tongue was German and she lived in England. Her parents also felt isolated:

> I don't think my parents coped with it terribly well . . . were very reserved. Didn't want to . . . put their heads above the parapet . . . so things that

other people took for granted . . . accepted in the culture . . . they'd be so uncertain, unconfident about, that they wouldn't want to have anything to do with.

Claudia's parents spent time with others who had been in prisoner of war camps. Even before the endemic racism in England of the late 1960s and 1970s, just being different could generate conflict in childhood.

Immigrant children and the children of immigrants developed a heightened awareness of the potential for everyday conflict. There was a need to be wary. This wariness was encouraged in the family and protective strategies developed where there was shared understanding, ' . . . having to learn a different way of being and to be very wary about things like giving people eye contact, it didn't seem to take much' (Apara).

Chomsky (1994, cited in Joly, 1996) argues that people are granted entry to a nation on the basis of what narrow national interest they serve. Certain factors influence policy and in turn the reception migrants (and their children and grandchildren) experience. Periodically relations with particular groups are more hostile and this contributes to their persecution, isolation and fear. It involves the need to socially withdraw and build links with others who share memories and experiences, ' . . . what is special about place is precisely that thrown togetherness, the unavoidable challenge of negotiating a here-and-now' (Massey, 2005, p. 140).

Bonds grew among newcomers. Some were a continuation of bonds that already existed in communities of origin, some were new. Links and communications between new-comers from similar places or with similar experiences developed. For example, Paulina's and Madhi's families used their homes to provide lodgings for people from their former places of origin in the Caribbean and India respectively:

Dad used to take in lodgers, mainly people who had come from the Caribbean . . . as a way of surviving . . . most of them really friendly . . . mostly black people . . . She was like a Latin-American . . . I remember her really, because she was so tiny and she wore really nice, even from then, I loved clothes, I must have loved clothes, 'cause I remember her, for her clothes. She was a lovely woman as well. (Paulina)

When we were all little kids, our parents owned the house, and there were different people living in the house as well, so it was my mum and dad downstairs, then somebody that they knew from the village at home lived in one of the rooms, and then another family had two other rooms at the top . . . that was just how it was. (Madhi)

For both Paulina and Madhi, everyday childhood at these times involved close ties with non-kin and continuously changing living arrangements in the home, as people came and went. This included significant and memorable encounters with particular residents:

> He . . . was like a brother to my father . . . in India, where my grandparents had their house . . . There were a family next door and he was their youngest son . . . My dad did treat him like a little brother . . . I don't think he had a lot of family, so he stayed with us. (Madhi)

These new social connections may have strengthened their ability to manage transition in difficult new environments. This process is encapsulated by Henderson et al.:

> the cosmopolitan is distinguished by competence, 'Possessing both a generalized and specialized ability to makes one's way in a different place via listening, looking, intuiting, reflecting'; displaying a willingness to engage in difference, 'yet always knowing where the exit is in the alien culture'. (2007, p. 102, quoting Hannerz, 1996)

Continuing Ties to Other Places

As argued earlier in this chapter, the everyday life of children in the research was touched by migration, whether or not they were migrants themselves. Former family migration gave Lara strong ties to Italy and some of the best experiences of her childhood during regular and lengthy stays with extended family, including lots of cousins:

> Oh, it was wonderful . . . you used to hear them in the streets, selling figs and sweet corn . . . shouting from six in the morning, and our flat was above . . . You'd drop the basket down, with the money, tell her how much you wanted, and she used to pop it in the basket, put your change in, and you used to pull the basket back up again. So that was wonderful, and it used to thunder every night, every single night there was a massive thunder and we used to like to lie on the balcony and watch the rain. (Lara)

Martin, whose parents had moved from Scotland to England, also happily spent every summer in Scotland with relatives and developed strong ties. Claudia travelled to Germany to visit her extended family every 3 years.

These continuing ties resulting from past familial migrations were formative experiences, including the excitement of travel and new encounters:

> Leaving the house, getting the train to London, then the train from
> London to Harwich . . . picking up the boat, the ferry that went across . . .
> that was a six hour trip . . . A bad storm one year . . . people were being
> sick and I wrote an essay about it, for which I got the highest mark in
> the class! . . . Then getting the train . . . through Holland, through
> Germany . . . following the Rhine. . . . going over the Loralie [a rock jut-
> ting into the River Rhine] . . . which is where there's supposed to be
> spirits that drown sailors in the river. (Claudia)

Further back in time, Tessa's maternal grandfather had emigrated from
Wales to England and Tessa visited Wales as a child, 'He was very proud
of being Welsh . . . there was a male voice choir, and going back to Wales
to meet everybody . . . I couldn't speak Welsh and they had such different
accents'. Visits such as this were accompanied by storytelling and the sharing of familial memory, including cultural and political perspectives and
related values. The social memory of the place being visited was shared
with the child and provided a new framework for understanding. Migration
generated stories of other places that were shared with children even when
they were not on the journey themselves. Familial stories of departures,
arrivals and change informed childhood as vividly as stories read in books,
for example, this story about her grandmother's journey from Canada
alone was very significant for Rachel:

> My grandmother hated it so much, 'cause they were literally on the
> plains, in the middle of nowhere. She could not bear it . . . her mother in
> law was a tyrant by the sounds of it . . . So she somehow managed to earn
> enough money to earn her passage back . . . In the 1920s, managed to get
> herself across Canada, and then get on a ship and sail back . . . on
> her own.

Such stories from the past were reconstructed by families in particular ways
with particular emphasis related to overcoming adversity. It was not just
knowledge that was transmitted and adapted in these ways, but a particular
education about familial resilience and the potential of the child.

There were also significant continuing ties related to material and cultural resources and tools. The processes of migration generated these

resources for families and communities through the giving and receiving of gifts and remittances:

> My Aunty . . . went to America . . . my memories were of getting exotic Californian books and things sent . . . and my mother's kind of disdain for that, cause it was foreign. (George)

> Grandfather had a business in East Africa . . . different quarries . . . it was actually quite important for the development of our little village at home [in India] because he used to bring the building stuff back to the village, so then it was a time when the village was expanding so people had the material to expand. (Madhi)

The significance of this cannot be underestimated. Far more is sent in remittances from migrant workers back to their countries of origin than is received by way of international aid (Hayter, 2000).

Encounters with Incomers

Migration shaped everyday childhood in complex and multifaceted ways. As well as their own experiences of migration, many experienced encounters with newcomers where they lived, and all became very aware of social discourses related to 'outsiders'. For some children rational explanations were lacking, and hostility was nurtured. The children in the research drew on different points of reference at different times and at different ages related to the wider social and political context (and the spaces around them). Stories such as the *Arabian Nights* may have deepened the fascination and attraction to darker skin colour in some White children in England:

> I think, my second year of infant school . . . he was my first encounter with somebody whose skin colour was not the same as my own, and I never spoke to him, but I remember being fascinated by him and wanting to go and talk to him but not having the courage. (George)

> I always remember her name [Saima] . . . Being entranced by these children, just thinking how . . . how delightful they were and how beautiful they were to look at. Got really vivid images of picking up these young kids, just as if they were dolls. (Cathy)

As they became older, children became aware that some children not only looked different but were socially positioned differently, 'I remember the Asian girls in particular . . . being in the C and D groups [in school]' (Julie).

Children's responses to this growing awareness varied in relation to the wider social discourses about immigration, 'foreigners', social respectability, nation and class. For some children, social inequalities were taken for granted; unquestioned fossils in the landscape (see Chapter 2). Sometimes children were taught to judge these differences harshly and justify them:

> [My mum] . . . told me about her time in the war, that she never went to a dance with an American air force man, 'cause they were considered to be a 'bit low'. It was always English boys, and then, later on, I discovered that my auntie, from my dad's side, had married an American Air Force man and gone to live in California. (George)

Ideas about gender, class, 'race' and nation combined here in the maternal effort to maintain social respectability. Sometimes children began to question the fairness of the inequalities in front of them. This related to their political education. In the 1960s and 1970s, the social construction of Black young people as 'outsiders' took hold (Solomos et al., 1982):

> When I was growing up there were newspaper stories on the threat of the Black community in the neighborhood; that they were the ones doing the crime and likely to get in trouble, and taking drugs. At the time . . . the Asian community weren't seen to be problematic, were seen to be quite hardworking, seemed to be quite valued. (Madhi)
>
> We had an Asian boy in my primary class and I remember . . . [the teacher] was obviously very intrigued because . . . to have an Asian face in an all white school, and she said, 'Gosh, where are you from?' and he said, 'London'. (Rachel)

Some children feared conflict they witnessed or heard about and began to associate particular groups of people with particular threats:

> There was a family who came from Northern Ireland . . . somebody they knew had been killed in Northern Ireland and they had children. But I do get a sense of seriousness. It was a very different kind of feeling around them. (Cathy)

Children who were already vulnerable to or subject to racism themselves might try to distance themselves from others in a similar situation in order to be safe and accepted by their peers (Candappa and Egharevba, 2002), 'My cousins started treating her as something inferior . . . "You were born in Africa" . . . [She] used to get quite upset' (Madhi).

Through emotion and reason, children compared and connected events, stories and explanations, weaving threads of influences from past and present times to imagine a better future (Adam, 2006). Martin grew up resisting hostility to immigrants from the former Empire:

> [Father] trying to . . . give us the experience of different cultures . . . we had some people from Africa come to the house . . . When [racism] really became apparent was around the late 1960s, Enoch Powell . . . [I went to] a very white middle class school . . . it was a very Conservative environment and I was probably the one who didn't take that stand . . . I remember certainly having an argument with a couple that . . . lived down the road about immigration . . . the fact that they thought 'They should be sent back to where they'd come from'. (Martin)

The political hostility to immigrants (and their children) again intensified under the New Conservative Government in England (1979–1997) and, at this stage, the doors nearly closed to migration for settlement from the Commonwealth countries. This period was nearly coterminous with Madhi's childhood (the youngest participant) and her response is discussed in more detail in Chapter 7.

Conclusion

This chapter has examined how migration influenced all the children's lives through the family archives and continuing ties. Many of the children in this research experienced complex geographical connections through past migrations (of their parents and grandparents, as well as themselves). There were particular challenges for children with direct experiences of migration. Some children, such as Richard, became more privileged in the place of arrival than others, such as Apara. Community links were significant in connecting past and present and building survival strategies as Paulina's and Madhi's experiences of their homes providing lodgings to others, demonstrate. Ideas about destinations were constructed and distorted in particular interests, for example, the ideas about Great Britain shared in the former colonies perpetuated myths of grandeur and privilege that led to disappointment for Paulina and Rehana.

Children were engaged in carving out space and time for themselves from the complex space–time relations of migration. Migrations and the mixing of different people were a vivid part of their experience. As well as their own personal movements as migrants, they experienced extended familial ties across regions and continents relating to past movement. Lara, Madhi and Claudia, all born in England, spent very significant times overseas as a result of migration ties. Martin spent every holiday in Scotland, the country of his parents' heritage. In these journeys and visits different and familiar people were encountered and new stories shared. This provided a rich tapestry. Paulina shared these images and questions from her early childhood, aged at most 5, in St Kitts:

> When I was in the Caribbean . . . the different colours . . . seeing Asian people and talking to my mum about it . . . She would tell us about the slave trade and then after the slave trade, . . . how people from different parts of Asia was brought to work, and with them, they brought their different culture and food . . . My early remembrance, was seeing people that were different, as I recall, 'Coolies' and all sorts of names that you wouldn't repeat now, but, asking 'Why?' And obviously white people, so asking questions, 'cause apparently that's what I was like . . . so my mum used to tell me. (Paulina)

Migration is part of the landscape of childhood. It is not only the concern of those newly arriving, although their concerns must be a priority. The idea that migration is 'pioneering' is passed down in family and community memories (see James and Rachel above) but this contrasts starkly with some of the social attitudes to 'incomers' and their children. Different migrations inform children's lives differently, close up and at a distance in time and space. Nevertheless migration is formative and significant for all children in complex ways; whether they are consciously aware of this or not.

At the time of writing the social and political attitude to newcomers are hostile in England. Those entering the country are often presented as a burden on the economy when, in reality, immigration has greatly benefited the economy (Harris, 2000). The costs of the schooling, health care and so forth of those emigrating are borne by the country they leave. The benefits are gained by the countries of destination (ibid) hence the costs of childhood are a central part of a quite mercenary equation as to whether a government encourages or deters migrant workers and whether they are allowed to bring their own children with them or not. This is one of the key areas of silence about migration and childhood in the social memory.

In the United Kingdom children and their families entering have been detained rather than welcomed (Refugee Council, 2010) and politicians continually exploit these divisions. It is essential that social understanding of migration is broadened from the focus on those entering. Clearly their well-being must be ensured. However, each child, needs to know their own complex migration heritage and the journeys through the generations that have brought them to their particular homes. The continued geographic connections that shape all childhoods need to be understood in their migration context. This should build more resilience and tolerance.

Chapter 4

Children and Home

Introduction

The last chapter considered the wide geographical connections that inform childhood. This chapter focuses on the micro-practices of home. Different areas of home life are discussed, for example, bathing, eating and sleeping. The focus is on routine domestic practices and uses of space. The chapter also includes some discussion of the ways domestic routines change and are disrupted and the ways domesticity is first experienced by children in institutions such as pre-school, school and hospital. This chapter addresses the intimate sphere of childhood and is positioned early in the book as it helps to further introduce the children in the research. As the research is concerned with wider social influences on childhood, home is discussed in relation to wider social space and time; considering the ways in which it provides shelter from the unpredictable environment and is informed by wider social expectations of family life. The social role of the family is an important element in the chapter although familial memory and experience is a theme throughout the book. Families are involved in the development, education and socialization of children (Hill and Tisdall, 1997). They sustain, reflect, challenge and seek to overcome inequalities.

Shifting ideas about social respectability, cleanliness, hygiene and 'good' parenting shape home life. Kenway and Bullen (2001) discuss, for example, the medicalization of infancy in the twentieth century and the way that mothers were constructed as ' . . . the front-line defence against germs' (p. 40, quoting Cunningham, 1995). Brannen explores the new 'liberality' related to childhood in the latter part of the twentieth century including the focus on the development needs of children and their rights. Parents began to see themselves as 'actively involved in creating their children's childhoods' (2004, p. 420).

Different forms of home and domestic practices have emerged over time and space. Williams (1987) explores historical changes in the social construction of home. The withdrawal of a lot of production from the home in industrialized areas was linked with the development of rituals of correct behaviour and sexuality within the home and shifting ideas about ownership, privacy and rights of control. Families became re-conceptualized as sites of consumption rather than production, and home was romanticized as a private, intimate place, primarily concerned with the care of children. Divisions within families were overlooked (Delphy, 1995; Pahl, 1995). Although considered a private sphere, public temporal practices regulate home time (Whannel, 1998). Feminists have identified the way ideas about 'public' and 'private' spheres of influence have involved the social subjugation of women (Gamarnikow et al., 1983). Childhood researchers also challenge 'what is proper to the private domain' in relation to childhood (Mayall, 2006, p. 207). Disability activists and feminist researchers have challenged normative assumptions about 'care' in the home. This concept has complex meanings. It may be associated with providing an income for the family, with the daily practice of 'looking after' and with feelings of love (Land, 1991; Dalley, 1996). It may also involve patronising attitudes, abuse and enforced dependency (Morris, 1991; Bornat and Johnson, 1997; Davis, 2004). Home based work and the tasks of child care are imbued with shifting ideas about appropriate femininity, masculinity and parenting in relation to time and place.

The chapter is in four parts. First, some of the children's homes are introduced, considering aspects of their geographic and social mobility and the wider environment. Secondly, several routine domestic practices are discussed, with reference to wider ideas of the time and material resources. Thirdly, some of the disruptions of home life are considered (such as children's illness) as these aspects were more vividly remembered and may deepen understanding of children's perspectives. Fourthly, social silences are discussed, considering, for example, some of the distance and tension between children and adults in the home.

The Children's Homes

Details of where research participants lived are included in the children's cameos (see Chapter 1). They experienced a wide variety of different housing in different locations, mostly in the England but also elsewhere. These included flats in high-rise blocks, small terraced houses with yards, lodging houses, semi-detached and detached houses, farm cottages, a flat above a shop, a house on stilts, a bungalow, a flat roofed courtyard house and a 'back to back' terraced house. Some properties were owned by the family, some rented and one was bought on rental purchase. One child, Martin, attended boarding school. Julie and Pamela spent some time in hospital. The domestic routines related to home were relevant to their experiences there.

When asked to remember where they lived as children, participants compared different settings. Rehana compared her home in Pakistan, with her new home in England, '[In Pakistan] we had a courtyard in the middle and rooms around it . . . and a big veranda. [In England] . . . very small, very closed in, very next to each other'. Similarly, Apara compared, ' . . . this quite privileged house in . . . Nigeria with indoor plumbing and hot and cold and servants, to a tiny upstairs flat in [north-east England], with an outdoor toilet and no bath'.

Memories of home could not be separated from memories of the quality of life there. Moving homes might involve a better quality of life for children but sometimes a dashing of expectations. It related to critical events and turning points such as bereavement, unemployment, inheritance, separation and opportunities for better paid work. Remembering home in childhood involved focusing on these events as well as the places they were associated with. Moving to a new home or visiting other people's homes, cast new light on everyday experiences, for example, George said, in relation to the home his mother was paid to clean, 'We only ever had broken biscuits from Woolies . . . but Mrs Smith had biscuits, like Penguin biscuits and I used to get one with milky coffee'. He mapped the geography of social class and home in the neighbourhood where he grew up, in a small through-terraced house with yard in a city in north-west England:

> There was [Castle] Road, which is all back to backs, then behind them, there was an entry, and there was more back to backs and then there was just streets of back to backs. On the other side, you had the beginnings of semi-detached world. So our street was almost, almost heading towards semi-detached world where they had gardens, so yes, there were people there who were seen to be posh. (George)

When she went to grammar school, Cathy, who lived in a similar house to George, became more aware of the relationship between home and her social class position through comparison with the home of a school friend:

> That was the occasion that I really got a sense that not everyone lived in a terraced house with a back yard; the rooms being huge. I think it was the space that was the thing that struck me . . . the kitchen the size of our

whole house really . . . being shocked by it . . . Going to that school, did move us into a different world.

Moving homes reflected social as well as geographic mobility. For Claudia, the physical quality of home improved over time. She moved from a home with an outside toilet to a home with a bathroom and inside toilet. For Paulina, moving from a house raised on stilts with a separate kitchen in St Kitts, her new home, in England felt like a come down:

> We used to have to go down three flights [of stairs] . . . we all used to live in one room in the attic . . . we had to eat there . . . sleep, everything was in that room. There was no alternative.

The Routine Domestic Practices of Home and Uses of Space

Domestic practices varied in relation to social ideas of the time which in turn related to times further past. They varied in relation to the roles of parents and carers, dominant ideas about childhood and divisions of domestic and paid labour. Areas of daily life were associated with different parts of home. Tessa spoke of the domestic weekly routine she experienced at her grandparents' home, where she spent a lot of time. This routine had evolved from a time before she was born and continued in her childhood. It was from a time when there were less domestic appliances and more domestic labour: 'We did set things through the week, so if it was Tuesday, it was washing day and Wednesday it was baking day and Thursday we went shopping . . . It wasn't really the house as such, it was the relations'.

The layout of domestic space in the home also provided a template for how home life should be lived, including where family members should sleep, eat and bathe (Foucault, 1980a). For the purposes of hospitality and to present home in an acceptable light to the outside world, parts of some homes were kept 'best' for visitors (Hirschon, 1993). These parts then became the public face of home; as were the grand reception areas of the large houses of the wealthy in previous times:

> The other room, especially in every black family, was your best room. . . . It was only visitors that went in there. Your best furniture and my responsibility to clean it . . . but certainly wasn't to go in it. (Paulina)

The front room was always a bit damp and was only used when posh people came, or people who were deemed to be of a different social standing. (George)

Some parts of home were occupied more by those who looked after the children, mainly, but not only, women. Looking after children and other aspects of domestic labour were interwoven, hence these were places for children (Davies, 1990), 'The kitchen was my mum's territory . . . when she was baking . . . helping, sticking fingers in' (Martin). Domestic routines were adapted to accommodate the changing times of day, the changing seasons and the development of children, which meant the space of the home was experienced differently in relation to these influences. Rachel remembers herself and her mother before she was old enough to go to school, 'My mum ironing and me watching "Watch with Mother" on the telly. We had a big old couch . . . just me and my mum at home'. Pamela remembers the shifting uses of space related to her father's comings and goings to and from work, 'In the evenings . . . we went to bed early . . . when my father came home from work. This was after tea, the living room was more his and my mum's space.'

At home, children experienced particular boundaries related to the ownership and control of the environment and artefacts there. Some things were theirs to play with; some things were off limits. In the spaces of childhood institutions different limits were imposed:

We had slates, chalks and mini-board rubbers. I had a slate and chalk at home but not a board rubber so I took one home. My mum told me I couldn't do that and took it back and I was embarrassed but no-one ever said anything. (Kate)

When children first attended institutions, some were shocked at the domestic practices as compared with home. These practices were designed to cater for large numbers. The personal needs of the individual child could be overlooked (Goffman, 1961). At home, the circularity and repetition of the domestic routine might be more easily modified to the needs of individual children. In hospitals and schools the needs of the system frequently displaced the child. The services to which the institution related (health or education) and the rigid timetables were the imperatives (Habermas, 1981/1987; Adam, 2006).

Domestic routines were a means of managing everyday home life and weaving complex and multiple temporal demands and influences (Davies,

1990; Adam, 1995). Women were more likely to 'manage' this sphere, sometimes with few instructions but always with particular standards to maintain (Delphy, 1995).The management of home related to the changing seasons, the need for food, health, sleep, cleaning, cleanliness and 'care'. Children's time and time for children were woven in to these routines in different ways. Children carved out their own time to different degrees and in different ways.

The Times of the Changing Seasons

One purpose of home is to provide shelter from the outside environment. This aspect was vivid in the memory of childhood. Participants described how routines were adapted to the changing seasons and how the uses of space changed. In the heat of Pakistan:

> In the summer times . . . we all used to come from our siesta and sit around on the chairs on the veranda . . . until evening, and then we'd go back to the rooms to sleep. In winter times . . . the families used to sit up at the rooftop all day . . . the whole activity to take place in the sun. (Rehana)

In the colder English climate, 'In winter, [the living room] was a place where we used to get changed and ready for bed, 'cause it was coal fire there' (Pamela).

Extremes of weather caused children great discomfort, 'I always remember being cold. Coming in, cold, as a child and having to wait until the fire was lit' (Julie). Hence the protection from harsh weather might be experienced by the child as an act of love from adults:

> My grandma . . . would somehow cool the room, spray water or something, then have fans and have siesta. (Rehana)

> That feeling that we were in our sanctuary, in our little cave and you could hear the weather outside but it was all kept away from us and we were together and snuggled. (Apara)

> My dad used to get up before anybody else in the house and he always used to make sure it was warm when I came down and they used to warm my socks by the front of the coal fire. That was nice. (George)

In the institutions of childhood such as pre-school and school, the weather was experienced in different ways because of the different layout of space (for example, the toilet block in the school playground) and the numbers of children to cater for:

> freezing cold. What seems like hundreds of children crammed together in a room . . . great big stove . . . all sat round the edges of a room . . . water dripping through the ceiling. (Claudia)
>
> There was a stove that heated the room and it had a big fireguard round it. (Kate)

The timetable of the day (class, play and lunch times) determined the times in the open air. The layout of space in the school determined the degree to which children were exposed to the weather. The institutional regime could afford less protection from the elements as, for example, children had to travel some distance to outside toilets (see below).

The Times of Eating

The routines of eating were formalized differently in different homes but to standards of the time and place. Rachel and Martin describe the domestic routines associated with mealtimes in their relatively spacious homes. Family meals were governed by the times of employment and school. There were gendered expectations. Particular parts of the home were associated with different meals:

> The breakfast room was weekday eating together and Sunday lunch and high days and holidays was the dining room, cause that was all set out with the big table in it . . . Mum did all the cooking . . . big sister washed up, middle sister dried up, I had to do the cutlery, or what was left . . . the horrible job that nobody else wanted. (Rachel)
>
> We ate in the dining room and the whole family sat down to tea together, and also lunch, cause my father used to come home from work for lunch . . . we all had our respected seats around the table. (Martin)

Different meals involved the presence and absence of particular adults, 'I can remember that we had a round table, chairs . . . dad [who did a lot of overtime] was hardly ever there' (Richard). Patterns of gender and age differentiation in the mealtime routine (and what was eaten) related to wide social expectations of respectability. Meals were important in 'sustaining definitions of home life'; a housework responsibility (Murcott, 1995, p. 89).

Meals became symbolic of and essential to a family's 'health, welfare and happiness' (ibid., p. 91).

Time, place and household structure made a difference. Warmer weather enabled more fluid use of inside/outside space. Where adult sisters shared the home, there was less isolated domestic responsibility (Wilson, 1978). Rehana described mealtimes at her home in Pakistan and the shifting uses of space, related to the seasons and times of day:

> We had a big room, which was used as the dining kitchen. . . . in winter times . . . breakfast we always used to sit there . . . evening meals, again, would be in the little room, with the coal fire. But in the summer time . . . we used to eat in the open air.

As children grew older, so times moved on and new technologies developed. Ideas about childhood also changed:

> All my relatives ate on their laps in front of the television on trays and I hated it, really hated it. So you wouldn't talk at meal time . . . When we were very young, we were still eating at the table . . . in the sixties, the movement onto laps and trays. (George)

Tessa's mother engaged with new ideas about children's rights (Brannen, 2004):

> Mum had been brought up very much to have to help round the house, and to cook from being little . . . I think she felt that it had affected her childhood . . . She was very keen that we had a childhood. (Tessa)

Not only were the rights of children relevant, but those of girls in particular, because of the unequal distribution of labour and consumption in the family (Delphy, 1995). Not only were her daughters relieved of the sort of domestic pressure she had faced, Tessa's mother also felt it important to keep children apart from 'adult matters' and tensions between her and their father were concealed. It is hard to distinguish the relative influences on the new mealtime routine that developed when Tessa was a teenager. These included the changing parental relationship, social attitudes, technologies and her age and greater freedom to roam outside the home:

> When I was fourteen or fifteen . . . we stopped eating in the dining room, we used to eat more on our knee . . . Mum used to cook and if you were

in, you ate, and if you didn't, you'd heat it up . . . It was never a set time.
It was when we were ready. (Tessa)

Even the design of eating places in the home reflected the new informality
and new forms of inclusion and separation associated with childhood,
'We'd sit at the breakfast bar and have breakfast' (Tessa).

For many research participants, the aspects of mealtimes that were most
vividly remembered were the multiple sensations (images, tastes and
smells) associated with food. Deciding what to have to eat related to food
resources, age and gender (Murcott, 1995):

> We used to sit in the sun on the rooftop and munching oranges, clemen-
> tines . . . carrots, moulis . . . sugar cane. (Rehana)

> [Dad would] always make sandwiches that had tomato in them . . . He
> wouldn't take the ends of the tomato . . . the ends would always be left,
> and I would be allowed to have the ends of the tomatoes. (Claudia)

Lara's long stays with her maternal family in Italy were deeply associated
with food, including the processes of food preparation, eating, the related
seasons and agricultural cycles:

> hot chocolate, little biscuits . . . figs . . . that was breakfast . . . go to the
> beach and the meal that they'd cooked the night before, they used to
> add eggs to it and make one big . . . frittata, wrap it up . . . put it in the
> sand, so as the sun got hotter, the sand would get warmer and so would
> the food . . . They used to put fruit in the wine . . . then pour all the nec-
> tarines and peaches and when they'd finished drinking the wine, they'd
> give us the peaches . . . soaked in alcohol and it was one way of getting us
> to bed at 8 p.m. (Lara)

Meals were deeply physically and symbolically associated with nurture, sustaining the family, giving and receiving (Murcott, 1995). They were also
associated with tension and conflict. Mealtime routines were remembered
by Julie less positively. Her childhood was more isolated. Her brothers were
much older than her, her father was working and her mother poorly. She
died when Julie was 14 (see Chapter 6). Food was associated with some difficulty, with convenience and more commercialized processes:

> Food wasn't a big thing for me . . . I used to have chips and something for
> lunch . . . cheese and onion sandwiches for tea . . . I remember going to

the fish shop for fish and chips. I taught myself to cook . . . I remember cooking a Christmas dinner when I was fourteen or fifteen and burning the custard. (Julie)

George sometimes resisted eating. The pressures on children to eat appropriately could be intense. Mealtimes could be a battle of wills as well as a source of entertainment, where a child felt able to exercise his or her will, 'I used to refuse to eat lots of things . . . sitting at the table in the living room, with [mum] feeding me each mouthful of fish, telling me this story to make me eat the fish' (George).

Mealtimes were structured in relation to the times of work and school. In institutions they were also constrained by time and numbers and confined to specific places. Menus were restricted, 'I couldn't eat the food . . . we'd not been brought up with English food. We'd always been brought up with either Italian food or West Indian' (Lara). Both Lara and Julie refused to eat institutional food and were subject to and observed bizarre penalties and abuse (children were not immune from this at home):

There was a little boy, and he wouldn't eat it, so the nun squeezed his mouth open, and forced the fork into his mouth and she stabbed his tongue. (Lara)

This silly cow of an old fashioned teacher tried to force me to eat rice pudding again, and took my water away *again* – I tried to do my best to conform, and then just got stubborn and wouldn't. (Julie)

The regulation of meals both at home and in institutions could involve this sort of repression. Mealtime regulation could signify and maintain different patterns of the consumption of food. Children could be forced to eat food they hated. This sustained the authority of adults, rationed resources and maintained gender, class and age based ideas about social respectability in relation to food (Delphy, 1995).

The Times of Cleanliness and Cleaning

The routine cleaning of the home took different forms. Cleaning was more than the task of maintaining an hygienic environment but a process influenced by ideas related to health, efficiency, gender and class, and involved visual signs of respectability (Davidoff and Hall, 1995), 'You had your carpet, but you never used to walk on the carpet 'cause you had runners that went across the carpet, from the hall to the kitchen, to prevent wear, so you never actually saw carpet' (George). Cleaning was generally, but not always, associated with women in the family, whether they were taking responsibility for servants or doing the work themselves. Men also cleaned but this was more exceptional. For some women, the routines of cleaning dominated, a duty and burden on themselves and others (including the children): 'My mum was a cleaner. She was always wanting the house cleaned, on a daily basis' (Cathy). Cathy and her sister had to do this cleaning. The demand to clean might be greater where space and money were less and the pressures to live up to class-based social expectations felt more deeply. Cleaning was to maintain 'standards' and protect children's health. In addition, where there had been illness and children had died (as was the case in George's family – see Chapter 1) the pressure to clean intensified, 'My mum used to clean the room every day'. Where homes were particularly hard to keep clean, coupled with lack of appliances, the demands on poorer women were intense:

> My mother hated it, she thought the farm was dirty . . . 'cause you had to walk through a yard to get to the house . . . Her main focus was . . . moving out of that place and going somewhere clean, new, modern, whereas for me, as a child, it was the most amazing place. It was full of nooks and crannies. (Claudia)

The cleanliness of children was also a priority. Particular places were set aside for bathing, according to space, place and cultural practices related to hygiene and health. When they were small, Claudia and George bathed in portable baths in front of the fire, 'I had a plastic bath which was pale green . . . I would have a bath in front of the fire, and my mum and dad had a metal bath that they would bring in and fill . . . ' (George). In the Caribbean, Paulina used public shower houses by the sea. These were a community resource; hence, bathing a more public affair:

> We used to have to go to the seaside to get a shower . . . they had public, little shower houses . . . we didn't have running water in the house . . . that's where you'd go and get your wash . . . I remember it being cold . . . but, yes, yes actually, having fun, cause we did it as brothers and sisters . . . remember splashing each other. (Paulina)

Memories of bathing and water play also blurred in Rehana's account:

> a bathroom, which had a cemented built in wash tank at the top . . . water used to collect to it from the main pipes . . . and we had a tap

underneath, and it also used to lead to a showerhead . . . I remember we used to wash our courtyard at night . . . several buckets of water we used to throw on it, and then mop it out. Sometimes we used to slip on it, or swim on it; we just had great fun.

Techniques were developed by adults to facilitate the movement of children from playing to bathing, '[Dad] . . . used to play hide and seek and the thing was, if he found us, you had to go in and have your bath, so bath time was the time he found you'. (Richard)

Cleaning a number of small children required multiple adult efforts. Dad bathed Lara and her three siblings in the kitchen sink when they were small:

> It was easier to boil the pan and pour into the kitchen sink and we were all so little . . . he used to put a towel on the drainer, then he'd plonk the first one of us in the sink, wash us down, then we'd sit on the drainer, and while the other one was in there having a splash, he'd dry you off, and then you'd go and get the talc off your mum in front of the fire, your pyjamas were laid on the floor, then we'd get us 'jamas on.

Memories of being bathed involved memories of love, care, control and vulnerability, of excitement and pleasure. This depended on the particular adults involved and their attention to the needs and desires of the child. The responsibility to maintain the child's cleanliness sometimes overrode the well-being of the child; sometimes protective measures were taken:

> My first memory of being in a bath was in Nigeria when the housemaid was supposed to be washing my hair and I really thought I was going to die . . . she would just get a big bucket of water and empty it over my head, without any warning, to rinse it . . . I hated it. (Apara)

> I remember having a halo to wash my hair to keep the shampoo out of my eyes. (Kate)

Hence bath-time could be a time of conflict as children tried to assert control through tears and games. As they grew older they became aware themselves of different social standards and new forms of respectability. They could feel shame and disrespect for the domestic practices of their own homes:

> I used to hate was when my Grandma used to grab me and start washing my hair with yoghurts and egg yolks . . . I could never tell anybody, if they

used to ask me how [my hair] was so shiny and silky . . . I was so ashamed . . . 'cause younger people would think 'Oh God, what an old-fashioned thing to do, what a disgusting thing, to put yoghurt in your hair'. (Rehana)

In the institutions of childhood, the cleaning of children could be even more rigid and still mainly managed by women. In Martin's case, at boarding school, children's cleanliness was supervised by, 'Matrons . . . the people that made sure you washed, got clean clothes and things, made sure you washed your hair regularly, inspected your nails to make sure you'd cut them regularly, and that sort of thing'. Bathing happened in, ' . . . shared bathrooms. Rooms with three or four baths in . . . It wasn't something that particularly bothered me . . . perhaps it was something they got a bit more conscious about as they got older, went through puberty'.

Limitations of water and time meant that the cleaning of children at home had to be effectively combined with the cleaning of clothes. Nevertheless standards and hygiene had to be maintained:

the Saturday ritual of washing my hair or giving me or my sister a bath . . . then doing all the washing of the clothes afterwards . . . You'd fill a bucket, wash your-self with soap then rinse yourself off with the water, and then again, shampoo your head and wash that off with the water. So a little bucket out of the big bucket and that's always just how it was. (Madhi)

So the routines of cleaning incorporated different expectations related to who should manage the process and what was hygienic and socially acceptable.

The sort of toilet a family owned might become symbolic of their achievement of particular standards of respectability, hygiene and related morality. George's family had an outside toilet when he was younger and his mother took responsibility for managing the night-time pots, 'Before we had a toilet, you'd pee in pots during the night and then my mum would be in charge of emptying the pots . . . ' Who is responsible for particular aspects of personal and intimate care will vary according to time and place (Twigg, 2000). George pointed out that to have an outside personal toilet at that time and in that place was one step up the social ladder of respectability, because:

Some of the houses had shared toilets and shared washrooms, but ours had its own outside toilet and then we had an inside toilet . . . some people still didn't like that, cause I remember my Great Grandma would not have a toilet in her house because of the germs. (George)

Claudia, living in a rural area, explained:

the toilet . . . you had to go outside the back door . . . it was part of the house . . . like a store outside . . . I can remember going to see friends of ours . . . where the toilet was a long drop, at the bottom of the garden, and it just had a wooden bench, seat over the top of it . . . so having a toilet . . . that was actually part of the house, was probably quite a big difference. (Claudia)

At a similar time, but in a more privileged home, Pamela remembers, inside the home, ' . . . a separate toilet from the bathroom. That was considered very hygienic'. Hence, there were different moral, social and health rationales associated with the elimination of human waste. Moral, social and institutional concerns could sometimes override concern for children's health (Davidoff and Hall, 1995). The most vividly remembered aspects of first experiences of school in England were the toilets. Most of these memories were very unpleasant. Children had to seek permission to go to the toilet; they had to travel across unfamiliar outside spaces; many of the buildings were deteriorating, there were bad smells, dirt and cold, compared with home:

The toilets for the infant school . . . you had to ask, and then you had to go across this playground . . . They were dreadful . . . there were wooden doors with sliding bolts, which were stiff and rusty, so as a little child, you could lock yourself in, but you'd be worried that you couldn't unlock it . . . Sometimes I didn't bother going . . . had the resulting cystitis and all the rest of it. (Pamela)

Apara's first day at a new school in a new country was marked by walking, with another child who was showing her the way to the toilet, across the playground:

It was an open doorway and then you had lots of doors off to one side . . . this horrific smell and this constant drip sound, and the child just turned around and left me . . . I stood there . . . pushed one of the doors open and saw this horrific Victorian toilet, with a cistern, up the top . . . I can just remember at that point thinking 'Oh my God, what have I come to?'

Nevertheless, despite these generally dreadful conditions, Tessa and her friends were able to turn the toilets into a central part of a playground game:

> We used to play chase, in and out of [the toilets]. They smelled, so you didn't want to go to the toilet in them, but they were safe, because at playtime, toilets were base. So if you were in the toilets you were safe, but if you ran out, you could be got . . . the smelly toilets were the place.

The Times of Sleeping

The places for children to sleep were also places where they were awake, where they played and read, listened to music and thought about past and future times. Children slept alone, together, 'top to tail', on mattresses on the floor and in different sorts of beds. The places where they slept could be places where children felt fear and lack of control, as well as pleasure and being in control. Sleeping alone could be both a privilege and something to be feared:

> My own room, when I was little, it was always a bit scary and I never liked going to sleep . . . then when I was a teenager, it became a place of colour . . . I'd colour the ceiling orange . . . I used to spend a lot of time up there reading, so then it became a good place. (George)

Whether children slept with others related to the numbers of siblings, the amount of space, cultural expectations, health, children's desires, the weather, visits and holidays. Sleeping together was part of complex sibling relationships. Lara gave a rich and detailed account of how she, her siblings and her parents managed the sleeping arrangements in a restricted space:

> There [were] four of us children . . . We had one room and it had a double bed in it and we used to top and tail . . . It depended . . . which way we ended up being put into bed, whose feet you had, or who would kick who, or who would pull somebody else's hair . . . you never have your own space . . . You never had a fear of the dark . . . you always knew there was somebody in the room with you . . . you could feel them and hear them.

Even when the family could afford separate bunk beds, Lara and her sister continued to sleep in one bunk bed out of choice, 'Me and my sister still used to share the same bed. The top bed was for our jewellery and shoes and clothes and the bottom bunk was for us to sleep, so we still slept top and tail!'

On her visits to family in Italy, sleeping was even more complicated, 'There were about twelve of us in one room . . . we all used to lay on little mattresses on the floor'.

New sleeping arrangements could be a source of interest and play. Rachel remembers visits to the much smaller home of her grandmother. Here sleeping together was different, exciting and mysterious:

> They had something called "The Mountain Bed" . . . a big double bed that we all got to sleep in . . . it was dead exciting . . . I remember it being just the most exciting bed to ever sleep in.

The places where they slept might also have provided more autonomy and control for children, away from the adult gaze, creating opportunities to carve out space and time for themselves. This was both a physical process, 'I used to read with the crack of the light coming under the door...We had to share a room ... we had a barricade down the middle ... a line of furniture' (Tessa), and also involved the imagination,

> If it was hot and humid we used to sleep in the open air . . . I sometimes used to wake up in the middle of the night . . . looking at the stars, looking at the sky, and thinking, 'What's the purpose of all this? Why was this made? What was God doing, doing all this? Why is it so strange, the sky up there, the stars, there's people here down here?'. (Rehana)

This border land between sleep and waking could involve reflection on past events and questions about the future. The imagination could allow entry to all sorts of different thoughts and feelings. This is how sleeping may also become associated with particular fears:

> [I was] scared about things under the bed, and jumping in the bed so you didn't have to go near the underneath of the bed . . . bending over to see what was there . . . [The] moon used to shine through a landing window . . . it used to shine against the wall, and I think it must have been a tree or something . . . there was a silhouette against the wall, and to me it was like a man, with a hat on. (Claudia)

Despite the relative freedom from adult surveillance, children's space and time for sleep was regulated by adults and the wider social and industrial calendar. There were sleep related taboos; for example, different sex siblings over a certain age may not share bedrooms. Pamela and her brother undermined these taboos in relation to their own sleeping arrangements:

> I'd have been nine or ten, so they probably thought it'd be a good idea to have a separate room . . . My younger brother hated that. He used to have nightmares and things, and used to sneak in and sleep with me! It used to be a little secret pact, that I wouldn't tell my parents that he'd come in.

The regulation of sleep was likely to be more rigid in institutions. Children's sleep was organized around staff work rotas and the need to maintain surveillance. The needs of the institution quickly overrode the wakefulness of individual children (Goffman, 1961). Children developed strategies to overcome the institutional (and home based) regulation of sleep:

> Strict light's out. No speaking after lights out. Cane if you did . . . Even up to the age of probably thirteen we were in bed by 8 o'clock at night. In senior school it was half nine, ten. Even the sixth form it was like 10.30 . . . We had ways round it . . . by that age . . . people used to go out after lights out, out the window . . . sometimes there'd be about ten of us that went out. (Martin)

The Disruptions of Home Life and Domestic Routines

During times of illness, the routine uses of space in the home were adapted. George and Claudia remember being taken into their parents' bedrooms, for warmth, to be watched and treated carefully and perhaps also so that the professionals who subsequently entered the home saw the best of care:

> the moment I was ill, I would go into their bed and when the doctors came . . . then you would be seen in their bedroom . . . It was a really comforting safe place.
>
> I was very ill when I was about eight or nine . . . I was allowed in my mum and dad's bed – when the doctor came to visit . . . it would be important to her to make the right impression.

In looking after these children's health needs, boundaries were crossed. The private adult bedroom space was breached. More resources were spent and effort went into comforting the children with pleasures and entertainments to ameliorate discomfort and anxiety. Children's health needs also involved them in staying in health related institutions, where some of the personalized attention of home was lost, ' . . . what a wrench to be torn away. I don't remember it being cruel . . . I remember it being austere and I remember it being routines and not being home and being homesick' (Julie). Even where the regime was less austere, separation from family was hard:

> It was quite big, airy, the nurses were lovely, there were lots of toys and books and things. You weren't allowed to have visitors out of visiting hours, and they discouraged other children visiting, so I didn't see my brother, and that I missed. (Pamela)

Martin experienced two health scares while at boarding school:

> it was actually quite supportive, and you know, after-care . . . I was back at school with my arm in a sling, and they dealt with things like changing the sling, making sure it was okay and getting me back to the hospital for x-rays and things . . . they did look after us . . . some were more comforting than others.

In relation to ill health and recovery in childhood, what was remarked on was the break from the everyday routine, the delight children took in particular treats and their own command of time, away from the rigid clock led demands of home and school:

> I used to quite like being ill . . . I got lots of attention and presents . . . I'd get sweets and I'd get colouring books . . . I used to like reading a lot, so I'd sit in my bed with my books and colouring books and my mum would come up and sit by the window and tell me what was happening in the street outside. (George)

Participants remembered other moments when domestic routines were disrupted and home based activities and events came together in different or unusual ways, enabling comparison and new understanding (Misztal, 2003 citing Schwartz, 2000). Memories crystallized where domestic routines were disrupted, for example, the home was supposed to be a source of shelter from the weather and intended to prevent entry to wildlife. Children recorded with excitement and trepidation when this security was breached and strange things that were supposed to be 'outside', entered the home:

> I can remember the invasion of the ants . . . seeing this mass of little black insects all over the floor . . . they'd gone in, underneath and come up through the cracks between the concrete floor and the floorboards. (Pamela)

> In my bedroom . . . there was an old fireplace with some cracked tiles and I found earwigs under them. I remember watching them and talking to them. (Kate)

Children heard, read and watched stories involving 'outside' (Christensen and O'Brien, 2002; Hallden, 2002; Rasmussen and Smidt, 2002) and Pamela feared the entry of some of these fictional creatures into her home:

> This toilet, underneath the stairs, had this tiny little window, which looked out on the side passage . . . and I imagined this would be an access for . . . Daleks, to come down, so I was terrified about using that space. (Pamela)

Other surprising, disturbing and entertaining things entered the home and were remembered because of the new slant they placed on the everyday, for example, George was entertained by a fall of soot into the living room, ' . . . one day we came down and the whole room was covered in soot and that was really funny, 'cause my mum was meticulously clean'. The imposition of mother's rigid cleaning routine had been usurped by this fall of soot. Hunt refers to the 'desire for a relaxed attitude towards order and spruceness' (1995, p. 303) as a form of resistance to women's authority in the home. George also remembered being disgusted at the idea of eating the bits of animals' bodies that his grandmother brought to the house to be cooked, 'Then when my granny used to come . . . she would have been to the pork butchers in Prescott, so she would bring the most horrific things into the house, like slavery ducks or bits of bulls' brain, terrible things . . . ' Claudia, exhibited the same disgust when she remembered a rabbit being gutted by her father, and was deeply concerned that she would be expected to bathe in the same tin bath:

> I can remember my dad being given a rabbit . . . he was gutting and cleaning this rabbit in this tin bath and I was completely horrified by

seeing him do that, because we would then have to have our bath in the same tin bath, and I thought it was awful, absolutely awful.

Turning points and critical events like this enabled children to make comparisons and further their understanding what was acceptable and respectable, drawing on their available bank of experiences and cultural beliefs. Ideas from home life, fiction and religion might combine to explain mysterious and sometimes traumatic events. Of her first home in England, with its dark and gloomy atmosphere and confined uses of space, Paulina came to believe, 'It was haunted . . . we remember seeing things . . . people that we described and neighbours would say they lived there years ago. Shadows . . . they passed us, left you feeling cold and your hair standing on end . . . so we . . . definitely hated it'.

Silences in Childhood Memories of Home

The selectivity of memory leads to social, familial and personal silences (see Chapter 2). The unequal distribution of power in families may be taken for granted. Important aspects of home life may be concealed from children, meaning that they experience these at a subterranean level. On the one hand, Tessa enjoyed lots of play and relative freedom, on the other, her parents' relationship was breaking down:

> As a child I wasn't aware of it . . . he was trying to keep the family together . . . all blown up one summer when we weren't at home . . . it was the time when the horses became much more central and we stopped caravanning . . . we were very protected from it . . . kept at my grandparents for a lot of summers . . . it was very covered up . . . on the surface it all looked very, now, you look back on it and it was all, if somebody says to you 'How was your childhood?' 'Aw it was great' . . . but a lot of it was an illusion. (Tessa)

The home and family were not necessarily 'safe havens' for children (Mullender et al., 2002). Children witnessed the breakdown of relationships and sometimes domestic violence, 'In bed, he's back, deep shouting banging, again, wish it would stop, not really scared but want it to stop to sleep' (Sylvia).

Lara encountered racism in her own extended family:

> My dad's family . . . we didn't see them very often . . . they didn't really approve of . . . mixed marriage . . . They used to always identify us as 'The

Ugly One', 'The Pretty One' and 'The Little Boy'. . . . I was 'The Ugly One' . . . My Dad used to go mad 'cause I was his pride and joy. (Lara)

Apara experienced difficulties with her father on access visits:

> He would wait until my mum was out of the room, and then he would ask me questions or say things that put me in a really difficult situation . . . saying to me once, that I should come back . . . to live with him, 'cause he was on his own . . . it really upset me . . . I felt such guilt, such guilt. This idea that he was on his own.

Paulina also experienced a great harshness from her father (see Chapter 7). Children experienced the tensions related to unequal social relations in their home lives:

> Although we had family meals, we weren't usually encouraged to talk . . . my father had to listen to the television, not to us chattering away . . . We used to build an awful lot of dens. They used to always have to be tidied up before my father came home from work. (Pamela)

Their everyday home lives related to and responded to these tensions, whether they were aware of the related events or not and whether they had a framework for understanding these events or not. These silences cast shadows in their memories of home life.

Conclusion

In this chapter, home has not been considered a fixed place, but an outcome of a series of material and social relationships, expectations and events related to the wider social world (Massey, 2005). As homes are constituted through interaction, so is childhood. Children in the research were involved in their own process of constructing home. They had a variety of choices, directives and temptations (Lefebvre, 1991).

Home was connected in complex ways to the wider society. The wider environment and home were deeply connected, through the design of the properties. See for example, the difference between Rehana's homes in Pakistan and England. Homes were also situated in landscapes that were differentiated by social class and led to children, such as George and Cathy, making comparisons. Domestic routines were influenced by gendered expectations and ideas as well as material resources. Martin's and Kate's mothers were remembered in kitchens and Richard's father was often absent from meals. Mealtimes and cleaning rituals clearly had symbolic as well as material value. There were shadows in the memories of home related to anxious and uncertain times, for example, the return of Pamela's potentially angry father from work which guaranteed things were tidied up first.

Space in the home was marked out in particular ways. The social ideas about respectability informing this might have come from another social class and time. To attempt to reproduce the home life of an elite group who have wealth and resources in confined spaces could be a burden. Keeping one room empty for visitors (see Paulina and George) was an example. As well as being class-based, ideas about home life were also deeply gendered and the home could be rife with conflict at particular times although children might be sheltered from this (see Tessa).

Use of space in the home and the routine boundaries of home were breached where there was illness, accidents (such as the fall of soot which caused George such amusement, but not his mother) or cramped conditions. Rachel vividly remembered the mountain bed where she and her sisters slept together when visiting grandma. Turning points and disruptions were remembered as these breached the boundaries and routines of home creating interest, enjoyment and uncertainty. The enjoyment and trepidation associated with creatures entering the home was an example. Children's behaviour did not confine itself to the regulated routines of home life. As Davies (1990) argues, many time spans shape everyday experience; domestic routines provide frameworks for experiences that may be simultaneous. In the memory it was hard for Rehana to separate playing from bathing. Pamela and her brother undermined the sleeping taboos of the time. George refused to eat. Kate educated herself in the kitchen, 'I remember getting the hang of reading in the kitchen when I was about four – there were packets of washing powder, OMO, on the shelves and it suddenly made sense' (Kate).

The research participants remembered home in relation to such turning points and strange connections. They experienced home in relation to significant events; a coming together of time and place. Where domestic routines were disrupted and challenged, memories crystallized. This is where different threads of social memory met, and the conventional social expectations of home were challenged and contested. Children engaged with the daily domestic routine and the comings and goings of different adults in the home. They experienced the way domesticity was modified in institutions. They observed different arrangements in other people's homes as they grew older. They viewed media representations of home (see Chapter 9) and saw creatures and people entering their homes from outside. They developed their own interpretation of what was socially and personally acceptable and what was not. In these ways children engaged and interacted with the familial and social relations that structured their home lives. It is these wider social influences and relationships that may be underestimated when professionals and academics consider the quality of children's home lives in order to improve these. The attempt to separate home based from wider social influences is difficult.

Chapter 5

Children and Employment

Introduction

This chapter draws on children's experiences of the spheres of employment, exploring the ways parents' employment informed everyday childhood as well as the impact of their own first jobs. It positions the 'public' sphere of employment as highly influential in children's daily lives. In poorer economies children are more visible in the spheres of employment, including agriculture and the production of goods and services. Sometimes children's work is paid, sometimes not. In richer economies, the focus is often on employment as one outcome of successful transitions to adulthood rather than as generating complex experiences throughout childhood (Morrow, 2003).

The nature of employment comes through the relations of production and reproduction and employment practices ' . . . crush time, by reducing difference to repetition and circularity' for example, the home based tasks of caring, cleaning and/or preparing and serving food became more repetitive and routine in the paid workplace (Lefebvre, 1991, p. 18). Hence, the structures and relations of employment influence the everyday experience of children in particular ways related to class, ethnicity, gender and ability. The working hours and ethics of work influence experiences outside work. This chapter examines how 'public' employment practices form part of the everyday and more 'private' landscapes of childhood.

The employment of parents outside the home was experienced at a visceral level by children from a very early age. Children's knowledge of paid work was gained in a variety of ways, including from the physical impact on parents, from what they said, from their absences, their moods, from children's visits to work settings and children's own engagement in work. This range of complex experience in childhood suggests that public and private worlds merge in complex ways. Absences, presences, inside, outside, travelling, smells and tastes and a sense of social class, place, ethnicity and gender were involved. Sometimes parents were present in the home, sometimes working. Sometimes the children were present in their parents' places of work, in factories, mental health centres, laboratories, shops and fashion shows or watching mothers cleaning the school, or cleaning 'posh' people's houses. Memories of feelings of anxiety at times of unemployment, redundancy and job transition were common. These were not mere descriptions of events outside the home but fields of intense human relations and energy that entered the child's world. This shaped expectations, involving feelings of pleasure, anxiety, uncertainty and pride, but above all providing a complex tapestry of experience in childhood.

McDowell (1997) argues that the spaces of paid work are gender coded, reflecting relations of power, control and dominance in the social construction of concepts of work and worker. Such codings also reflect wider social divisions such as age, class, 'race' and ability. Children's experience provides insight into how, ' . . . the spaces created by market relations . . . ' (Massey, 2005, p. 100) are experienced in the family and how their own position, experiences and expectations relate to this.

The chapter is in three parts. First, the places of work are discussed and the ways that children began to understand and experience the world of work from an early age. Secondly, the relationship between family time and work time, considering the way familial memories of work were shared with children and the way work and family time were interwoven. Thirdly, the chapter focuses on the ways that children gathered the 'tools' for work. This part of the chapter draws on Bourdieu's (1986) ideas about material, social, cultural and symbolic forms of capital and the ways these shape social interaction. The chapter considers this through children's experience of money, schooling, social networks and the status, esteem and discrimination related to work.

The Places of Work and the Meaning of Work in Childhood

The Places of Work

The places where family members worked are discussed in the children's cameos (see Chapter 1). They worked in a wide range of occupations from cleaning to inspecting schools, reflecting their social class, gender, ethnicity, place and time. Accounts of work remembered from childhood were stories of transition and change, of geographic and social mobility, of economic flux and the associated emotional and material upheavals of family life. These were snapshots of ' . . . multiple routines, rhythms and well worn paths . . . ', influencing children's lives (Massey, 2005, p. 112 citing Jacobs, 1961). A summary of occupations would give only a glimpse of those realities and fail to convey the flux and change in children's lives and the weaving of paid and unpaid work in families which is necessary to sustain family life and care for children.

Gender and class differences in parents' employment were evident; nursing, caring, cleaning, catering and shop assistant work were usually associated with mothers. Cousins argues that the development of industrial capitalism and process of urbanization led to, ' . . . functions provided by the family in the past, such as recreation, leisure, security and emotional needs, (becoming) commodities, as too did the care of the young, the sick' (1987, p. 66). Some working-class fathers worked as manual workers, labourers and engineers. Many were obliged to spend long hours away from home. Administrative, technical and professional roles (such as teaching) appeared to be less gender differentiated, but even within those areas, particular roles were different, reflecting vertical and hierarchical differences within each occupational area (ibid.).

The intermittence and flux of work related to the demands of domestic time and children's time on the family. It also related to parental education, class background, social networks, health and fluctuations in labour demand. In relation to this combination of factors, some families experienced more marginalized and insecure employment than others, but all experienced flux and change. When children began to work themselves, occupations tended to be intermittent, marginal and insecure.

There were major shifts in patterns of employment, related to critical events such as redundancy, dismissal, migration, bereavement, separation and inheritance. The sphere of employment was part of a narrative of social change in childhood that was evident in Rehana's account, 'My mother was an inspector of schools [in Pakistan] . . . she worked for the United Nations and Dad [for] the British army'. Major changes affected her family. Her mother tragically died when she was 4. Her father moved to England and the children followed. In England, Rehana's father then had to work in, ' . . . a bakery . . . on the buses. Then he bought his own business, minimarket. Couldn't run it . . . sold it after a few years. Then he worked in one of the textile mills'. A high status and professional career in Pakistan was replaced by a number of manual jobs in England based on a belief that opportunities for the children and wider community would be better.

Children work more where there is low family income (or no family), where there is a strong ethic of work in the family and where there is less child-related welfare or statutory schooling (Montgomery et al., 2003). However, nearly all the children discussed in this study experienced some employment, whatever their economic background. This first employment did not necessarily reflect their future trajectories because of its marginal, insecure and temporary nature. They filled a place in the employment market associated with flexibility, low training and low pay. For some children, the earnings from work were essential to their families (see below). Nevertheless, for all the sample, their first paid work experiences were important in many other significant ways, in particular in accruing a range of resources for the future and introducing children to new patterns of collective organization (social memories) and social discipline that informed the world of work. These experiences altered children's expectations and relationships. For example, George's early experiences of working at the gas board, provided more than just ready cash:

> All the men used to sit in one area of the canteen and all the women used to sit in another area of the canteen and they would not mix, even husbands and wives would be separated like this. And I remember asking my dad, 'Why is that?' He didn't have a clue; it was just the way you did things . . . then you'd go back and work, but all your leisure time was in separate gendered spaces.

This separation of the sexes emerged from past cultural practices and beliefs related to gender and heterosexuality. These practices had become so fossilized in this workplace that the original reasons for them were perhaps no longer clear (Halbwachs, 1925/1991). George wondered how this separation related to his own life and gay sexuality.

The Meaning of Work

However, children learned about employment from a much earlier age than this. Early memories of parents' employment included the smells of soil, potatoes and manure from land-work, the grease from haulage, the chemicals from the laboratories and hospitals where parents worked. These smells were carried into the home by the parents returning from work and provided intense early memories:

> where everything is being milled. It's not a floury smell, but animal feed's got a really distinct smell . . . That's dad when we were little . . . it was the smell of dad when he came home from work. (Tessa)
>
> We did go down to the docks occasionally . . . there was that kind of, aware of the smells, that oily burny smell. (Richard)

When I get potatoes now, that are fresh, I have the most vivid memory, it just throws me right back . . . and I can smell the field . . . it's got the most wonderful smell for me, of potatoes, with soil, coming straight out of the dirt. (Claudia)

This is how the external world of work entered the home world of the very young child, who was curious about the differences. The smells became deeply associated with particular experiences, emotions, places and people.

Later when children got their own first job, the experience was also visceral and vivid, grounded in sensations and feelings, focused on critical events and new experiences related to people and places. Rachel, for example, remembered working with the milkman:

I do remember wanting to look like the proper milkman and carry lots of bottles in your hand and then realising my hands were too small and dropping one and smashing it. That was really embarrassing 'cause it was full . . . I'd meet him in . . . the working man's cafe . . . he'd have his egg and bacon and I'd sit there and have a piece of toast and a cup of tea, and be chatting to all his . . . friends . . . and I found that quite interesting, 'cause I suddenly found myself in this other world.

Rachel attempted to model herself on the 'proper' milkman in the process of learning the new work system and relationships. The dropping of the milk bottle signified a temporary failure.

Another way children experienced work throughout childhood was through visits to their parents' work places. George's and Claudia's mothers worked as cleaners. George came from an urban and Claudia from a rural working-class community. Claudia's godparents provided domestic service, to a wealthy man in the village. These everyday connections provided interesting experiences for the children. George accompanied his mother while she cleaned a 'posh' semi-detached house (see Chapter 2), ' . . . sitting in her house, going through her Woman's Realm [magazine], reading it, while my mum was cleaning, and she had a dog called Shandy . . . it was a bit exotic, going to a semi-detached house'. Claudia visited the house where her godparents provided service:

They 'lived in' . . . going to the loo . . . you had to go out of the kitchen area . . . which involved going through a door which had green baize on it . . . You'd go down this corridor, and it had, lining the walls, heads of animals, stuffed animals, deer and foxes and badgers and grandfather clocks . . . This dark long corridor, with animal heads and tick tock, tick tock.

The class relations structuring these children's lives were becoming apparent through the process of visiting, moving from working-class to middle- and upper-class homes. The children were captivated by the gardens, the artefacts and the relative space in the homes they visited. Through these experiences they developed understanding of other class positions to their own and of their own social class (Lefebvre, 1991). The children were curious, nervous and enjoyed these experiences which cast light on their own social place and raised possibilities for play and for the future. George's mother also worked for a time in a motorway café:

Oh it's all to do with treats and food . . . I was allowed to have . . . strawberry milkshakes . . . that was a bit posh too, 'cause it was attached to a pub and the people there had a colour television . . . I used to go and watch colour television . . . work was associated with posh people and with treats.

Children also visited other institutions and organizations, factories, laboratories and so forth, where their parents worked. They experienced different forms of social organization and occupation related to health, social care, industry and retail. Lara and her siblings visited the mental health centre where her mother worked:

We used to sit in the staff room . . . she used to make us hot chocolate, and it was like a real treat . . . to go to work with my mum . . . I remember one time when we were at work, this man came into the staff room, totally naked . . . I remember my mum's face, coming in and going 'Ahhh!' . . . I think we all looked up, glanced and carried on what we were doing.

Martin regularly visited his father, a consultant bacteriologist, in the lab:

There used to be animals there . . . the things that they were testing . . . we probably weren't very aware of what was happening to them. That sort of grew later . . . mice, rabbits . . . white lab rats, guinea pigs, all sorts of things . . . I soon had a feel of his sort of work.

As well as food treats, animals and artefacts, the places of work provided contacts with different people, sometimes of different colour:

> From the age of two I remember going with my mum to these little villages . . . whenever there was an opening of the school . . . I remember once, this [White] American . . . 'cause it was a United Nations program. (Rehana)

Through repeated visits, and over time, children developed understanding of the spheres of employment and wider social organization; including, some of the personal and moral issues, the way other people lived, their own social place and different potential futures.

In childhood, however, those zones that Halbwachs (1925/1992) terms 'personal' or 'technical' and that society would try and differentiate, as home and work related, in fact merge in many complex ways. Work may be experienced playfully, as care but also as hardship. For Claudia, potato picking was both a pleasure and pain, 'It was quite common for children to be there with their mothers . . . you'd help, you'd get stuck in; collecting potatoes . . . it was a pleasant memory, although it wasn't very nice when it was cold'. For Martin, agricultural work also provided pleasure whereas, for his uncle, it was probably a hard daily round, 'Harvest, planting potatoes . . . milking cows, collecting the eggs . . . driving tractors, my little legs wouldn't reach on the combine harvester, but you know we used to ride around with my uncle all day on it'.

Cathy sometimes travelled with her father in his lorry. His work became her play and her care melded together. His work provided huge excitement, a different experience, taking her out of the everyday. It was also a way for father to look after her while her mother was working elsewhere, 'I remember one of the journeys . . . sitting in the front of this huge lorry . . . being queen of all you survey . . . rattling round in this great big cab . . . thinking it was marvellous . . . it was an adventure'.

Family Time and Work Time

Familial Memories of Work

Children were also introduced to the sphere of employment through work related stories passed down in the family. These stories included examples of personal resistance, struggle, hardship and great achievement in relation to work. They contained complex and ambiguous messages regarding the importance and value of work, about who controls work and the child's

potential place in the work order. A common theme, even in more privileged homes, was achievement against all the odds and with little resources
(in terms of education or finance). Of her father, Rachel said that when he
was a child:

> He got evacuated during the war and had an interrupted education . . .
> very working class parents sent him out to work at fourteen . . . so the fact
> that we had a company car and he was a sales director . . . very scant
> formal education.

Rehana shared a family memory of her mother's work achievements for
the United Nations in Pakistan, before she died in her twenties, 'She was
so dynamic . . . [relatives] find it very hard to believe . . . that she [was] even
a human being . . . not so many people can achieve so much in such little
life'. Stories of her mother, when she was a child, gave Rehana a sense of
pride and future possibility. Familial memories of work that were shared
with children were about overcoming social barriers, social class mobility,
the importance of education and the low expectations of particular social
groups. Through these stories social expectations of particular groups
were both reinforced and challenged; for example, Martin was told a story
about his mother, '[Mother] was one of the first . . . [women] to do physics at
university, which from a farming background is actually very remarkable'.
Such stories taught children the ethics of working hard, of getting educated and of challenging social expectations, in relation to themselves and
their families. They taught children that some work is more satisfying (and
better paid) than other work. They were stories about overcoming adversity
and of achievement in the context of potentially hard life conditions. They
told the children that they too had these capacities if they behaved in particular ways. Such stories were repeated to children in both working class
and more privileged homes; they were imbued with the public ethics and
structures of collective memory related to work (Halbwachs, 1925/1992,
see Chapter 2).

The Weaving of Work, Childcare and the Domestic

The weaving of work, child care and domestic responsibilities were also
key features of family life. The creation by Tessa's mother, of a play group
at home was a prime example. Other better off families (e.g., Martin's and
Rachel's) were able to create more home based space to fulfil domestic
obligations. The choice to stay at home related to the social expectations

of class, ethnicity and gender at the time (Edwards and Duncan, 1997). Rehana's mother presumably was able to sustain her high status and time consuming job because she lived in an extended family with women relatives who helped her care for her children, coming from a society where, at that time, the expectation of practical care for particular children did not fall solely on the mother (Wilson, 1978).

Children's experience of employment therefore was also informed by the daily comings and goings in the home, through the absences and presences of particular people and through who provided their everyday care (if that was provided). Usually children had little involvement in negotiating routines in the home related to the balancing of family time and work time. However, George's mother actively involved him in negotiating the everyday routine when he was 6:

> She said, 'Now I could stay at home and be there when you come back from school, or I could go out to work and I'll do what you want.' So, I think I said, at that age, 'I want you at home', and then she asked me again, two years later, and I said, 'I don't care', or something like that.

The clock times of the workplace (and school) structured the children's days (Adam, 1995). Father might eat breakfast alone and earlier to get to work:

> I remember vividly him getting up at six and sitting in his dressing gown having breakfast on his own. (Rachel)

> Dad used to work very early . . . I can remember him making his sandwiches in the morning, and me being around . . . and the smell of percolated coffee, 'cause he'd always take a flask of proper coffee to work. (Claudia)

The long daily absences of particular parents meant their limited presences became memorable. The day might be structured around their comings and goings. The demands of parents' work could also interrupt the child's day and night in other notable ways. Tessa's father managed a mill, 'I just remember him being called out at two or three in the morning, 'cause the mill had broken down or machinery had broken down, so he was always going out late at night and coming back'. Claudia's father, when a farm labourer, ' . . . used to work very long days and long hours and long weeks as well. So often he'd work at the weekend'. The demands of the workplace on the home related to the degree of responsibility the parent carried, their level of wages and the degree of exploitation they faced. Absence from home created qualitatively different relationships with children; perhaps more distant, perhaps more exciting, 'My mum was always there and my dad . . . who drove to work, would come in later, just before I went to bed, so it was always quite exciting my dad being around . . . special time' (George). The disruption caused by unemployment did not necessarily mean that the former worker became more committed to home time. Sometimes distance remained between the unemployed worker and the child, 'He just happened to be around when my brother and I came home from school' (Pamela).

Some parents fitted around each other's work to care for children and the degree of their involvement in everyday care influenced the quality of the relationship as a whole:

> My dad used to take me to school and then we used to go to somebody's house, and then my dad would pick me up . . . so a lot of my early years were with my father, because my mother was [working] early mornings. My father's involvement in my life when we were young was really significant. (Madhi)

The demands of employment meant that some children were taken to other places to be looked after, 'We had to go to a child-minder, which was a woman in the community, who looked after us' (Paulina), or other people came to care for children in their own homes, 'My mother went back to work when I was just a few weeks old, so I was cared for by . . . a series of maids, it wasn't always the same one' (Apara). Where possible, extended family took on more caring responsibility, 'My grandparents would always pick me up from school and look after me' (Tessa). These relationships with different adults were significant for the children in different ways. See, for example, Apara's fear of being bathed by the maid and Tessa's deep involvement with her grandparents which are discussed in Chapter 4.

Where money was short and childcare expensive, there was sometimes less everyday care for the children, 'One of my brothers said that I brought myself up, to a large extent because people were busy in the shop' (Julie). Cathy and her sister,

> were very much on our own. Our mum and dad were out most of the time . . . You didn't have any buffer between you and what might happen. I can remember one lunchtime, coming home from school, and for some reason we were frightened of something and we were in an upstairs bedroom and we'd barricaded ourselves in, with wardrobes. I don't know

what we were frightened of, but we were terrified of something . . . but there was no adult there, to mediate, to say, 'Actually this is a small thing'. (Cathy)

In addition, more domestic demands fell on the children. Cathy's mother's experience as a paid cleaner informed the home life of the children. They too were expected to clean, to replace the loss of mother's labour in the home and to replicate the ethic and system of cleanliness at home:

We were 'domestic' . . . hoovering every day, dusting every day, beds, making the tea every day, and it was quite a monotonous kind of round, and it caused quite a bit of friction between my sister and I . . . 'Well I've done this, and I've . . . ' you know, that kind of thing, and then we'd both rush towards getting it done, 'cause we would sit around, not doing it, and then it would get to the point where my mum was coming in, from work, so we'd have to run around the house, madly, trying to do all of this stuff.

The differentiation of space between work and home was sometimes very blurred. The separation of work and home (see Chapter 4) was mainly physical but not social and emotional. In some cases it was not even physical. The weaving of work and the domestic involved the creation of solutions that met complex needs (Davies, 1990). Tessa's mother developed her paid work from home, creating a playgroup there, which involved the re-designation of family space in the home. The playgroup was based in the back living room. Everything to do with her own children's 'home life', therefore

happened in the front room and the gardens . . . our toys were in the bedrooms so they were ours and mum was very careful to keep it very separate so that we did have our toys which weren't playgroup toys.

Tessa's mother created clear markers to distinguish 'work' from 'home'. Such distinctions were more blurred for Julie, who lived above a shop and who said:

Work surrounded me . . . insurance business always came home, the paperwork . . . the shop was always on the doorstop until I was eleven . . . surrounded by work for six years . . . maybe I did serve children with sweets. I remember weighing sweets. (Julie)

Parent–child relations were caught up in the ebbs and flows of the employment market and expected and negotiated familial roles. Children developed significant bonds and sometimes hostility to carers other than their parents. Sometimes they were left to their own devices to carve their own pathway through the day. Family time was structured by work time and the spaces of home and work could become blurred in everyday childhood.

Gathering the Tools to Work

The ability to get and sustain employment relates to opportunity, capital accumulated and discrimination faced. Capital may come in a variety of forms including money, social networks, education, language and the means to assert status, authority and power (Bourdieu, 1986). Without sufficient resources, young people may abandon the search for formal work (Barry, 2006). Families and children developed the means to access and navigate employment in different ways. This section considers the significance in childhood of these messages and experiences related to money, selective schooling, social networks and social status.

Money

Regardless of social class background, in capitalist economies, the significance of money is stressed to children. They learn about the importance of working hard and earning money and that this will improve or sustain the quality of their lives. Of her parents Claudia said, '[They] were very keen to work a lot, as much as they could so they could save and buy their own house, which is what they aspired too, and which they succeeded in doing'. Children in the research learned about the risks associated with financial fluctuations through what was selectively told to them and through fluctuations in their own experience of 'necessities' and 'treats':

> When he moved jobs, we were acutely aware of cutbacks . . . if we ever went out, we could only have small drinks, not large ones like we used to have before . . . there was this shift . . . we had to tighten our belts, everything was bit less and a bit smaller. (Richard)

Pockets of prosperity and poverty, insecurity and change marked some children's lives more than others (Jordan, 1998). They experienced very different living standards. Although adults decided how their finances were spent and this spending did not always benefit their children, there is no doubt that more money created more opportunities for children in relation to education, leisure, health, well-being and career opportunities, 'The cementing of class inequalities begins at an early age . . . ' (Novak, 2002, p. 65).

What was common in these children's experiences was that they all learned the value of money. The power contained in money became enmeshed in their everyday lives. The pride in handling money was evident in Pamela's account of her first job:

> It was working in accounts, doing the payroll . . . I realized that I could actually do it . . . I had all this responsibility of working out these pay cheques for all these hourly paid workers . . . I actually used to go to the bank, collect the money, bring it back and sort it out . . . I had to work out what change I needed to put it in . . . the pay packets.

For some of the poorer children, the value of money was learned even sooner. They highlighted their financial contribution to the family through work:

> My first job . . . I got £23.50 a week. £10 went to my mum for board. £7 went to my driving lessons and the rest went on bus fare. (Lara)
>
> I remember the first thing I bought when I got my first full time job, a washing machine for my mum. Got it and paid bit by bit. (Paulina)

Julie had her first child at 16, got married and lived independently from her parents; she also quickly learned the value of money:

> His parents supported us . . . then we managed on his first wage, when he was articled clerk . . . £9 a week . . . being really frugal. . . . I can remember [baby was] a year old, before I bought her any clothes . . . then gradually I got bits of jobs cleaning or working in the local factory.

The value of money was a lesson passed on to children of all social classes through their formal and informal education, their experience of treats and necessities, fluctuating earnings in the family and their own experiences of work. In all these ways they learned the importance of gathering financial capital to ensure the quality of life. Habermas (1981/1987) argues that in 'advanced' societies, money is a 'steering media' providing system integration and social regulation. The power of money is understood in childhood, but the origins of this symbolic system of social transaction are less clear to them. The financial system may appear like a fossil in the social memory (Halbwachs, 1925/1992).

Selective Schooling

Depending on which generation they were from, children were put through different forms of formal and informal selection to enter particular schools related to different prospects for employment. This applied even where state systems were intended to be comprehensive (Welch, 2008b). Martin was sent to a private school in England; Rehana and Apara to small private schools in Pakistan and Nigeria respectively, and then state schools in England. All the other children were completely schooled in state run institutions. But whether private or state, school groomed children for their future place and future imagined employment.

Those children growing up in the United Kingdom in the 1950s and 1960s learned that to enter particular schools they needed to pass the 'eleven plus' examination. Depending on their results they would be divided into the 'academic' and 'vocational' schools which deeply reflected and reproduced social class divisions and led to differentiated patterns of employment. Girls were sometimes deliberately marked lower than boys because there were less grammar school places for girls (Thomas, 1990). Children learned that those who passed the examination should be proud and that there was some shame or disappointment attached to not passing. Consequently, they learned something about how they were socially valued as human beings. Contrast Paulina's and Pamela's experience of this divisive examination:

> I didn't pass my 11+ . . . my reputation had followed me, they put me in 2D rather than 2C and the idea was that they'd see how I behaved, before they'd move me up. (Paulina)

> I had been so proud, because I'd got to grammar school. (Pamela)

James described the different forms of division shaping schooling in his community in Northern Ireland, where, during his childhood in the 1960s and early 1970s, social class, gender, religion and political allegiance all influenced where children were placed and their consequent routes to employment. At this time, work was also segregated along similar lines and

Fair Employment legislation was introduced in 1976 (Equality Commission for Northern Ireland, 2010). Families knew that the different schools provided their children with different expectations, resources, beliefs and education, tailored to particular futures. They knew also that in some schools their children would be physically and emotionally safer than in others:

> I did the 11+ so I passed and went to the Grammar School. The equivalent for the girls would be . . . High, same; 99.9% white Protestant . . . People who were Roman Catholic would go to two of the other schools. If you didn't pass you went to . . . Intermediate, which was a Comprehensive . . . slightly more, but not much more, mixed in religious terms. (James)

The importance of selection for the 'right' school concerned more than the quality of the education, but was also about securing pathways to future well paying work, social mobility and 'keeping out of trouble' and 'in' with the 'right group'. No wonder then, that for all children there was

> an anxiety that was closely related to school . . . the options for schools were either we went to . . . High School, which was by selection . . . or you went to . . . Secondary Modern and that was the place this trouble was going on. So the whole issue of where you went to school . . . was very fraught. (Cathy)

The schools provided different curricula and training and invested time differently, with higher academic expectations for some than others. Some of the children emerged from school with very limited qualifications, others with many and high expectations of professional careers. Employment futures were imagined differently for children in their families and in the wider society based on their sex, religion, ethnicity and colour (see Chapter 7) as well as their social class.

Social Networks

Familial social networks also created opportunities to gain better paid work:

> That was [father's] first job [in England] . . . baked bread or something. Then one of my brothers worked [there] as well. (Rehana)

It was only through knowing some people who were in this kind of work, [mother] kind of fell into it, she wasn't really looking for it. (Rachel)

My mother had got a job as a technician in a large secondary school; locally . . . [father] joined her as a technician at the school. (Pamela)

These networks and contacts benefited the children themselves when they come to look for work and were highly significant, creating pathways to better paid or 'nicer' employment for some; including Tessa, with horses and George at the gas board, where his father worked. Through her mother's work contacts, Rachel got fashion work which was exciting and interesting, providing an entry into the world of celebrity:

You're showing the next seasons collections . . . sorting out the clothes, getting them in the right running order . . . getting clothes ready and putting them in the clothes . . . it's all very fast and frantic, and all the designers are kicking off and being dramatic and unreasonable . . . Great fun for me at the time . . . sometimes you meet famous people, which was nice.

At a similar age, Paulina experienced the physically cold and tiring work of a hand carwash:

It was wellies, buckets and your cloth . . . I can remember one particular day . . . water was going in my wellies . . . they weren't particularly well fitting wellies and my feet feeling like lumps of ice.

Paulina may well have obtained this work through her social networks but the employment provided a very different experience and more limited potential for future work. Social and familial networks were very important in relation to the work opportunities for children and were one of the vehicles for passing on benefits of class and position. The equality legislation of the 1970s in the United Kingdom was concerned to put a stop to such informal and unequal employment practices (Williams, 1989).

Status and Recognition

Children measured their own prosperity and status in comparison to those nearby, whether they themselves were from better off or poorer homes:

We were classed as the rich family of the street, 'cause my dad used to get £8 a week . . . 'We can pay our own rent' . . . we could have our own TV, you know, instead of renting. (Lara)

They measured their prosperity in comparison to other social groups who appeared to be positioned differently. Madhi spoke of the Muslims in the area of India her (Hindu) family came from, which she visited as a child. She spoke of the work they did and where they lived:

cleaning of the streets . . . I'd never really noticed them, until when I was 16 . . . we were going round the cricket grounds . . . it was almost underneath the earth . . . there were these little hidden shacks . . . almost living in dark . . . and very close together.

Richard spoke of the Black labourers, who worked with his White father in South Africa during apartheid:

[The White workers] all had . . . helpers . . . black guys . . . the labourers . . . and the culture was . . . you called them 'Boy' . . . but my dad always used to call them by whatever their name was.

Sivanandan (2001) writes of the racist rationales used to justify the exploitation of workers, which he argues historically demonized particular groups of people; in the first instance to justify slavery, then colonialism and then the movement of workers under global capitalism. The colour hierarchies of South Africa were part of growing up there, particularly during apartheid. Children had a strong sense of what their place was considered to be in the employment order related to their colour and skin tone.

Children quickly became aware of the relationship between work and social reputation. They took pride and pleasure if their family gained social esteem:

I was quite proud of the fact that my mum worked for the police, 'cause I was very law abiding and thought that was good. (Apara)

He . . . actually figured on the BBC news at six o'clock when he was interviewed. We got a special dispensation from school to watch television on that day . . . Oh I was very proud of him. (Martin)

I knew that my dad was always respected by our family and our community, 'cause when we'd go to social functions, people used to call my dad 'Master' . . . People would come to our house . . . my dad would help them fill out papers and forms . . . He was different to other people's dads. I knew that . . . it made you feel proud 'Oh look at my dad!'. (Madhi)

Children were also deeply affected by the insecurities and loss of status and reputation that were generated, for example, by unemployment. When Pamela's father was made redundant:

> There was a lot of anger . . . I can remember feeling confused about who they were angry with exactly. I mean, who had actually stopped my father working? . . . The fact that he was unemployed and not going to work and hanging around the house all the time, really upset our routines and he was very upset. (Pamela)

Children became aware of the varying quality of work, that work could physically hurt and was tiring, or that it was considered of low social value. Madhi became aware that her mother's cleaning work was of low social status:

> I went to the school where she was the cleaner . . . we all knew . . . especially the Asian community, that our . . . parents were doing jobs that were not very well [paid], or well thought of . . . cleaning up other peoples mess, whereas other people's parents were working in offices or whatever . . . I do remember this really funny time, when my mum was walking past me in the corridor and one of the boys in my class pipes up to my mum, in this stupid accent 'Hello Auntie' and my mum just looked at him and said 'Hello', and I had this moment 'Should I tell him to Fuck Off, or should I just ignore it, but then if I ignore it I'm dissing my mum', and in the end I said, 'Oi, that's my mum you're talking about' and . . . the boy, was 'Oh Sorry . . . '.

Lara and Paulina's fathers were involved in dangerous work in factories:

> He ended up going to hospital and having an operation . . . to restructure his hand . . . it was actually crushed in the machine . . . his arm was in the air and he had a blue bandage on it . . . so badly crushed. (Lara)

> He took me to work . . . it was a big industrial firm . . . big machines, furnaces, and just lots of people working, the noisiness of it, the darkness, the grimness . . . that was my very first . . . image of work . . . 'This isn't a

place I want to be' . . . although the people were nice, feeling sorry for my dad, that he had to do that. (Paulina)

Their parents' lack of choice, but to do unpleasant and hard work, became clearer to children as they grew older, and some developed a deeper understanding of the exploitative relations of work and the unequal sharing of profits:

> A ship would have something wrong with it . . . would come into the docks and would need to be worked on . . . as many hours of the day they could, to get it out as quickly as possible . . . to increase profit, 'cause it cost them money the longer it stayed in the dry dock. (Richard)

The gendered nature of work also became increasingly visible. Although her mother's work was less physically dangerous than her father's, Paulina saw it as hard and monotonous, ' . . . going one day with her to work and seeing rows and rows of people just sewing away' (Paulina). Claudia remembered the women involved in potato picking, 'It wasn't very nice when it was cold, and clearly hard work, back breaking work for the women that were doing it' (Claudia).

When the children commenced work themselves, unless they were properly supported and trained to cope with the complex, profit related routines (Lefebvre, 1991) the experience could be quite traumatic and damaging to their self-esteem. Madhi got a job in a shoe shop:

> It was a nightmare. I didn't know what I had to do . . . all these shoes fell on me in the stock cupboard and I just had to pile them back up. . . . I was run off my feet, and a lot of the kids . . . weren't very nice . . . You had to sell as many shoes as possible . . . at the end of the night, when they did the tilling up, they'd say which member of staff sold the most shoes.

Apara had a similar experience in a department store:

> Horrible . . . Spent my days encased in this brown crimpelene dress . . . my first day . . . I was just so incompetent. I was put on . . . the raw meat counter first, but I had to be taken off that very quickly, 'cause I couldn't catch the bacon . . . They put me on the sticky buns counter and you were supposed to add it up in your head and I just kept getting it wrong.

Young people's vulnerability to low pay and exploitation was nowhere clearer than in the case of Rehana, who at 16, worked in a chemical factory, where the health and safety issues were clearly ignored, 'It was things like anti-freeze and petrol patch . . . car sprays. We just had to bottle them from the big containers . . . we were supposed to wear masks . . . I used to get blisters on my fingers'.

From these experiences and their observations of their parents' work, children learned what work they did not want to do in the future. Some developed acute awareness of the risks associated with work:

> I didn't want to know a factory . . . when I left school . . . I [wasn't] going in a factory. That was one thing and I think that was because of my first images of, definitely my dad's place, but also my mum's. (Paulina)

As Haug (1992) argues, the social rules and relations related to social class, ethnicity and gender, represented in the structures of employment and related occupations are more than just external They are internalized by people, not least the children who are newly introduced to them. Children in this research took pride if they benefited socially from these work relations. They also felt humiliation, confusion and shame related to their own and family experiences. They questioned these social rules when they or their families were looked down on. Through these experiences, children discovered their own potential social place in the work order and something of the social relations of work that they might engage in. The relationship between work, social status and self-esteem shaped their experiences every day.

Conclusion

This chapter has considered how the wider social sphere of work informed children's everyday lives from a young age and how they engaged with work in many ways. In childhood the meaning of work blurred. At times it was experienced as play and at times as hardship. It connected children with new people and ideas and informed social expectations. This happened through stories from the past shared with children as well as everyday experiences. Work involved relationships and learning, and related closely to social position and geographic place. Work shaped how the child was looked after and by whom. Hence work in childhood was associated with many different aspects of everyday life.

Through their engagements with work, both inside and outside the family home, children learned about the social value and priority of time spent working. Money was accepted as the driver to a good quality of life. The value of money was learned. However, there were also many silences about employment, particularly during childhood. The wider social relations of work including the power, pursuit of profit and exploitation involved were less visible. Some work experiences, such as unemployment, accidents, mistakes, lower status positions, were therefore felt as personal and/ or familial failures. See, for example, Apara's and Madhi's first negative experiences of work systems and the way Pamela remembered reacting to her father's unemployment. Some children, such as Lara and Paulina, did learn early about the associations between danger and hard physical work; Lara through her father's injuries, Paulina through her observations of grim parental workplaces. Other children never experienced these aspects of work life.

Stories from the family archive that were shared with children sometimes stressed individual work related achievements of particular kin, less so the influence of collective struggles against discrimination. Martin's mother's entry to higher education, for example, would have been secured both through her own ability and through earlier feminist pressure to widen access to universities (Moss, 2006b). Richard was taught something about the exploitative relations underpinning work. Apara was taught of the working-class struggles that had improved working conditions. Other children learned that work involved confusing expectations and demands and that they needed to position themselves with a questioning eye to their own safety.

Employment in childhood provides a place for a range of experiences from play, leisure, learning and work that are hard to separate. Childhood is involved with the sphere of employment. Employment informs play. See how care, work and play are blended in Cathy's journeys in her father's lorry. Schooling leads to differentiated employment and transmits employment ethics. It led some of the children such as Martin and Sylvia straight to university, others, such as Paulina and Lara, straight to fairly low paid work. Domestic life is riddled with work related stories and practices. The blending of work–play and work–home in children's lives is hard to disentangle. The 'public' sphere of employment penetrates everyday childhood and provides children with more understanding of themselves in relation to others. Children journey through the complex space and time of employment both inside and outside the home and carve out space–time for themselves accordingly, with an eye to their own imagined future. This may echo the one imagined by adults but have particular and important adaptations – see how Paulina said she would never work in a factory. Children's everyday movement through space and time involves weaving different influences. This is important to understand. The conceptualization of childhood as involving transition to work is limited. Work penetrates the everyday lives of children continuously and in complex ways. At the time of writing, many people are losing their jobs as political decisions are made to support the banking system and cut public expenditure (Elliot, 2010). Children will experience the material, social and emotional consequences of this directly and in all the dimensions of their everyday lives discussed in this chapter.

Chapter 6

Children and Religion

Introduction

This chapter discusses religion in relation to children's everyday lives. This is conceptualized as involved with childhood in complex ways, whether children come from families that actively practice religion or not. Long time spans of collective religious memory continue to shape children's present times,

> although religious memory tries to isolate itself from temporal society, it obeys the same laws as every collective memory: it does not preserve the past but reconstructs it with the aid of the material traces. (Halbwachs, 1925/1992, p. 119)

The religions that influenced the lives of children in the research included Hinduism, Islam, Christianity and Judaism. Atheism and Humanism are also considered, as they emerge from and/or in relation to other belief systems and were mentioned by respondents in relation to memories of religion.

This chapter does not consider the way children conceptualize religion in relation to their development. This development has been characterized as children moving from 'more concrete imaginary and literal belief' in the early years through to more abstract religious thinking in adolescence (Bridges and Moore, 2002, p. 3). Nor does the chapter attempt to distinguish different types of 'religiosity' in terms of 'intrinsic' versus 'extrinsic'. The former is considered 'a search for the spiritual, as it is undertaken within a collective' and the latter 'participation in a religious community to reach goals that are not inherently spiritual' (ibid.). Such distinctions, related to a contested concept of spirituality, are difficult to make. Childhood in this chapter is conceptualized as experienced within overlapping religious and secular landscapes and involving a range of complex engagements that cannot easily be separated in these ways. Religions structure the childhood calendar in particular and overlapping ways. The chapter looks at

the interplay between religious times and the times of childhood exploring different influences. It explores the way that children in the research
engaged with and resisted different forms of moral regulation, carved out
space and time for their own childhood and practiced religion in their
own way.

Religions transmit particular images of the world and how children
should behave. They may warn against materialism, conceptualize work as
furthering God's will, see material wealth as a blessing, see hardship as a
consequence of sin or a route to salvation. They may value reciprocity and
they may value individual enterprise (Weber, 1948/1991a; 1948/1991b).
Religions may value the roles of men and women differently and transmit particular ideas about what is sanctified or not in relation to sexuality (Foucault, 1980b). Religious functionaries are granted the status and
authority to propagate and interpret these messages and mete out sanctions and rewards in different childhood settings.

Religion, particularly in more secular societies, may be seen as separated from other spheres of experience when it is closely connected.
Religious images and concepts are woven through the spheres of education, work, politics and war. Concepts from Puritanism paved the way for
modern capitalism through ideas about individualism and the thriving
self (Weber, 1948/1991a). Hence children's experience of religion may
be direct and indirect and involve complex threads of social memory that
inform several different aspects of their lives.

The chapter is five parts that consider different dimensions of children's
experience of religion. First it considers how participants themselves distinguished between 'doing religion' and 'being religious'. Following this,
the second part discusses children's sense of belonging to a particular
belief system. Thirdly, it explores children's experiences of freer movement
between diverse religions. Religious institutions and practices are deeply
associated with major personal loss such as bereavement and the fourth
part of the chapter considers this. Finally, the chapter considers religious
and 'moral' discipline in its subtle and far less subtle forms.

'Doing religion' and 'being religious'

When asked to remember experiences related to religion, memories were
evoked of visits to religious institutions, encounters with religious people
and involvement in other formal, family and community based events.
This included conversations about faith, feelings, participation in rituals

and the experience of religious and moral discipline. Respondents distinguished between involvement in religious practices and personal beliefs. For example, Madhi, who had not been made to attend the Hindu temple on a regular basis, distinguished between 'doing' religion and 'being' religious. Her friends had been forced to go to temple as children and they accused her of not being a real Hindu. When she was a young person she began to read about Hinduism and found some relevance to her own life. She distinguished between genuine and enforced religious practice. Richard and Apara also drew distinctions between beliefs and practices Richard's family were 'token Church of England' but in practice 'Atheist' and sought rational explanations for events which they shared with their children, ' . . . I think they were quite happy for us to understand the story of Jesus and all the rest of it but would balance it with, "You need to bear in mind, it's a fable." ' Apara's grandparents and mother were 'Humanist' and drew distinctions between the humanity of some religious messages and the corruption of religious power, ' . . . thought Jesus had some nice ideas but organized religion was a thing they did not approve of . . . they reckoned that it was always subverted for the benefit of the male power base of whatever country'.

In this chapter the ideas of 'doing' religion and 'being' religious blur. It is hard to categorize the ways children identify themselves, the beliefs they engage with, their treatment and other experience in these ways. In this context, abstracting 'being' from 'doing' becomes difficult. However from 'doing' to 'being' does indicate a temporal process of becoming more deeply engaged, which distinctions between 'intrinsic' and 'extrinsic' religiosity (see above) may fail to convey. Maintaining the visibility of space and time gives visibility to the process, drawing attention to context and the complex nature of action (Sayer, 1992). Memories in childhood provide a lens to the wider landscape, drawing attention to the complex and different ways that religion and childhood interrelate.

Religion formed part of the social landscape which each child in the research experienced in different ways, 'It was very obvious, 'cause there was a mosque nearby our house and you could hear the call for prayers five times a day . . . You grew up with that noise in your head' (Rehana). Religious practices structured the childhood calendar, marked important transitions to adulthood and provided frameworks for other experiences:

recruited to be a Sunday School teacher . . . an automatic thing, so . . . I had little five year olds to draw pictures with and read them a bible story . . . then taking them to church, so you sat through the service . . . I

think I was interested in it . . . I never got moved by it as a child, but I kind
of quite liked the ritual, and the song singing. (Rachel)

going to church . . . on Sunday, was a regular part of being a child . . .
went to church primary school . . . the boarding school . . . Church of
England . . . a regular part of the daily life of the school. (Martin)

Belonging

Some of the children felt a deep sense of religious belonging, others, were
less interested and engaged. James, who grew up during the conflict in
Northern Ireland in a Protestant community, described belonging to an
interpretation of faith that comfortably informed many different aspects
of his everyday experience:

> I was very happy to be very much a part of [religion] . . . through Sunday
> school, church, confirmation . . . The school I went to had a very high
> Christian moral ethos . . . steeped in the curriculum . . . the local com-
> munity boys brigade . . . church services, marches, bible classes.

Protestant religious practices marked his transitions and structured his
childhood calendar. Rehana also came from a community where religion
provided such a framework and came to influence and shape her desires:

> I used to see these little girls with their little scarves on their heads, and
> carrying a little Koran, wrapped up in a little cloth . . . walking to the
> mosque . . . I wanted to keep the fast for the whole day, and I wasn't
> allowed to because I was too little.

Whether this sense of belonging and the desire to belong to a religious
community was a sign of developing spirituality is hard to say. In childhood, a feeling of spirituality is involved with the desire to be included
and to share in a wide range of practices related to sociability, festivity,
clothing, music and food (Henderson et al., 2007, also see Chapter 10).
This is evident in Paulina's account of early religious experience in the
Caribbean, where religious practices provided special time away from the
daily routines,

> it was 'Hearts on Hands', and they dressed in black and white and tam-
> bourine and singing . . . the jolliness . . . the starkness of this . . . it was
> out on the streets . . . remember it being a happy time.

Later, Paulina said she chose to renew her Christianity which she referred to as being 're-born'. Again the memory is associated with a particular outdoor place, music, festivity and a sense of inclusion:

> It was the place I gave my life to Christ and I was re-born . . . 16/17ish . . . by the seaside . . . bonfire on the beach . . . used to sing 'Work for my Daddy-o' . . . I loved the beach and the night scenes and the singing.

Researchers have tried to identify how and why such religious attachments develop in childhood, relating this to the nature of parental beliefs and the quality of familial relationships (Kirkpatrick and Shaver, 1990). The wider religious landscape and the way this is involved with everyday experience is also very significant.

For children in communities where religion explicitly informs their everyday lives (education, meals, social calendar), belonging to the community involves belonging to a particular faith. It is hard to disentangle these. For children growing up in more secular societies, religion too may provide a deep sense of belonging and a framework for experience. Kate remembers that religion provided an anchor at a time of emotional turbulence and transition:

> The church was important during my teens. I would sit at the back and enjoy the service. I also had a crush on one of the choir boys and would try to smile at him when he processed . . . Sunday School . . . I remember our group being asked why we needed to say special prayers that week and answering that we had nearly had a nuclear war.

Kate's memories demonstrate how the experience of religion in childhood is particular to the social landscape of the time and how the child's position and desires (related to gender and age, for example) inform the relationship.

A sense of deep belonging in childhood may involve the identification of 'others' (people and things that do not belong). Religion is involved with social conflict (see Chapter 8). Habashi (2008) interviewed 12 Palestinian children and explores their conceptualizations of 'self' and 'other'. These concepts are rooted in historical narratives about resistance, honour, traitors and oppressors. The idea of the 'religious self' and the 'religious other' are part of their understanding. The lines of division in the social landscape that children encounter may be delineated in relation to different faiths and different interpretations of particular faiths. When (Protestant) James remembered Catholicism in Northern Ireland, he said,

> As a child, it was certainly one of two parts – we were one part and it was another part and everything associated with that was not for us . . . The messages . . . they were about a different sort of religion, a different relationship between clergy and congregation. The message to me was such that Catholicism was about indoctrination more so than worship . . . you don't sit on the fence. You're either one or the other . . . there's a security. (James)

When the interplay between religion, family and community involves ongoing conflict, the choice or desire to retreat from the family's religious base is less possible. Religious differences become threatening (see Chapter 8) being part of complex historical divisions. Halbwachs (1925/1992) argues that social conflict and the movement of peoples underpins all religious development (see Chapter 8).

Hence, familial and community memories delineated the boundaries of religious belonging for particular children. In the midst of conflict and war this process was intense and loaded with emotion. When conflict settled, the narratives of religious difference carried on, creating a sense of appropriate and inappropriate beliefs for the child but also tinged by retrospective humour and some critical distance. George heard tales about 'inter-religious violence' and political conflict in these ways:

> My great Granny used to have to be boarded into her room, because she would go out and do violence against the Catholics and one of the stories that I was told was that she emptied the chamber pot over the crowd when they came past.

Kate, who lived in northern England, was warned about listening to her father:

> Although my dad was a lapsed Catholic he had a sense of support for the Catholic community in Northern Ireland and listened to John McCormack. I remember my friend's mother . . . saying that [he] was a rebel and we shouldn't listen to him. (Kate)

At a different time and place, away from direct conflict, familial and community memories may be less likely to reinforce a religious position in the child and a sense of belonging to a particular faith, but they are still highly significant, and continue narratives of division that may be accentuated when other forces are at work (such as unemployment and economic inequality).

Feelings of belonging are associated with many spheres of experience, not solely religious, and with similar degrees of intensity. Cathy remembered the passion and commitment associated with being a football fan throughout her childhood (see Chapter 10), 'The belief is in a God, or in a team: both are there to perform, bless, lead and bring victory to the believer' (Percy and Taylor, 1997, p. 40). Madhi said that participation in sport (see Chapter 10) replaced religion as a source of meaning for her:

> Throughout my teens I just stopped praying, I stopped doing everything and my mother just gave up . . . at that time, I got really into sport and stuff, so that was quite a big part of my identity and who I was.

Despite designated religious pathways, children made their own choices and interpreted religion in relation to their personal experience, position, desires and needs. At 11, Pamela rejected Christianity for Humanism because a pathway in that direction opened up:

> [My school] was quite high Anglican. Father . . . always wore his priest's cassock . . . My form teacher . . . was ex Roman Catholic . . . quite open to discussions and debates . . . so I joined the Humanist society when I was 11, in that first year.

Clearly such choices were much more possible where different pathways were available and were considered legitimate for particular children to follow.

Diverse Religions and Strange Encounters

In cities, many different religious practices leave their mark. Different social boundaries related to religion shape children's movement. Children may cross these boundaries. Strange and new religious encounters generate questions, uncertainty and excitement. Memories of religious conflict continue to shape events. Cathy and her sister (technically Protestant) moved through a complex religious landscape (see Chapter 2). They visited and were welcomed to a convent with a Catholic neighbour who they called Aunty:

> [The nuns] knew we weren't Catholics . . . but 'They're nearly Catholics cause they know Mary!' . . . She'd say, 'Go and tell [the nuns] this' . . . helping serve the lunches. They had an old peoples 'club' . . . I remember

that being an exotic world . . . It was a bit like 'Alice through the Looking Glass' . . . we'd walked past this wall for years and no idea in the world of what was behind it, and then to go in, and because of the religious imagery, it looked very different to what we were used to. (Cathy)

Several children crossed religious boundaries in this way and were involved in strange and different religious encounters, particularly in the city, where the movement of different peoples in and out created a complex tapestry, 'One of my friends was Polish . . . my friend . . . she was a Methodist or something . . . and I had Jewish friends. So I experienced lots of different religions even though we were never religious ourselves, I always went' (Julie). George remembered a regular visitor to his home who wasn't allowed in but stood on the step:

'Funny Joe', and he was a Jehovah's Witness, and in the words of my mum, he was 'A Bit Simple' . . . one of my early reading experiences was 'The Watch Tower'. So I associate religion with, you know, 'Armageddon' and 'saved and unsaved'. (George)

These encounters with religious difference also shaped children's families historically, as forming a family may involve the coming together of people from different religious traditions. Religious restrictions on inter-faith marriage limit this process. Children in the research therefore experienced a number of different religious influences within their families, for example, different versions of Christianity:

My dad [from the Caribbean] always supported that we had a Catholic religion. [Mum was an Italian Catholic] but he was Evangelist, so he always used to go to [Evangelist] churches . . . on a Saturday we used to have to go to . . . my dad's church, and we used to go and learn and sing and praise and dance . . . and get taught my dad's teachings and then on a Sunday, my dad used to get us all up, get us ready, in our best Sunday clothes, and we used to go to Catholic church. (Lara)

The form different religious influences take in families relates to the relative power of family members and the status of particular faiths in the wider community and country. These influences are involved with other areas of consensus and conflict within families. Sylvia remembered the way that domestic violence in her family (attacks on her mother by her father) was informed by religious differences. Her father was a German Jewish refugee from the Nazis and her mother, English born of Christian heritage:

> I was in bed, he'd come back from work. I could hear deep shouting and banging . . . I wanted it to stop, to sleep. She called him a 'Dirty Jew' and I knew that was a bad thing to say as I knew bad things had been done to the Jews in the war. (Sylvia)

Such experiences leave their mark and influence children's future expectations of both religion and family. Children listen, watch, question and sometimes hide. Each new religious encounter (in the broadest sense) introduces new threads of collective memory from the past.

Bereavement and Social Anchors

> You've got strong memories of little things, which I think you wrap all the other things round. (Julie)

Here, Julie was describing how she coped with her mother's illness and death when she was young (see below). Bereavement is a normal part of childhood as many children lose significant kin before they are 18 (McCarthy, 2007), but the loss of a parent is much rarer.

Because religious influences are deeply implicated in children's everyday experience, they are associated with a wide range of emotion. Respondents recalled feelings of intense pleasure, boredom, inquisitiveness, uncertainty and fear. The form religion takes and its particular attention to matters of life and death however, means that some feelings may be more intensely associated with religion than with other spheres of experience. Feelings of desire, belonging and uncertainty (see above) may also be shaded by fears associated with death, dying and the afterlife and the grief related to bereavement. Apara's family were 'Humanist':

> I was worried because what would happen to Auntie . . . when she died, and I said 'I understand that if you are good and you believe in God, you go to heaven, but if you've been very bad, you go to hell, but what if you're good but you don't believe in God . . . will she just stay in her grave?' . . . My mum saying 'Well, nobody really knows . . . ' and I said, 'Well I've thought about it and I've decided that I'm not going to believe in God either because I don't want Auntie . . . to be alone for ever in her grave,

so if we bury me next to her then I can talk to her and we can keep each other company so that she won't be all alone when everybody else is up in heaven.'

Apara's delightful logic, as convincing as any religious fable of the afterlife, was structured around religious ideas and practices she had encountered, concerned with life, death, afterlife, rituals of dealing with the dead, morality and a need to adhere to her family's beliefs (in this case, not religious).

Religious practices provide systems and structures for dealing with grief and loss. Ritual ceremonies related to bereavement may ease the process through the confirmation of community and familial bonds. They may provide a sense of future continuity and emotional comfort and they may not (Cohen, 1985; Driver, 1991). Mysterious, deeply upsetting and inexplicable events, such as the death of a close family member, may become deeply associated with particular artefacts that become symbolic containers of children's hopes and fears. Religious practices may provide such artefacts.

Both Julie and Rehana experienced the deaths of their mothers. Rehana was very small (4 years), Julie older (14). For both, the memory of their mother's death was vivid:

> My mother . . . died of a brain hemorrhage . . . very dedicated, a very accomplished woman . . . every minute of that day I remember so vividly . . . from the time she was taking her last breath . . . me going to the grave yard, seeing her burial and right up to the next day, and some of the events that followed . . . and what everybody said, who was there, what was happening. It's like minute by minute by minute, memory, like a film in my head . . . not realising the finality about death. (Rehana)

> She had cancer . . . I think she should have had a hysterectomy when I was little, but she didn't want to leave me . . . I remember her dying and I saw her when she was dead . . . She was in the front room, as they were in those days, on the funeral day . . . Somebody else took me in to see her, and it was a really good thing, because the last time I saw her . . . she looked like a skeleton. They'd made her look nice and peaceful in death. (Julie)

The raw descriptions of the deaths were accompanied with comments on the goodness of the mothers they had lost. Research has shown how a continued narrative about the person lost informs memories of their death (McCarthy, 2007). There were stark images of the processes of dying and death. Julie and Rehana remembered the ceremonies through which the transition from death was managed. These memories clustered, 'wrapping around' the events (see above) which were very hard for the children to deal with. Both remembered a critical event which was laden with significance and symbolism. Before her mother died, Julie visited her in hospital:

> I must have picked a lily of the valley out of the garden . . . I was walking by myself from the house . . . to the hospital . . . I somehow dropped all these lily of the valley all over the street, that I'd picked for her, and this kid at the other side of the road laughing at me, and being tearful, 'I'm going to the hospital without' – not picking the flowers up, just left them – being mortified.

Rehana remembered standing by the funeral:

> There was . . . one of these mystic, beggar type women who . . . just come from the street to have a look and she had all these big massive beads . . . she almost looked like a white witch . . . like a magician almost . . . I'm thinking in my head . . . 'This woman's gonna perform magic and my mum's gonna wake up and everything's gonna be alright.'

Many other events and associated emotions clustered and were wrapped around these memories. The flowers in Julie's memory and the woman with beads in Rehana's memory carried emotion and hope for the children. They were drawn from the ritualized processes related to sickness and death available in the religious culture. The flowers were customarily taken to the bedside or funeral in Christian tradition. The mourners with beads, from outside the family, attended the burial as a sign of respect in the Islamic tradition. Julie's momentary inability to cope and isolation came together in the dropping of the flowers. Rehana's inability to understand the death of her mother, and the grief around her, came together in her hope for a magical solution. Death is hard in any culture (McCarthy, 2007).

From those times, Julie's and Rehana's experiences of home were deeply affected in different ways. Rehana's childhood was woven with familial stories about her mother and her own personal memories. Julie was more isolated and reliant on her own skills:

> She'd always been ill and I brought myself up . . . I think I was doing housework and bits of cooking. I remember ironing my tie for a speech day and burning it – big heat mark on my tie.

McCarthy (2007) discusses young people's isolation within family relationships and how the grief within the family may limit support to the child. This seemed the case with Julie more so than Rehana, whose kinship support was much more extensive.

Other loss and bereavement, less immediate but very powerful, shaped the lives of others in the research. Claudia lost her sister when she was a young adult and there is no doubt her memories of their shared childhood were deeply coloured by this later loss. George's parents lost two babies before he was born. Their memories of loss affected his home life and were influential in the way he was very carefully looked after, loved and protected (see Chapter 4). In addition,

> I was a difficult sleeper . . . probably not helped . . . by the fact that my parents kept my dead sister's toys in and behind the wardrobe in my room . . . So I used to make them sit in the room, while I fell asleep . . . I could see the light of the cigarette. (George)

The collection of toys and other memorabilia related to the loss were kept in the family archive. This served a purpose. Halbwachs explains the power of religious memory in the family, particularly in relation to the attention to departed kin and the relationship between familial and social practice:

> the cult of the dead allowed the family to reaffirm its bonds, to commune periodically with the memory of departed kin, and to reaffirms its sense of unity and continuity . . . following roughly uniform rites . . . they participated in a totality of beliefs common to all their community. (1925/1992, p. 65)

This may be a depressing and/or an uplifting experience for children. It may be felt as oppressive because the child might be burdened with expectations through comparison with the person lost, but it may also give them comfort and develop their understanding that this is both a personal and shared human experience. The child may be fearful of their own death. McCarthy (2007) has argued that research into bereavement has given poor visibility to the relative power, responsibility and involvement of children and young people. Religion and death are associated and this association comes to be understood by children. This association attracts and deters children according to their experiences and desires. For Kate, this association was formative in the way she imagined her future:

When I was about fourteen I remember spending time in bed planning my orphanage in Africa. I also had a hymn book and would sing favourite hymns, particularly 'Love Divine' which was sung at my brother's wedding. Religion was very important to me and influenced my thinking about the future. (Kate)

The religious future she imagined concerned the bereavement of children; it concerned doing good and gaining salvation (Kate would save the orphans and in turn be 'saved' by God) and it concerned the dissemination of Christianity to an imagined place in 'Africa'. In other tales of the time (in England in 1950s and 1960s) this place was represented as 'less civilized', where the people were considered to need 'conversion'; a religious narrative from further past that justified empire building.

Religious Discipline and Abuse

Enduring throughout is my conviction that a focus on children's geographies articulates how places, institutions and mechanistic notions of justice teach young people how to behave and how young people resist this kind of disciplining. (Aitken, 2001, p. 26)

Aldridge (2006) discusses the Durkheimian perspective that religion provides social cohesion, social control, meaning and purpose to life. But the social and moral regulation associated with religion may be experienced as abuse. Consider Lara's experiences below, in the context of divisions related to her social class, gender and ethnicity. This treatment reinforced pre-existing divisions and reproduced inequality. Here religious discipline transmitted certain dogma and operated in the interests of those wielding it:

We had to learn this Catechism, and you had to recite it in class . . . I remember really struggling. I used to have to write . . . put my finger between . . . to make a space, otherwise I'd just continuously write without a space and she always used to rap me on the knuckles for putting my fingers between, but it's the only way I could . . . nuns were dreadful. (Lara)

As religion is socially legitimated in relation to the regulation of children's moral behaviour, this is source of fear, respect, anxiety and rebellion in childhood. Halbwachs distinguishes between the mysticism and dogmatics informing religious practice. Dogmatics, 'are not preoccupied with reliving the past but with conforming to its teaching' (1925/1992, p. 103). Within homes, schools and religious centres, children are told moral tales about good and bad behaviour, sinfulness and punishment, intended to regulate their behaviour. These may be explicit stories from the sacred texts. They may involve different sanctions and rewards related to behaviour management (the concern to control greed, waste and rudeness in the child). They may be concealed within citizenship or other forms of 'moral education'. They provoke strong emotion, enquiry and resistance (both passive and active). In addition, children repeat these moral tales, 'I remember a family tea when I was about four. My nephew was sitting next to me and didn't eat his ice cream and I told him he shouldn't waste it and everyone laughed' (Kate).

Children fear the moral sanctions. This is where 'The eye of God or Satan' (Saadawi, 2007, p. 9) merge in their experience. See how Madhi echoed the feelings of Saadawi:

> I've got vivid memories of being a really young girl . . . being frightened of this thing called 'God'. Frightened that if I did something wrong, I was gonna get punished . . . if you're not good, something bad's going to happen to you in the future, that Karma stuff . . . Sometimes when I'd done anything bad, I remember going to sleep thinking 'Oh my God, I'm going to get punished . . . and God's everywhere, and God's gonna know that I've lied and God's going to see everything that I've done.'

Sanctions against children's behaviour may be abusive, they may be internalized so the child regulates their own behaviour, they may be repeated by children themselves and they may be resisted. Punishment may involve the exclusion of children from religious spaces:

> I was doing a Frankenstein impression from down the aisle [of the church], just trying to chase this friend around, arms outstretched. I have no idea why I was doing it, but we were yanked out and basically told never to darken the doors of the church again. So that was the last time I went to church. (Apara)

The ritualized repetition of what is perceived by some to be meaningless dogma could create resistance in other ways, such as boredom and disengagement. There is a deep boredom associated with enforced (rather than willing) religious practice in childhood. Boredom in itself is a complex feeling that is also associated with fear, lack of confidence and emotional resistance. In childhood, boredom involves the denial of play, 'My dad's church, we used to find it really boring . . . wanted to play out. You didn't want to be in your Sunday clothes' (Lara). Tessa's mother experienced boredom through enforced religion when a child. She made sure her own children had a more secular experience: 'We're a very non religious family, generally . . . the reasons why, I think, mum had been made to go to chapel when she was little and thought it was very boring, very dull, very plain.'

The capacity to choose secularism as an alternative to religion did not happen in social isolation. It reflected wider social change, where religion was being accorded less social authority in England in the 1960s and 1970s. In the early 1960s, the most significant aspect of Martin's 'confirmation' appeared to be that, 'We got the rest of the day off, so it was actually worth it for getting the rest of the day off' (Martin). The creativity of children to make the most of things is evident in the way Apara handled religion:

I didn't want to do Brownies, mostly 'cause I had such an aversion to the colour brown . . . being brown was the bane of my life.

So I went, [to the Girl's brigade] and there was this clause, that in order to be in the Girls brigade you also had to go to the Sunday school . . . I persuaded mum to let me join, cause it all seemed to be dancing and having a go on the vault and stuff like that . . . Went to a bit of the service . . . [My brother] came a couple of times, until one Sunday when I painted his toenails before we went, and it was really frowned upon, and so we didn't go back and mum didn't have any nail remover and he had sandals on.

Religious institutions may be like fossils in the landscape, providing frameworks for what are considered more pleasurable activities, but where child abuse may go unchallenged.

Saadawi (2007) writes of her own physical mutilation as a girl which was sanctioned by religion and carried out by adults in the family. Her life's work has involved political struggle for equality which has led her into much danger and imprisonment. Religion may claim the social space for the moral regulation of children but in so doing the spaces for abuse may be increased and legitimated. The 'single eye' (God and Satan) was evident in Lara's experience of punishment by the nuns and in Madhi's feelings of guilt. Haug points out how, 'Adults seem, on the one hand, to be in complicity with the judges. On the other, they appear as comforters, as beings who act as a force for both reconciliation and regimentation' (1992, p. 45). The authority socially granted to religious functionaries to discipline children means that much associated violence and abuse of children has gone unchallenged (Butt and Asthana, 2009).

Themes within religious discourses may become naturalized as representing good behaviour when they work in the interests of powerful social groups (Aldridge, 2006):

> I can remember being told off once . . . we used to do jobs round the house when we were staying in the summer and we'd get 5p and 10p for something . . . I'd done something and obviously thought that I was going to get 10p for it and I remember [Grandpa] telling me vividly that you didn't do something to get something. You did it because you wanted to do it for somebody and you shouldn't expect something at the end and that vividly stuck with me that actually you do things *for* people, not to get something back . . . Church of England, very strong – do the right thing. A sense of you did the right thing for the right reasons. (Tessa)

Here, the desire for money was associated with the moral bad; as 'materialistic' rather than involving self-sacrifice. A link was made between godliness and the importance of working for the common good (and future salvation). In these ways religious ideas are transmitted in the family. Some children, as they grow up, perhaps learn to accept low wages and identify struggles for acceptable pay as associated with selfishness and greed. However, such religious messages might also emphasize the need to share and the importance of reciprocity (see Madhi's experiences on the Ganges, Chapter 2).

Conclusion

The sphere of childhood and the sphere of religion interrelate in complex ways. Both are involved with other spheres of experience discussed throughout this book. Religion is significant in Chapter 8, concerned with war and conflict. It is also relevant in Chapter 6, concerned with the state. Madhi thought that migration (see Chapter 3), being in a minority combined with her mother's isolation, might have influenced the nature of religious commitment in her family:

My mother used to actually make us sing hymns and pray to God every night . . . It was her way of trying to give us something that would be meaningful . . . something that was quite important for her and in England, kept her going. This sort of faith and also something to maybe pass the time, because, I guess sometimes she was very isolated at home. So reading religious books and scriptures, gave her some sort of faith and she would tell us that reading this helps you, in the future, decide between right and wrong. (Madhi)

The influences of religion in children's lives are diverse, complex and difficult to disentangle from other spheres of experience. Religion provides children with family and community biography. It presents different pathways through childhood for children to choose from. It provides moral reference points, some of which are explicit, some taken for granted, their historical origins having lost visibility. Children from religious and secular societies and from practicing and non-practicing families are all profoundly influenced. Religious stories are transmitted through familial, community and national memories. Some relate to conflict; some to its resolution. Children construct possible futures for themselves and identify their own position in relation to other positions (Habashi, 2008). Each new religious encounter introduces children to new threads of social memory. Children are inquisitive, excited and fearful in relation to how they are positioned and the level of conflict in the wider society.

There are many silences in the social memory related to religion and the power of religious functionaries. These silences may involve the abuse of children such as Lara. They may involve the dissemination of dogma that leads to the continued oppression of a low-paid social class, or caste or minority faith. They may perpetuate war and conflict. Children carve out space–time for themselves from these complex religious landscapes and make individual choices in these contexts. They perform religious practices in their own way, with their own interpretation. They draw on religious engagements in multiple ways. Like Madhi, they may try and resist imposed categorization in terms of religious beliefs (Moinian, 2009), sometimes choosing different pathways, sometimes feeling boredom and disengaging. 'Belonging' manifests itself in different ways in childhood, but the sense of belonging has to be associated with the will to belong.

The complex religious influences in childhood need more disentangling to deepen understanding of children's everyday lives. Religion is too often associated with conflict, and the 'othering' of particular groups (see Chapter 8), rather than being recognized as part of the social fabric that all children engage with (whether 'believers' or not). The assumption that children belong to one faith or none, leads to the social 'locking in' of children in particular ways. On the one hand, children may be automatically assumed to share particular beliefs with adults in their 'faith communities', on the other, the ways that religion shapes the lives of more 'secular' children remain less visible.

Chapter 7

Children, State and Civil Society

My grandfather was very much aware that education had been withheld from the working class . . . been given as a right after a considerable fight . . . He said 'There are certain teachers who don't want to teach you – they might not want to teach you because of your class, they might not want to teach you because of your colour, however legally, they can't help themselves, they've got to . . . so don't give them any ammunition and take everything they've got to give you . . . '.

(Apara)

Introduction

This chapter explores respondents' experiences of different state processes in childhood. This is a complex area and is touched on in most chapters. The state intervenes and regulates migration, home life, employment and leisure. States engage in war and civil war, sponsor particular cultural and technological change and involve changing allegiance with particular powerful interests. The form of state intervention at a particular time relies on certain constructions and expectations of children and families (Moss, 2006). In this chapter, the state is conceptualized as part of the relations of everyday childhood involving institutions, state functionaries and different forms of intervention and regulation, 'The state is not a "thing" but a process, that in its shifting boundaries and ensembles provides the arena for the organization of social forces, continually recodifying as well as drawing upon "public" and "private" interests' (Coleman et al., 2009, p. 9). The state involves complex relations with the civil society of which children are a part. State processes involve selective social memories, reflect powerful influences and involve struggles over resources. The state generally views children in relation to their future contribution rather than viewing them as participants in these struggles (Mills, 2000). The social interests of children and of some of the communities to which they belong may be considered marginal in comparison with other influences. The different faces of the state may be disciplinary, supportive and neglectful in relation to different aspects of childhood experience (Fox-Harding, 1996). The state provides services, enforces responsibilities, rewards, sanctions and may ignore certain behaviour, for example, what happens inside the family may be sometimes considered outside the power of the state the intervene. It often perpetuates the assumptions and interests of powerful social groups at the expense of those less powerful. Some families may be labelled as 'less deserving' of support than others. Limits may be placed on support based on the countries where people come from (Williams, 1989; Jones and Novak, 1999). The 'criminal' behaviour of some better off groups may be ignored (Coleman et al., 2009). Although the state may be considered a unitary entity, it involves a complex web of powerful relationships and influences and may be best conceptualized in terms of the powerful governing social processes that inform everyday childhood.

In this chapter, first, the focus is on children's early experience of state processes through school, where they learn the power of state functionaries such as teachers and are positioned in particular ways related to their social background. Second, it considers the different faces of policing experienced, including, policing as a protective force, conflict between the police and young people and the policing of sexual identity and the family. Third, the chapter considers children's growing understanding of civil society movements, including feminism, Black consciousness, animal rights, labour movements and party political interests. Finally the chapter considers the ways that children navigate complex state relations including the ways they accept, resist and try to change their position.

Schooling and Children's Social Place

Selection for schooling and the implications for self-esteem and future employment are discussed in Chapter 5. The aspects of schooling that are considered here relate to the ways the children in the research began to learn the rules of engagement with the wider society and their social 'place'. When they entered school they were required to behave differently from home and to adapt to the collective of children and the interests of the institution. The changes required of them were more difficult for some than others. They had to move in particular ways through the space and time of the school day and learn the unique repetitive rhythms and routines of each institution (Lefebvre, 1991; Gallagher, 2006). Previously learned behaviour and routines from home were challenged. New sets of sanctions and rewards were encountered, intended to modify children's sense of who they were, in line with the requirements of the institution (Goffman, 1961; Illich, 1973). These were applied differentially as pupils conformed (or not) to wider social and institutional expectations. Children entering new schools entered new fields of selective social memories involving expectations for their future (in relation to family and work) (Welch, 2008b).

Some children in the research felt more comfortable at school than others. The reasons were complex and related to their home life, social position, the school and the connections between these influences (Edwards, 2002). School life was easier where there was an easy fit between the practices, values and beliefs encountered at home and school. Children quickly learned the hierarchical relations and social values attached to certain groups and in what ways their own lives were socially valued. They felt unease in strange settings and some children had to cross a chasm of difference and disrespect and did not feel easy with the manners, customs and abuse they encountered.

Julie was funded by the state to attend a private grammar school, where most of the girls were from more privileged homes. She felt her social class difference there. She never settled comfortably and started to play truant. She learned the hierarchies of social class that shaped the classroom hierarchies of the school and her place in those:

> I did feel like I was out of my class . . . there was a posh class, ours was an average . . . then there was another class that seemed to be more noisy . . . I was aware that they had a completely different lifestyle to me and that when I wanted some skates for my birthday, I arranged to buy second hand skates off somebody in my class.

In addition to reproducing social class divisions, Richard's school in the South African apartheid state was deliberately colour (and gender) segregated, ' . . . all white . . . all boys':

> We were shown a film at school . . . a white family living in a rural part of the country and they are attacked by some blacks . . . I remember the teacher at the end of the film actually being quite upset and saying 'That film was obviously made by a bunch of Nationalists'. (Richard)

The influences of school as an arm of the state were not straightforward. The teacher used her professional status to undermine the apartheid framework of understanding presented to the children. Nevertheless, the curriculum was developed in relation to eugenic ideas about the 'naturalness' of 'racial' difference and the threat to the social order from the oppressed and exploited Black majority.

Gender segregation in schools also took deliberate forms. In the United Kingdom, until the Education Reform Act, 1988, the curriculum varied in relation to gender (Welch, 2008b). In addition, Tessa experienced a particular form of gender segregation:

> a row of girls, a row of boys, a row of girls . . . We had years one to three boys' playground . . . one to three girls' playground and then when you got to be years four and five . . . were allowed to mix and speak.

Some educational consensus was achieved through professional acceptance of what were assumed to be 'natural' differences between boys and girls. Deep-seated gendered inequalities were also reproduced through this sort of spatial segregation. Sexualized differences were relied on, advanced and reconstructed in ways that suited particular political, economic and professional interests (Kristeva et al., 1981; Haug, 1992). Teachers and students were able to draw on different social ideas about the potential of girls, depending on time and place. At her grammar school, Pamela took up

> the classical Spanish guitar . . . [taught by] a music teacher at the schoo . . . in our first year there, free additional music lessons, if you took up an instrument . . . There's no way my family could have afforded me to go and have music lessons . . . my world opened up at that point.

The cultivation of girls' musical abilities were provided for in this (and Julie's) middle-class grammar schools. Different social divisions informed the everyday management and education of children:

> They'd walk past you to see if you were singing properly . . . We used to go in height order into the school, so there was me and two friends who must have been small . . . whether we became friends cause we were all the same height or not, I don't know. But walking past us once, and we were all three of us told to mime in future in assembly. (Julie)

One wonders whether it was flat notes in the singing that were being concealed, or the children's working-class accents; either might have altered the image the school wished to present.

School catchments were also different, related to social class and ethnicity. This sometimes led better off parents to move house, in order to secure a particular sort of schooling for their children. It was common knowledge that it was likely to be the better off children who achieved more academically. Some working-class families might have accepted this as inevitable, but others, like Cathy's, saw their children into the 'posher' schools. This led to her experience of ' . . . two separate worlds running alongside each other'.

The hierarchy of social values related to a child's considered social 'place' was reproduced in the playground, where children mirrored and resisted these divisions. Apara experienced abuse when she moved from a small private school in Nigeria to a predominantly White working-class state school in north-east England:

My colour was an issue . . . people who'd beat me up because of it and people who would tolerate me but still call me names when they felt like it . . . if you ever tried to assert what you wanted out of . . . friendship, then they would quite easily just turn around and call you a racist name.

Child against child hostility could be more intense in the playground where there was less supervision. Children learned that it may be safer to distance themselves from those who got bullied, in case they were bullied themselves (Candappa and Egharevba, 2002). Rehana, as a child, distanced herself in relation to class and ethnicity:

I just thought 'Why am I sitting with all these immigrants, all these dumbos?' . . . People who didn't have as good starting point as we did . . . 'Typical Asians', 'people from the villages' . . . We were bad.

Despite Pamela's enjoyment of some school based opportunities (see above), and her pride in being selected for a 'grammar' school (see Chapter 5), the school nevertheless required conformity and some stripping of prior identity:

uniform that was too big for me . . . long grey socks, dark bottle green serge pinafore dress thing, hat . . . velour in the winter and a straw one in the summer . . . lace up brown shoes . . . hated, loathed . . . 'cause the hat used to fall off, the socks used to fall down.

Uniforms were modelled on clothing from more elite schools and from past times. In order to sustain conformity and discipline in the school; children's behaviour was rewarded and sanctioned in particular ways. On Paulina's first day at school in the Caribbean she was brought home, 'Apparently there was some lad or something that was annoying me, and wasn't listening or something and I went and told him what to do and whopped the slate over his head!' Later, the complexity of rewards and sanctions baffled her at school in England, 'I won an award for not missing a day at the school, but I remember spending a lot of my time, still, outside the classroom doors'. Paulina's most positive memories of schools were that they were bases for friendship and play. She had a vivid memory of winning the award for attendance, but she also remembered being deliberately 'kept down' a class because of messages about her behaviour that followed her from a previous school. Particular imposed 'standards' were apparently more important than educational achievements.

Claudia and Richard conveyed their fear and anger in relation to the attitude and behaviour of particular teachers, ' . . . she used to shout at us. She was miserable and nasty . . . I remember standing next to her . . . the window was open, thinking "God, I'd love to throw you out of that window!"' (Claudia).

> We used to give teachers nicknames, according to their characteristic. This one teacher, if he used to hit you, he used to take great relish in the fact that he'd drawn blood, . . . so they used to call him 'Butch', short for butcher. (Richard)

Lara, who was used to being told off by teachers, subverted expectations through the use of humour, 'We were doing about sex education and it being a Catholic high school . . . so I promptly decided I'd ask if we could have a demonstration and I'd be a willing participant . . . and I got detention!!!' Through nicknaming teachers the children warned each other of the potential threat. The use of comedy subverted the system and elicited the collective support of other children. In these ways they refused to accept what they perceived to be poor treatment (Overlien and Hyden, 2009).

School was also remembered positively, where friendships were strong and pathways through, relatively smooth. Several of the children including Martin and Madhi, talked of school and friendship in positive ways. School could provide child friendly opportunity and education and many of the teachers were committed to children's well-being (as well as fulfilling the targets of the state and school), ' . . . listening to

"Magic Faraway Tree Stories" . . . a nice classroom and some playtime . . . reading . . . "The Big Red Bus Went up the Hill" . . . playing outside and paddling and things . . . ' Praise from teachers was vividly remembered, 'We were asked this at school, "How often do you read?" . . . I just kept putting my hand up, and I went off somewhere to do this selection of books, I was chosen' (Julie).

However, through schooling, the state could easily override personal needs and desires and children in the research worked for a more personalized and loving approach, 'I used to have a lovely, lovely, class teacher . . . getting there in the morning and watching to see whether my teacher's car would arrive and if not, that horrible sinking feeling' (Richard). 'Miss . . . walking past me, I was standing up to go to assembly and holding somebody else's hand, and she walked past me and winked at me . . . Made me feel all nice inside' (Rachel). The state institution distorted the domestic routines of home to another more collectivized template (see Chapter 4). For Lara this involved a new awareness of self and the loss of familial protection from racism during the long school day:

It was the first time in my life I noticed I was different, because at home, we were a mixed race family but then suddenly I went to school and I was the only dark skinned child and got hurled lots of abuse.

In different school settings, while well-being may have been addressed in different ways by committed professionals, children also learned of the wider social expectations of them and the roles that they would be expected to fill in the future (Welch, 2008b). Their education involved the disciplinary state (Jones and Novak, 1999) and for many it was their first direct experience of this. Claudia conveyed the complexity of her journey through school where everyday pleasures and pains were experienced through the social discipline and framework provided by the institution.

In the first year . . . being excited about doing subjects . . . getting your books and cover them in wallpaper, and starting your bestest handwriting, which would always end up in disaster . . . You'd get an ink block or something . . . I remember doing things like English literature . . . we did Midsummer's Night Dream, and I've got positive memories of that play, 'cause it was just magical to me . . . and I remember my first French lesson . . . she had a great big bouffant hairdo and sharp pointy shoes . . . and a tight skirt . . . I can remember us going into this room and

she spoke to us in French for the first half an hour . . . Not understanding
a word she said . . . at all . . . and actually scaring the living daylights out
of us I think.

Here she conveyed her commitment to learning, her excitement in the
preparation, her very real pleasure in some of the learning opportunities
as well as how her expectations could be disappointed and her feelings
of fear. For many of the children, school was one of their first and most
intense experiences of the complex social expectations of them and the
power that state functionaries would have in their lives.

Policing and Children's Social Place

Children experienced different faces of policing, as protective, to be
respected, as a source of amusement and to be feared. The balance of
experience was weighted in different ways for children at different times
and from different backgrounds. They all developed understanding that
the police, as state functionaries, had some social status and an established
social role. Cathy said, 'I had a positive image of the police . . . police were
people who would help you' and George, '[The police] used to come in
and do the cross [road] code . . . I won a colouring competition for the best
colouring in of a Belisha Beacon!' This aspect of policing involved safety
and protection from 'outsiders', 'My father was always very worried about
burglary and robbery. We . . . referred to the front door as the . . . draw-
bridge . . . there was always a very routine performance, every morning
to unlock it and every evening to lock it up' (Pamela). When their homes
were burgled, the police could act in helpful ways reinforcing children's
respect, ' . . . the detectives trying to find out where this [burglar] had gone
after he'd left our house . . . there's a patch of land at the end of the street
and searching in there' (Martin).

In Northern Ireland, James was surrounded by conflict in a place where,
at that time, the police were more allied to his own community's political
interests. His perception of the police therefore involved:

They are the guardians of 'You do not do' . . . a respect and an aura that
surrounded the police force and the people that wore the uniform . . .
Uniforms were quite significant in my childhood . . . There were badges

and emblems associated with certain things . . . signaled a particular allegiance to one side of the divide.

Apara also found the police supportive. She and her family experienced racial attacks for many months in the late 1970s and got police protection for a while, helped by the fact that Apara's mother worked in the police station:

> There was a note wrapped round [the brick] that said, 'Pakis go home' . . . every night . . . there'd be a barrage of stones and bricks thrown at the window . . . I remember the curtains billowing and there was a brick . . . it had landed on my desk . . . For three months we had two police officers sitting upstairs in our attic . . . a brick did come flying out and they ran down stairs . . . I was so angry, I ran downstairs into the cemetery after them and my mum screaming after me not to . . . [The police] were usually nice guys and talked to us. (Apara)

But at this time in the late 1970s, the police were often much less supportive and there was growing hostility between some groups of young people and the police (Hall et al., 1978). The understanding that the police provided security and protection was tempered by a growing knowledge of their power, 'We knew if we did anything wrong they'd give us a clip around the head' (Lara). The understanding that the police enforced law and order created ambivalent feelings as children also feared what they respected. Their own behaviour might fall into the categories of 'good' or 'bad'. Even when they accepted policing as in their interests, as with God (see Chapter 6) there was a degree of uncertainty. The power contained in policing was a source of attention and also, as in children's stories, could became a source of humour:

> We had 'Bumbling Bobbies' . . . this police officer was hiding in a hedge and his legs were sticking out at the back of the hedge and he was trying to catch somebody . . . every time I saw this guy, cycling round the village, I used to think, 'What an idiot' . . . but he was in a position of authority . . . I took other peoples authority seriously. (Claudia)

Particular children became aware that some groups were policed differently. Paulina learned about the police killing of David Oluwale in 1969, a homeless Nigerian immigrant (Aspden, 2008); Apara, the police killing of Liddle Towers, in 1976 (Hansard, 1977). Paulina had seen David living rough. Apara's mother worked in the same police station where Liddle was killed. Apara, who was in junior school at the time, developed understanding that 'the law could be above the law':

> There was an enquiry into it and the verdict came back that it was justifiable homicide . . . That frightened me, the idea that you could be beaten to death and it was 'justifiable' and this idea that . . . some people were above the law and the law itself could be above the law.

Paulina, who has just started secondary school, developed deeper awareness of her own social place as a result of the killing of David Oluwale and subsequent events. She said she began to connect his killing to wider political events related to racism, to her negative experience in school and to her own skin colour:

> I had seen him . . . as a vagrant . . . being scared of him . . . and then seeing his pictures branded across the television . . . I used to be one of these who'd be in front of a mirror with a towel and imagine being [in the police] . . . I hadn't really begun to think about anything political, or acknowledging and understanding what was happening to me in schools, but it was his pictures and . . . what happened to him, especially when you heard the things about him being weed on by the police . . . at the same time, there was something happening in France, which was to do with peoples' colour . . . looking at my skin and thinking, 'What is it, what's this about, why?'

Richard, growing up in an apartheid state, also came to realize that the power invested in the police in an apartheid state was partisan:

> a very repressive police force, mainly white . . . completely armed . . . used to walk around with guns . . . sjamboks . . . rhino tails on sticks . . . frightened of the idea of them, frightened of them, being aware that they were unjust, that they were arresting people who were trying to change the system. They were using torture as a routine way . . . I was acutely aware of all that . . . [from] 12 onwards . . . the story of the Biko murder and others started to come out.

It became clearer that biased policing affected particular groups badly and others fared better (Coleman et al., 2009). In the 1990s Madhi became aware of the discriminatory use of 'Stop and Search', 'My young, black male friends . . . being picked up . . . especially the boys . . . they'd tell you about how they were stopped'. Behaviour was policed differently in relation to ethnicity, colour, social class, gender and sexual orientation and the more 'private' terrain of family and sexual relations. Some aspects, such as domestic violence, were poorly policed, other aspects related to developing sexuality were heavily policed (Radford et al., 1988; Weeks, 1977; Weeks, 1999).

In these ways ideas about heterosexuality, the power of men and adults in the family to exert authority, were supported by the state. Marital rape did not lose exemption from prosecution in England and Wales until 1991 (Lees, 2002). Aspects of family life and behaviour considered 'sexual' (even when violent) were considered outside the remit of state interference, more the concern of religious and moral sanction and there was a veil of silence over some of these issues (see Julie's experience of being 'flashed' at, Chapter 2). Paulina's father used to hit her. The state intervened when this became visible at school:

> They asked me about it, and I didn't think, I just said 'My dad beat me, because I did something wrong'. So they came to my mum when he was out at work and my mum, up till then, didn't know what her rights were, sort of just putting up with the violence really and they agreed to take us away . . . I was my Dad's favourite.

Overlien and Hyden (2009) point out that children experiencing domestic violence do not 'suffer in silence' but refuse to accept it in different ways, protecting themselves and attempting to rescue adult victims (mainly mothers). They also plan future resistance. Nevertheless, ' . . . the way that privacy is produced and maintained will tell us something about women's [and children's] social being, about their resistance and acquiescence' (Haug, 1992, p. 55). The absence of a social framework for Paulina and her mother to understand and take control of events in the home and to harness the power of the state in their own interests were clear. It is unclear which officials came to see them. She remembered saying she had been beaten 'because I did something wrong'. She knew that it was possible to be her dad's favourite and also to be hit. These were not alternatives. To be 'loved' as a child also involved adult control in the home. Clearly there was some state intervention, albeit late and reactive rather than preventive, where Paulina may well have felt further powerlessness.

Children's experiences and perceptions of policing related to their social position, place, time and communities of interest. Their acceptance, amusement, fear and resistance varied depending on the degree they considered themselves and their communities protected or not. Some aspects of their experience were not considered the legitimate remit of policing. Authority lay elsewhere, for example, in the family or religious centre.

Children Engage with Civil Society

Inadequate policing in past times has led communities to develop their own ways of policing that lack the recognition of the state. Domestic violence is an area where there has been such community responses including 'stang riding' (Hammerton, 1992, p. 16) which involved the community banging of kettledrums or worse outside the offender's home. The importance of protecting a neighbour experiencing domestic violence was part of Lara's childhood and a local community response:

> Her husband used to . . . get drunk, every single day . . . They regularly had smashed windows. She was black and blue . . . [She] used to always have to come to our house . . . One time he came home and they had little white rabbits and for some reason he just slaughtered them all. If he was drunk, we didn't go near him . . . but when he was sober, kindest man you could ever meet in your entire life. He used to bring us lollipops and things.

Similar to Paulina, who connected her father's love and violence, Lara connected this neighbour's violence with his kindness. 'Kindness' may also be a means of exerting control.

However, other areas of interpersonal relations were heavily policed and sanctioned (Weeks, 1977). Aggressive policing intruded into the private life of young people who were gay, lesbian and bisexual. George developed understanding of the authoritarian face of the state, of laws that discriminated against gay men and of the power invested by the state in the police:

> I realized I was attracted to other boys from eight or nine . . . I soon realized . . . it wasn't legal . . . I was always frightened, 'cause I knew that it was 'bad' . . . the police were always tinged with that . . . When I was nineteen and I was driving in a car with my then boyfriend . . . four policeman, on motorbikes, drove up and started hammering on the windows of our car

and shouting 'Puff', so you know that's a through memory, from early sex play to police doing that.

In the late 1970s, the policing of intimate relations was riven with contradiction. Failures to police abuse inside the home contrasted with heavy state intervention in relation to consenting gay (and lesbian) relationships, while homophobic violence was ignored. This informed the direction of the feminist, lesbian and gay equality movements at that time (Weeks, 1999).

Particular children were drawn to and became aware of movements and organizations within civil society that related to their interests. It became clear to Paulina that the police represented certain communities and not others, reinforced by unequal recruitment (across gender and ethnicity). Shared memories of persecution generated communities of resistance, 'What makes recent memories hang together is not that they are contiguous in time; it is rather that they are of a totality of thoughts common to a group' (Halbwachs, 1925/1992, p. 52).

Paulina remembered 'Bonfire Night 1975' (Sivanandan, 1990) when friends and a family member were arrested:

It ended up a pitched battle between the police and the people in the community . . . I wasn't there . . . but my brother had gone . . . The year before that, people had said, 'That's it, If they come back next year and bother us, we're not going to put up with it', and I remember people being angry . . . and lo and behold, they came and people were ready.

In a different city, at about the same time, Rehana described the developing resistance to racism in which her younger siblings were involved. She went with her father to her brother's school:

Somebody called him 'Paki bastard' . . . Head teacher said to my dad 'Your son kicked her in the teeth'. My little brother turned round and said, 'Yeah, she shouldn't have called me "Paki bastard" then, should she!' . . . They wouldn't stand for it.

Patterns of unjust policing in relation to Black young people, reflected the re-emergence of a form of state that has been described 'coercive, authoritarian and brutal' reflecting a crisis generated by capitalism (Coleman et al., 2009, p. 3). *Policing the Crisis* (Hall et al., 1978) was published, focusing on the moral panic related to the young Black people, their demonization and resistance. Similarly in South Africa, there was widespread resistance to the apartheid state among mainly Black and some White children and young people. Young Black people boycotted school and were involved in a wide range of organized and less organized resistance (Mzamane, 1987). White friends of Richard's sister joined the resistance, 'I felt proud, but on the other hand, concerned . . . some of the people she associated with, were actually arrested . . . interrogated. . . . made to feel frightened . . . there was always that edge to, that kind of darkness there'.

The strong 'law and order' state in the United Kingdom was underpinned by neo-liberal economic ideas that led to cuts in public spending, less welfare intervention, the deregulation and privatization of work and a more authoritarian state to regulate discontent (Coleman et al., 2009). A 'return' to family responsibility was promoted alongside archaic notions of what constituted 'real families' (Moran, 2001). In the late 1970s, Rachel was developing awareness of her lesbian identity, and was drawn to wider political and social struggles for state provision and protection which provided social anchors, new terminology and new questions:

I became very aware of the . . . feminist movement as soon as I could look outwardly enough . . . very early teenage years for me, because of very, very stark memories of injustice . . . There was a newspaper seller . . . I'd circle him about ten times before I'd pluck up the courage to go and ask for the gay newspaper.

She drew on this to understand her own experience and make demands of the state, drawing on state resources, 'I can remember . . . writing for the school newsletter . . . even in primary school I was campaigning for girls' rights to do stuff.' In the early 1990s, Madhi shared interests with wider Black and minority ethnic communities:

Malcolm X was released in the cinemas and going to my Afro-Caribbean friends' houses and seeing big pictures of Bob Marley . . . A lot of the black kids . . . were becoming aware of the civil unrest and the black political movement and there was this really strong desire to get back in touch with their roots . . . There was really a lot of tension around those black kids . . . These other kids, who were actually mixed race . . . they had more of a struggle, 'cause they didn't fit, and I remember some of the black kids to the others, 'You're a coconut'.

Different civil society movements and events touched the lives of children differently; closely or at more of a distance. Geographical place, family and community memories, education and friendship positioned children in relation to these struggles, and each struggle had a different relation to and demands of the state at a particular time. The feminist movement, for example, demanded more effective policing of domestic violence, the anti-racist movements, less hostile policing of the Black community. Children in the research had very different perspectives on such issues. These differences were apparent in considering three children's perceptions of the civil unrest in the early 1980s. A family connection and her experience of racial attacks made Apara (aged 13) acutely aware of the Liverpool riots of 1981,

> I remember it being in Upper Frederick street, and my mother had had a friend . . . who lived in Nigeria, but she was actually from Liverpool and we'd visited her once in . . . so that really felt like a real connection to it.

Working-class Cathy (aged 19) felt physically distanced but scared and confused by these riots, 'I remember when I was coming in to the parlour . . . and watching images on the television and I was thinking it was in South Africa and the next thing they said they were in Toxteth, [Liverpool]'. Rachel (aged 17) felt emotionally and physically distanced from similar events the same year in Brixton, 'I was a product of a typical middle class suburban upbringing, so it was almost like, I didn't need to know, cause it wasn't actually impacting on my immediate life'.

Different perceptions and experiences also shaped understanding of the animal rights movement. Two children, Kate and Tessa, shared similarities in relation to social class and ethnicity, but were born at different times and in different places. Kate, born in 1950, in an urban middle-class area, loved animals and identified with animal rights in her teens:

> We had to give a talk on something that we were interested in and I chose the cruelty associated with mink farms. I was incredibly nervous and thought my talk was boring as I didn't have anything other than what I said and others had visual aids. (Kate)

Tessa was born nearly 20 years later when the conflict had intensified. She was also passionate about animals, but was more caught up in struggles defending fox hunting in the countryside where she lived and where she participated in the hunt. As a child she was told the animal rights activists who appeared at the hunt had been paid to protest. This implied they were mercenary, without commitment to animals and only interested in violence, 'We used to call them rent-a-crowd, because . . . if you'd paid them ten pounds they'd have supported fox hunting'. At this time, fox hunting was legal and associated with a powerful rural landowning lobby as well as many workers in the countryside. The hunt was often protected by mounted police. Tessa remembers the routines and rituals associated with repeated encounters with protestors which were connected to wider competing social and political interests that she didn't understand at the time:

> It was this big three way game. The antis were trying to get to the hunt, the hunt were trying to keep out of the way and the foot followers and a couple of farmers, usually with big traps and trailers and horseboxes, would block roads.

She described the emotional impact:

> It was quite scary . . . especially if you were on a pony . . . 'cause they were trying to pull you off . . . They were grabbing at you . . . they used to attack you or that was my vision . . . I saw somebody being pulled off into a ditch, a big chap . . . well they pulled him so the horse came over . . . He was a local farmer who'd lost all his fingers in a farming accident and I can remember vividly thinking 'Well it's not fair cause he's only got one hand'.

She was uncertain of her memories but remembered those involved in the hunt were people she knew and cared about who were struggling with people she didn't know and had been told myths about. In this place and time that she grew up in, ' . . . it was what you did when you had a pony at that age'. Her allegiances become more uncertain in later childhood as the widespread nature of the social resistance to the hunt becomes more evident.

Children were drawn to and engaged differently with civil society movements related to the degree to which the state legitimated and policed different areas of their lives. This process was similar in relation to party politics.

Children Engage with Party Politics

Drakeford, et al. (2009, p. 247) ask how much children 'know and understand' about government and how it connects with their lives. Rather than conceptualizing children as ill informed and disengaged, they reveal children's interest and enthusiasm if questions are broached in meaningful ways. This part of the chapter explores respondents' memories of party politics in childhood. First, different experiences of similar social events are discussed in the context of the political messages involved. Second, the political influences of family and community are considered and third, children's growing political awareness and choice. This part of the chapter draws on some 'flashbulb' memories. Misztal discusses the power of such memories. These shared memories cluster around major social events; yet they are personally differentiated as they ' . . . allow individuals to . . . include themselves in the narrative' (2003, p. 81). Hence they provide particular insight into children's different perspectives and experiences of social change and the role of the state and civil society.

The Politics of Immigration

Rehana came to England when she was 11. When she first went to school, she was viewed as 'exotic' and 'clever'. At the time she said she didn't mind this attention:

> We were a bit of a novelty, 'cause we were the first generation [to enter the United Kingdom from Pakistan]. . . . There was no aggression in it . . . People had more curiosity than rejection, so it didn't feel so bad . . . [Later] I saw that disappearing. I saw that novelty or that kind of curiosity developing into rejection and resentment of the Asian kids and that was a very painful transition. (Rehana)

She became aware that her community was in a weak political position (lacking social influence). If elections were to go the 'wrong' way they and their families might be at risk:

> [I was] very aware of [the National Front] . . . and [Enoch] Powell . . . I remember his . . . 'Rivers of Blood' speech [April 20th 1968] . . . I knew that there was an anti immigrant feeling in the country . . . the elders always voted for Labour . . . All the Asians would ring each other up and say,

'Don't forget to vote Labour'. I don't think anybody ever voted Conservative. There was this thing that they were more anti-immigration. (Rehana)

Rehana was 8 years old and living in Pakistan when Powell spoke out, but knowledge of his speech informed her childhood. Powell was a Conservative Unionist politician, who, having been actively involved in recruiting immigrant workers to the United Kingdom but turned on them for political expedience and spoke publically, positioning them as 'outsiders' and warning of potential conflict (Dummett and Dummett, 1982). Although not directly affected in the same way as Rehana, Martin (aged 17) also remembered the 'Rivers of Blood' speech because of the controversy, wide publicity and being 17, he was old enough to remember events quite well. His father in particular had taught him not to discriminate (see Chapter 3):

There was a lot of anti-immigration feeling . . . I was probably fairly politically naïve at that point . . . I didn't have the real deep understanding of the reasons why the migration had taken place in the first place. That came along later, but I was certainly of the view that these people were actually contributing to British society and they had every right to be here as we did. (Martin)

George, however, grew up in a community that internalized the media and political hostility to 'immigrants' and 'foreigners' (Gilroy, 1987/2002), 'I remember there being a huge fuss . . . rumoured that there might be a chip shop on the corner of the street . . . it might be Chinese people coming to run it and this was felt to be terrible'.

The Politics of the Power Cuts

Several respondents remembered the power cuts and related industrial unrest of the early 1970s. In England, Scotland and Wales, these arose due to a miner's strike related to pay and conditions they worked under. In Northern Ireland, they arose directly in relation to the political conflict there. Although the children were of different ages and of different social positions, there were commonalities as well as critical differences in children's perceptions and political learning. Apara was about 5 and had recently come to England:

power cuts . . . a link to being in Nigeria in some ways . . . sitting around at night by the light of the fire in my grandma and granddad's house where we were living and candles . . . you had to be very careful . . . we'd all be in the same room together and it was cosy and the adults would talk . . . and you could eavesdrop.

The conversations in Apara's home were supportive of this industrial action, bearing in mind political allegiances and family history (see Chapter 2). Pamela's father however, in a more privileged home, politically opposed the action. Pamela (in her late teens) vividly remembered him loudly sharing his opposition. Nevertheless, she too found some enjoyment in the new experience:

> doing my homework by candlelight . . . my father saying . . . 'These people should not be going on strike' and 'This is disgusting' . . . I quite enjoyed them actually. I thought it was quite exciting and I didn't really understand why they were doing it.

Cathy's parents also expressed anger at the cuts and she too, at around 10 years, found events exciting and different, becoming aware that the lights going off involved the exerting of power:

> being in the dark . . . it seemed a really marvelous thing . . . I have happy memories of it . . . sitting round the candles in the dark . . . It was always quite exciting and different. . . . it was a change really . . . I remember, my parents . . . being very angry about it. . . . the feelings that it was a fairly cataclysmic thing, 'The whole country should have come to this.'

George, about 13, from a working-class community with a strong street culture, remembered these power cuts as an event that brought people in the community together, ' . . . people . . . would go into each other's houses with candles'. Lara, who was about 7, remembered fear rather than enjoyment. She feared the dark, mice and 'they' who had cut the electricity:

> Mum used to always leave a light on for us . . . we were scared of the mice . . . there was no electricity . . . One morning, it must have been only just dawn and I turned over and there was mice in my sister's hair and I never understand why they wouldn't let us have electricity . . . that went on for a long time. A long, long, time and the nights seemed to last forever.

In Northern Ireland, the power cuts took another form, being directly related to strikes organized by the Ulster Workers' Council. James, in his early teens, was very aware of the power involved. He knew that these actions were intended to protect his own community. Trepidation and excitement, underpinned this memory:

> The 'Loyalist Association of Workers' Strikes' . . . went on for three years . . . Deliberately wiping out the whole of the city lights, for days. . . . the schools were closed, nobody could get to work . . . zoning off the town . . . they only let in people they wanted, and they were very clear about who they wanted in and out . . . I remember lots and lots of times, sitting with candles and having meals . . . The scary bit was, there's somebody out there that's doing this and they are very, very scary people that control to such an extent as that, but at the same time, knowing it was sort of on the same religious side, there was no fear.

Families in the Nationalist community in Northern Ireland would have been positioned and felt very differently in relation to these events.

The power cuts created some excitement and interest for all the children of different ages who experienced them, except Lara. They involved the sharing of adult political perspectives and memories, whether directly, through the expression of emotion or through the struggle to cope. The absence of power (the cuts in energy) and the presence of political power were powerful learning experiences for all the children, taking them in varied directions.

Political Choice

Apara remembered the impact of Margaret Thatcher's Conservative election victory in 1979 and the way this was seen to be a direct threat to her family. She was 11:

> Quite frightening . . . It was the only time I'd heard my Grandfather swear . . . there was a news bulletin on about Margaret Thatcher . . . she was out for a certain section of the country and we weren't in that section, and even if we had been in that section, that still would have been wrong.

Children were introduced to different threads of political memory related to their position. Communities under threat and the need for political resistance was a theme within family memory and in the selective stories that were passed down to children. Rehana was taught to vote 'Labour' to protect her rights. Apara was taught that she was a socialist and was positioned with the working class (see Chapter 2):

> My uncle had been a member of the communist party . . . we always used to joke about how he was blacklisted from going to America . . . My grandfather was unemployed for 8 years through the depression . . . They always talked about the general strike and the fact that we 'bottled out'.

In the 1980s and 1990s, Madhi learned about anti-colonial struggles in India and the peaceful direct action politics of Gandhi:

> My mum and dad used to take us to these places . . . to find out about our history and culture . . . they used to tell us about the stories of Gandhi, for example, and the politics of really back in those days, where actually Muslim and Hindu politicians worked together and it was about the well-being of the people, regardless of religion.

For James, the political party his community supported was fixed. There was no possibility of personal political choice and changing allegiance:

> deeply intertwined with the Fence . . . no real interest, to be honest, of the politics of it . . . but very, very clear, you voted this, or you had allegiance to that, full stop . . . didn't really need to understand the politics . . . because there was no real choice there.

In Tessa's family, allegiances to the Conservative party and threats from the Irish Nationalists formed part of her childhood. She remembered being more immediately interested in playing cards:

> Conservative . . . [politician, Airey Neave] came to my grandfather's house . . . The bodyguards taught us how to play . . . "bodyguard patience" . . . He was blown up . . . not very long after . . . it was the first person I knew that had been killed.

This happened when Tessa was 10 years old, as the result of a car bomb in March 1979 (Hansard, 1979). Responsibility was claimed by the Irish National Liberation Army. The death of such a family friend would, in all likelihood, have anchored some of Tessa's political allegiance at the time even though she had little interest in politics.

However, as with religion, families did not always present a united polit-ical voice. The parents of several of the children had differing allegiances. Their political beliefs accorded with their different biographies, gendered responsibilities and power relations in the family. Rachel's father was a staunch Tory, 'Mother, just kind of went along with anything he said . . . that's the way it was', and George's parents

> used to deliberately vote to cancel each others' vote out . . . My mum used to vote Tory and my dad used to vote Labour . . . They didn't really talk politics, but my mum would generally be on Mr Heath's side and my dad wouldn't be because he was . . . a member of a union.

Some respondents such as Julie and Cathy had no memory of party politics ever being discussed. Whether this was because they were excluded from discussion or discussion did not take place is hard to tell. The most mem-orable aspect of party politics for some was that elections got them time off school, 'I was just aware of elections, 'cause they would close school, and that was a good thing, 'cause you'd have time off' (George).

Nevertheless, all children were influenced towards or against particular political positions even when these influences were not explicit, as family responses to the power cuts showed. Political parties represented a mixture of private and public interests that individuals, families and communities shared (or not). As they got older, some children were drawn into electoral processes, whether these were 'mock' elections at school, or real elections. Richard puzzled as to why, even in elections, friendship was considered more significant than wider political priorities:

> I helped with a count . . . There were three main parties . . . the Nationalists, who were basically the racists . . . Liberals, they were the most left wing and . . . the Democrats . . . The person [we] were helping was Democrat and . . . I remember saying . . . 'I feel a bit strange, because I feel like I should be helping a Liberal' and [my friend] said, 'Oh I know, well it's to do with friendships as well you know. I mean I don't agree with his pos-ition, but he's a friend, so I'm helping him out as a friend'.

Children sometimes chose to follow a parent or parents' political alle-giances and sometimes not. They made their own decisions, drawing on their experience and the threads of memory they had been connected to through family and community. Two remembered first voting, '[In 1970]

... My mother, my father and myself went to vote. My mother had voted Conservative, I'd voted Labour and my father had voted Liberal' (Martin). Rachel's father was Conservative. She first voted in 1982:

> out of rebelliousness but also . . . in terms of human rights, I was never, ever gonna go down that route . . . We had . . . Margaret Thatcher . . . the constant battles of the [Greater London Council] who were trying to do lots of things . . . I was only ever gonna be a Labour voter. Nothing else made sense.

Their independent engagement with civil society (Martin had been drawn to socialism and Rachel to feminism), facilitated their political choices. For James, it was not possible to divert from Unionism, 'Unfathomable to think that you countered that, or even worse, sat in the middle, or didn't vote . . . The person didn't really matter . . . just belonged to that group . . . that's all we needed to know'.

Party political understanding and allegiance in childhood was influenced by threads of political memory from family and communities of interest. These narratives might become more pronounced in relation to major political events (such as the power cuts). Children's political allegiance (or lack of this) developed in these ways in addition to any direct engagement with electoral processes.

Conclusion

Children's experience of the state involves engagement with complex struggles related to services and intervention involving different interests. Children themselves may be viewed as economic investments rather than as human participants in these struggles. Some of their 'less than human' treatment at school and by the police shows this. The different faces of the state may discipline, support and neglect them. These elements are weighted differently at different times and for different children. Sometimes the state may come down heavily, as George's experiences of the policing of his sexuality demonstrates. Such experiences lead children and young people to become aligned with related civil society movements and press for social change. At other times, the powerful forces influencing the state are more closely aligned with children's own interests, enabling some (including George) to gain university education and better paid work.

Children learn about the politics of the state in various ways, including through family, community, civil society and wider social events. They receive complex and competing versions of how the state should be harnessed to their interests. Their everyday childhood is woven with different threads of political memory. There are also political silences in relation to their childhood, as aspects of childhood are considered 'private' and therefore immune from too much state interference (e.g., domestic violence and the 'punishment' of children in the family).

The children in the research carved out space and time for themselves from this arena in many different ways. In state institutions such as the school, children like Rachel and Richard worked for a human response, looking out for the teachers that smiled and winked. Children took opportunities and made these pleasurable, for example, Julie enjoyed stories, Pamela, music and Claudia, covering her books in wall paper. Children such as Apara and Lara, navigated potential abuse at school and drew on family and community to do so. Julie refused to accept the position she was in and began to play truant. Lara and Richard harnessed the power of other children; Lara, by turning lessons into comedies, and Richard, by calling teachers names behind their backs. Rachel drew on school resources to press for change and greater equality for girls.

In relation to policing, the state was more problematic for some than others. For some (such as Pamela, Martin and Tessa) it was experienced as mainly protective, keeping 'outsiders', outside. Others (such as Paulina) were sometimes positioned as 'outsiders'. Members of her community became involved in wider civil resistance. The range of political choices for each child depended on their social position, where they lived, the time they lived, their experience and the political stories they were told. Out of these complex influences they wove their own political choices.

To understand how children come to engage politically, it is important to acknowledge their complex experience of the state and civil society. They engage with these through the institutions of childhood, family, community and country. There is often concern that children and young people lack political engagement. It is true that they may experience distance from party politics, but they are deeply engaged with state and civil society. Awareness of the forms this takes for different children gives visibility to their political engagement. This engagement is not at all marginal.

Chapter 8

Children, War and Conflict

I remember my granny reciting some prayers . . . while I was screaming and wailing . . . I don't remember feeling so scared in my life . . . I could see this rain of shells coming down on my head and I thought, 'That's it, we're all gonna die' . . . When everything stopped, there was no noise for about half an hour and everybody from the streets had come out, and there was lots of commotion going on and lots of people had died in our street.

(Rehana remembering the Indo-Pakistani War, 1971)

Introduction

This chapter explores the complex ways that children's everyday lives were shaped by war and conflict. This includes the lives of children with direct and traumatic experiences, like Rehana, and the lives of children whose experiences were more indirect. The chapter considers communications related to war and conflict including the sharing of photographs, relics and stories containing threads of family, community and national memory. They include dark secrets, hushed voices and things children heard 'under the table' discussed in Chapter 2, as well as repeated anecdotes of war.

Memories of war and conflict in childhood involved direct and indirect experiences, a range of people, including grandparents, parents, the children themselves, different communities and nations. The nature of the involvement remembered includes the experiences of civilians, observers, combatants and workers in the war industry. The influences on everyday childhood came through complex relations of space and time involving closeness to and distance from events. Nevertheless, for all respondents, the influences in childhood were palpable.

It has been argued that children's understanding of war varies in relation to their age, gender, the explanations they hear and their personal experience (Blankemeyer et al., 2009). In the case of the research discussed in this book, children's experiences were refracted through adult memory and understanding. These memories contained communications about the time of remembering as well as the time remembered. The experiences of war and conflict were altered through the processes of memory. For example, when George recalled his parents' stories of the Blitz in north-west England, the time of his remembering framed a past before he was born, ' . . . eight miles away, which to me as an adult is no distance, but to them, felt like another country almost. So they could see the red fires from the bombing'. George's memory was a reconstruction of events from stories he heard as a child. Nevertheless the image of burning is vivid.

This chapter is in five parts. First, the wars and conflicts remembered from childhood are outlined, including those directly experienced and those that children learned about. Second, the chapter considers the relationship between everyday childhood and war, including the need for shelter and the disruption of family life. This part explores how war was remembered in relation to childhood, through juxtaposition with 'the opposite of normal' in children's everyday lives (Blankemeyer et al., 2009, p. 231 citing Myers et al., 2005). Third, the creation and transmission of war stories from family archives is discussed. This involved the selective representation of war to children through the tailoring of war stories. This process also occurred at community and national levels and this is the fourth area of discussion. Children were positioned and childhood constructed in particular ways in wider social narratives of war. Particular communities and faiths were positioned differently. 'Others' were constructed as enemies and outsiders (Hobsbawm, 1983). Misztal (2003, p. 93) argues that the passing on of tradition has the effect of normalizing certain events and institutions, painting the landscape with particular meaning. Certain (sometimes brutal) forms of behaviour become legitimated. Blankemeyer et al. discuss how some children in the United States came to conceptualize war in Iraq as 'Helping the Iraqis' (2009, p. 240), drawing on national ideologies of 'freedom'. However, the identification of allies and enemies is not just a top down process (Habashi, 2008). Misztal draws on Foucault to stress the importance of understanding the, ' . . . interaction between popular and hegemonic discourses . . . between private memory and public memory' (2003, p. 64), and this is also considered in the section 'National Memories' of this chapter. Silences in the collective memory are also highly significant. Ericsson and Simonsen argue that national collective memory both preserves the past and is concerned with reconstructing the future, ' . . . mending painful and splitting issues and building a base for meeting the challenges ahead' (2008, p. 400). The fifth area considered in the chapter is concerned with how different threads of memory and experience were woven by children and families to understand and cope with events. Running through the chapter are the conflict related themes that were most resonant in participants' accounts, including fear, loyalty, excitement and humour; the importance of hiding, fighting, escaping, surviving; the significance of noise and physical devastation. The chapter concludes with a discussion of the ways children engage with such experiences.

War and Conflict Remembered from Childhood

Although, at the time of the interviews, the respondents were living in one region of England, the geography of their experience of conflict as children was far wider. Several were affected by the Second World War, for example, Claudia's father and uncles were, ' . . . in the German army, in different places and survived the war . . . my father came to England. On my mother's side, her brother ended up in Siberia, captured by the Russians'. Sylvia's father was a Jewish refugee from Germany and George's father, ' . . . served in . . . Afghanistan, in the Khyber Pass, and my mum worked in a local munitions factory'.

Rehana directly experienced two wars, the Indo-Pakistani War of 1965 (the second Kashmir War) which lasted 5 weeks and the Indo-Pakistani war of 1971, which lasted 2 weeks. Madhi did not directly experience war but learned from her family about British colonialism in India. When Apara was very small, she experienced the Nigerian Civil War (1967–1970) (known as the Nigerian-Biafran War). Richard was brought up in apartheid South Africa, as part of the White English community. As well as experiencing civil war, his childhood was affected by news of related wars in border countries involving South Africa. He also grew up with the knowledge that he was a potential future conscript to the South African army (which was avoided because his family returned to England). James was brought up during the conflict in Northern Ireland (1968–1998) (known by some as the 'Troubles' and others as 'war'). Other children experienced that conflict at more of a distance and other more distant conflicts were formative in children's lives, including the Vietnam War (1959–1975), the Six Day War (1967) between Israel and Egypt, Jordan and Syria and the Cuban missile crisis 1962 (the 'Caribbean' or 'October' crisis, during the Cold War).

Shelter and Disrupted Childhoods

The experiences of children were grounded in the landscapes of everyday childhood. Take for example, Rehana's experiences when she was small girl of 5 or 6 years, sheltering from the Indo-Pakistani War of 1965. In September of that year, the Indian army launched an offensive in the area of Pakistan where she lived:

> We used to be taken into . . . the store room . . . no windows . . . we used to eat by the candle . . . My dad had an army background. He kind of took over precaution measures . . . We used to sit in a hollow place all night . . . then my dad would say, 'It's coming' . . . My grandma, my dad, my mum (my second mum), we'd bury our heads in their laps and we'd hear this big canon going off and then there'd be silence and then another one. I think my dad could see a reflection of light before it happened . . . He'd say 'It's coming' and then the burying of the head, and then we'd hear this big cannon . . . or lots of cannons . . . That continued all night . . . I just remember being petrified. (Rehana)

This vivid, traumatic, personal memory involved clusters of events. It was multi-sensory and contained and conveyed strong emotions: of fear and being comforted in the family. Attention was drawn to the family's response. They sought shelter, avoided being near windows, avoided light and protected the children's hearing. The father's military background enabled him to predict attack. This family expertise in dealing with military attack involved memories of earlier wars. Rehana's father was aware of weaponry from his work in the army. Her memory also drew attention to the wider collective experience. The shelling raised important questions about who was shelling and why; the associated national and international struggles at the time, the relationship with British colonialism in India and partition (1947). These would be outside Rehana's understanding at the time. She did however become aware that this was a shared experience that went beyond her family, 'Some people had hidden in the graveyard, which was at the end of our street . . . it was an open space and every one of them died'. Memories of war in childhood were anchored in very strong emotion. Events were remembered (or buried) in relation to the associated trauma, 'The body and it's habitual and emotional experiences . . . both a reservoir of memories and a mechanism for generating them' (Misztal, 2003, p 79).

The memory of sheltering from attack would be a particular experience of children, who were usually (not always) more protected. Three children were a generation removed from the 'bunker' experiences of their parents when they were young, during the Second World War. They had a 'memory' of these events (prior to their birth) which was refracted through their parents' selective accounts and filtered through humour, 'They had a bomb shelter in my granddad's back garden . . . it was all to do with singing songs' (George). It is hard to disentangle the experiences and the way selective memory may reconstruct events:

> My grandparents . . . had one of these Anderson shelters . . . The kids thought it was great fun . . . It was a great thing to be got up in the middle of the night and dragged from your bed. It always seemed, as they told you, that they'd forgotten about the bombs. It was quite strange really, 'cause in the telling it was quite funny, but you imagine it wasn't that funny at the time, or maybe the children perceived in a different way. (Cathy)

The humour may have been associated with coping with distress and with the need to distract and calm children at the time of shelling. It may have been retrospective, as they had survived. It may also have related to the way stories are selectively edited for the next generation of children. As with first-hand accounts of sheltering, these family stories also drew attention to intense emotions, the protection of children, the collective techniques to survive and children's perspectives. However, some of the fear was filtered out:

> [Mother] used to tell a story about going into and L shaped Anderson type shelter at school . . . teachers standing in the corner, the elbow of the L, and one class down one side and another class down the other . . . It was huge wide piping with duck boarding and they used to be given things like knitting to do and they did spelling B's and . . . mental arithmetic . . . Dropping things down through the duck boarding and not being able to get them back 'cause it was all wet and muddy, and the darkness and the smell. (Pamela)

The detail in this memory makes it hard to tell that this was not Pamela's first-hand experience but a repeated story from her mother of events before she was born.

The processes of memory reconstruct events from different sources. Lara's account of a 3-day trip to Northern Ireland during the conflict was associated with a strong image, 'Everywhere you walked, there was rubble or there was, like, big fencing'. This image may well have been reinforced through television, as the conflict was constantly in the news. Apara thought she had a memory of the Nigerian Civil War from her very early childhood. She was 2 when the conflict ended,

> I think it's a memory of the noise . . . there was our boundary wall . . . then . . . jungle and a lagoon . . . I just remember the noise of planes shooting overhead, and being told they were crashing into the jungle.

It is not possible to tell whether Apara actually heard these explosions or was told later, however, there is no doubt she was there at the time and whatever the sources of the memories, they were grounded in real events, 'The past is neither subjective or a linguistic fabrication but a harsh reality' (Misztal, 2003, p. 68).

Experiences of war were understood in relation to everyday childhood. Clearly the duration of any conflict made a difference to the ways children were affected. James' childhood was influenced by conflict. He said he was 9 or 10 when he became more deeply aware of the forces external to the family:

> Being very aware of quite a threatening situation outside, of something which was bigger, inside of the oasis of where we lived and the closeness of the family . . . close enough to have an impact on my life . . . an impact that's still there today. In some ways it was direct and in some ways it was more indirect. But the directness I suppose would be in people . . . a bomb going off in the town and causing damage and I don't even know the loss of life. (James)

James juxtaposed the conflict with his family life, which he described as an 'oasis' in relation to a wider climate of fear, munitions, loss of lives and destruction. We know from other research that children during this period feared and respected the paramilitaries and were drawn into adult conflict (Leonard, 2010). Rachel's memory of a bomb scare and blast in London in January 1974, associated with the IRA (Bowyer Bell, 1997) contained her fear in relation to family separation:

> We were ushered out into the streets. There was a real sense of panic because my father couldn't find my mother . . . but we did find her . . .

That was quite scary. We were far enough away from the building not to be in danger but we heard glass break, so we heard an explosion.

Rehana's memories of being shelled in the 1971 Indo-Pakistani War were counter posed with images of home, including the house, family members and domestic relations:

> I could hear this tap, tap noise . . . some shells had fallen on our roof, but luckily they didn't come through the room where my granny was and where I was. They'd fallen on the other side of the house . . . You have rooms around in a square, then a veranda on top and a courtyard in the middle and the stairs leading from the courtyard to the top . . . Either my Auntie or my Grandmother had soaked some chickpeas in a big pot and put them in the sun . . . to heat the water, so the chickpeas get softened and I think a shell had fallen on it . . . I went upstairs to the rooftop and I saw this metal pot. It was all squashed up and all the chickpeas were all over the place.

The Cuban missile crisis (1962) and potential nuclear threat deeply affected children in the United Kingdom, because of the intense media coverage and preparations, 'That was probably sort of the first real time that there was any sort of period of threat – that affected me' (Martin). Such memories were also related to everyday childhood, in this case, for Kate, the importance of Dad being safe inside the house as opposed to in danger outside. Kate was 12 at the time:

> I was very scared . . . A talk we had at school about what to do in the case of nuclear attack. It included not letting anyone into the house and I was worried that my dad would come home from work and we wouldn't be able to let him in.

At the time of the Nigerian Civil War many images of children appeared in media in the United Kingdom and there was extensive fund raising involving children. Martin (who was 16) said it had a profound influence on him and Paulina (who was 11) remembered,

> lots of black kids with big bellies, big eyes, on the telly . . . You looked at them with the flies around them . . . We used to have envelopes to put money in, with pictures of Biafrans on the front . . . Putting some of my pocket money in . . . I must have felt pity for them . . . I didn't get a lot of pocket money.

Children compared their everyday lives with the lives of other children. Paulina also questioned why wars occur. She focused on the human consequences for families and the loss of fathers:

> Thinking, 'Why are we doing this to each other? . . . They've got families . . . on both sides' . . . and . . . saying similar, I can't remember my exact words, but saying them to mum, 'All the families . . . the children who've lost their dads'.

It is argued that as they grow older, children move from concrete to more abstract understanding of war. Those directly caught up (like Rehana and James) may provide more personal descriptions set in 'normal' everyday childhood scenes (Blankemeyer et al., 2009). Whether memories were based on first- or second-hand experiences, they were compared with and viewed through everyday childhood and they involved children's priorities.

Family War Archives

Familial memories of war and conflict were shared selectively. The experiences of previous generations were passed down to children in a variety of direct and indirect ways. Several respondents talked about the archives that were kept to aid recollection. Martin's father had a chest of war 'relics'. George liked to look in the photograph albums, ' . . . and get [my parents] to tell me about them'. Tessa spent a lot of time sitting with her grandparents, looking and listening, ' . . . medals and the pictures . . . big suitcase of old photographs and looking at the war pictures, of all the tanks lined up in Africa . . . Somebody famous, somebody royal . . . and granddad talking about that kind of thing'. These family archives were built to record turning points and critical events, to recollect the furniture of war, the position and role of family members and to celebrate or mourn events in partisan ways. These archives were developed during conflicts and added to subsequently. Rehana remembered her father bringing back a piece of shrapnel, 'One of our house walls had been destroyed and he brought back a big piece of bomb, as a memory, saying, "This was the one that went through. It was inside, in the middle of our house."' Such mementos provided an aide memoir for the family. Pamela's mother in the Blitz went, ' . . . to and from school . . . picking up shrapnel and bits and pieces'.

The family war archives contained repeated stories that transmitted particular messages to children. These were altered in relation to what was considered appropriate to share. In some times and places adults would assume that children have no interest in war or should be protected from such knowledge (Brannen, 2004; Blankemeyer et al., 2009). Pamela's mother told her many stories of the Blitz:

> going to school . . . my grandfather being an Air Raid Warden . . . collecting . . . for the war effort . . . her father coming back after raids, being very distressed . . . When she describes it, and she still does . . . it's not just what she saw, it's also what she smelled, heard, felt . . . Very vivid memories.

These stories began when Pamela was a young child but continued through her adulthood. They involved a blend of two childhoods, her mother's and her own. The stories would be tailored differently depending on Pamela's age at the times of telling. Sheltering, the journey to school, the role of grandpa and father would have been themes throughout.

The selectivity of family memory meant that some aspects of war were hidden from children, for example, the brutalities of combat. Martin's father was a medic and would have witnessed much injury and loss of life:

> It wasn't something [father] talked about much to us as kids . . . He was actually quite lucky to survive because the boat he was travelling on back from Africa was torpedoed . . . The German commander of the boat that torpedoed them allowed them to get off before they sank the boats. (Martin)

War stories were tailored and altered in particular ways. They were structured around significant turning points, strong emotions and reference points to everyday life. They involved the transmission of feelings anchored in sensory impressions. The emphasis was on survival rather than death. In this way a softened version of war developed for children. Events might be chosen to amuse children as well as to educate them about the need for resilience and to fight social injustice. Stories would be shared with some children and not others depending on age and whether or not they asked questions. Stories would be selected on the basis of what was happening in the child's life at the time of the telling. Stories continued into adulthood and it is difficult to distinguish what was learned when. Three respondents referred to these family stories as 'always' there in their childhood. The strategic use of family archives as well as more spontaneous sharing of memories in families educated children through softer accounts of events and indicated where they should be allied in relation to particular conflicts.

National Memories and Landscapes of War

Blankemeyer et al. (2009) argue that children's understanding of war is shaped by several levels of experiences including the wider social explanations they hear. In the case of Ericsson's and Simonsen's research with children of Norwegian women and the German soldiers who occupied Norway during the Second World War, 'The national narrative provided the lens through which war children regarded themselves' (2008, p. 404). The Norwegian mothers were thought of as less than human and traitors. The children experienced social silence, abuse and were burdened with negative national symbolism. National narratives of war and conflict altered the collective memory in inclusive and exclusive ways.

The communities (of place and interest) that children in the 'Pathways' research came from, also provided counter narratives to the national war 'archives'. This created a choice of perspectives for some children. Resistance to British colonialism in India was celebrated in a family story passed to Madhi in the 1980s (see Chapter 2). This created distance between her and the royal celebrations that she watched on the television in the United Kingdom. The long-standing divisions arising from the partition of the Indian sub-continent at the end of British colonial rule, positioned Indian and Pakistani people in conflict. During the Indo-Pakistani wars, Rehana said the national message was clear:

> You had to be against the enemy . . . 'They are bombing our country and attacking us and we must fight them back' and 'Support your troops' . . . Every song you heard on the radio . . . They were national songs, chanting, slogans against the enemy force . . . 'They are bad, because they are the enemy, they'll come and take us away or kill us.'

Similarly, resistance to Communism was a strong element in the versions of war transmitted through her family to Claudia in the 1960s, 'There were definitely things about the communists. There was a very negative vibe around what communism was all about and how cruel it was and unjust'. The threats of the Cold War and Communism ran deep and were reinforced by Western anti-Soviet rhetoric at the time, 'Just the sort of awareness that there was this sort of fairly serious threat to Western civilisation' (Martin). The importance of patriotism, loyalty, 'brotherliness', shared religion, 'race' and colour were reinforced. Richard's schooling was militarized in these ways:

> We had to be cadets. It was compulsory, every week, we had to wear an army style outfit which was dark brown khaki . . . We marched and we were taught to shoot guns . . . From the age of 11 . . . The phantom enemy that we were supposed to be shooting at were always what were called the 'Kafers' which was the derogatory word for black people.

These national narratives were contested and there were counter narratives from different communities of interest and political groups, for example, Richard's family were constantly critical of the apartheid regime.

The growing opposition to the Vietnam War in the 1960s, which involved many young people, facilitated Martin's growing scepticism about war. He was 16 at the time of the Six Day War (1967) between Israel and Egypt, Jordan and Syria, 'There were quite divided feelings in the school . . . Support for Israel, probably less support for the Palestinian cause . . . the Vietnam thing in the late sixties, probably what formulated my views on war'.

Patterns of inequality and difference shaped the experience of children and families in war and conflict. In relation to the struggle over Kashmir in 1965, Rehana learned that women and girls were a form of 'collateral', considered 'property' to be taken by the conquering side (Brownmiller, 1975):

> The enemy army had moved into the city . . . in the middle of the night, . . . their grown up, young daughters . . . the fear that soldiers are gonna rape them or take them away . . . I remember . . . without shoes even, we were just dragged by our arms . . . just running away, to the other side of the city, in the middle of the night . . . away from it.

Children also could be viewed as a form of collateral in war, perceived as continuing the blood lines of enemies (Ericsson and Simonsen, 2008). During apartheid in South Africa, 'racial' categories based on eugenic dogma and White interests imposed routes through the landscape, particularly restricted for Black people. Bridges and other channels for the movement of goods and people were highly significant. These reproduced and generated conflict (see Chapter 2, the apartheid bridge), forcing children into opposition:

> My brother, on the way back home from school got caught in a stoning of his bus, by a group of black youths, as a way of protesting that the whites, the rich whites didn't have to pay to go to school, but the poor black children had to pay . . . He got home in a sort of shaken state. That was mixed feelings really, because obviously we sympathized with them because we understood where they were coming from . . . but felt that they'd picked the wrong target. (Richard)

The family story of a curfew in Lagos during the Nigerian Civil War demonstrates how social class, gender and ethnicity interwove to create a differentiated experience:

> There was one story about [mother] sending . . . the maid, to go and buy milk . . . The maid coming back 'Have you got it?', ' No, no, no, I couldn't get over the bridge' . . . [Father] being 'Don't be so stupid' . . . My mum storming off to go to the bridge . . . She couldn't get across . . . There were soldiers on the bridge not letting anybody through. (Apara)

The power relations were such that the maid was the first to be risked in the journey to get milk. The father's anger and frustration then involved mother taking risks. The bridge formed a narrow passage where people passing were being identified in relation to the purposes of conflict, as Igbo or Yoruba, for example (Adichie, 2007).

Care for children and related domesticity had to continue despite the most dangerous conditions:

> Sometimes the only thing that would send me to sleep was being driven round in [mum's] car . . . despite the fact there was a curfew and you'd be shot on sight, she would just put me in the car and drive round Lagos. (Apara)

> My mother [as a child] . . . was evacuated to . . . [another city] which of course also got bombed . . . Her mother made the decision to bring all the children back . . . If they were going to get bombed, then they might as well get bombed at home. (Pamela)

The gendered landscapes of war involved the departure of more men than women as combatants. There were many silences related to men's experiences of combat. Dangerous experiences and their own role in the combat were touched on but there was a lack of detail. In the war stories shared with children there was more likely to be a sense of nostalgia, freedom and male camaraderie:

> My father was away for seven years during the war . . . he had a really 'good' war. Apparently he had a really nice time. (Julie)
>
> One of the best times of his life . . . he enjoyed it. He used to take out cloths that he had brought back and . . . a very beautiful knife . . . fiddling around with radios and doing Morse code which he taught me . . . Swimming and messing about . . . That was his war. (George)
>
> I don't think he had a particularly harsh war. (Martin)

Whether these fathers had 'good' wars or not, war was grim and survival cast a softer light on events related to killing and the threat of being killed. These silences may also have related for some to a sense of shame at the pleasure gained in combat. Such silences produced social clichés and fossils (see Chapter 2) that concealed and altered past events in partisan ways, 'Freud taught us that we were not so much the sum of what we could remember, as the sum of what we had forgotten'(Atwood, 2005, pp. 214–15).

In relation to the experiences of children in this research, such silences were threefold. The first area of silence concerned the absence of detailed accounts of the brutality of war on all sides. War games were designed with the focus on strategy. Memorials related to the crimes of enemies rather than allies. Unpalatable truths were edited from national records, in order to subordinate the past to present interests (Haug, 1992). In these contexts some children, such as Claudia (see below and Chapter 2), were made vulnerable, becoming aware they may be associated with enemies rather than allies.

A second area of silence was the invisibility of the wider political and economic purposes of war and conflict. These were outside the consciousness of many children, requiring specialist knowledge. Adults, remembering, tried to explain, for example, about apartheid, or colonialism in India. The most important influences would remain elusive for children, who understood war from their own standpoint and asked questions accordingly.

A third area of silence was generated by the selectivity of memory and of the research process itself. The researcher probed in particular ways. The respondents selected particular memories in relation to their vividness, but also in relation to subsequent events. Many aspects of the experience of war and conflict in childhood remained unshared. Two extracts from interviews related to war convey how such silences shaped children's experiences and the representation of these. In relation to the Second World War, the atrocities of the Nazis became public knowledge in England where Claudia lived. The researcher wanted to know how she coped, bearing in mind her parents been allied with the Germans:

Researcher: Was there stuff around the Jewish question?

Claudia: No, nobody talked about it at all and I haven't even asked, because I suppose deep down, I find it very difficult to believe that people didn't know what was going on. I do, I mean, I'm not sure about all of that, but I do find it hard, and I don't want to know what they think really.

In Ericsson and Simonsen's research, one schoolchild, the daughter of a German soldier, ' . . . closed her ears when they taught about the Second World War' (2008, p. 402). This seems to be Claudia's experience. In addition, silence was evident in the researcher's question. The phrase 'stuff around the Jewish question' referred to the Holocaust but minimized the issues. The researcher's father was Jewish. The phrase 'Jewish question' was the Nazi euphemism for the Holocaust and genocide which the researcher unconsciously reproduced. The polite phrase sanitized the process of genocide in Nazi-controlled Germany. The silence continued in Claudia's answer. She said her family never talked about this and she never asked because of the pain involved. Ericsson and Simonsen discuss how meaning 'saturates' the silences in their interviews with the children of Norwegian mothers and German occupier fathers, 'These silences were "absorbed" without knowing or understanding why they should feel what they felt: insecurity, inferiority, guilt and above all shame' (ibid., p. 403).

The second extract concerned growing up as a Protestant in Northern Ireland during the 'Troubles'. The term 'Troubles' itself conceals and minimizes a deep and brutal conflict involving much death and injury. The lasting sense of division and difference in communities ran deep and drew children in as combatants (Leonard, 2010):

James: You're either one or the other and that's the way . . . there's a security in that . . . but by the same token it's also putting you into one of two camps, and on many occasions . . . where there was conflict between me and another, the other religious sect, which sometimes you come up well and sometimes you don't come up well . . .

Researcher: So there were street encounters.

James: Absolutely . . . I had particular instances with a family . . . I sort of bore the brunt of their differences . . . You pick up cues and clues from environments . . . confrontations on a regular basis, with people of a similar age. So you're going through the teenage years and you meet somebody in the street and they asked you a question and the question has one of two answers and depending on how you choose to answer that, you get a response . . . It's called survival, growing up, you know and quick to ask the question or be aware of the cues that follow the question.

James said 'Sometimes you come up well and sometimes you don't come up well'. The details were not provided. This phrase might have related to victory or failure in physical combat or to a sense of responsibility related to this. The researcher continued to draw on euphemisms using the term 'street encounters'. James avoided naming 'the other' religion (Catholicism). He talked of how deep the conflict went and how he learned to 'read' silent cues and clues, in order to protect himself and identify combatants. Leonard's research into the contemporary experiences of young people in Northern Ireland, demonstrates the continuity of divisions. A Protestant boy says 'We riot because we hate each other' and a Catholic boy, 'We riot with them because they're scum' (2010, p. 44).

The silences in the research related to children's experience of conflict did not just relate to processes of personal and familial remembering but to the national and community narratives that sustained the conflicts and positioned children and their families as enemies or allies.

Children Weave Threads of War Memory

Blankemeyer et al. argue that, in order to understand war, children, ' . . . selectively piece together information from sources at various . . . levels' (2008, p. 241). In this research, children's understanding of war was informed through direct and indirect experiences and in relation to family, community and national war narratives. They viewed events in relation to their everyday childhood. Their questions drew on this experience, as they juxtaposed and compared different elements. Lara recalled a 3-day trip to Northern Ireland to Catholic relatives during the conflict, 'You didn't get ice cream vans hanging around, because we saw a tank go past, and I thought it was an ice cream van'. Rachel, juxtaposed spelling tests with a bomb scare and blast, 'Kind of scared at the time, but quite excited actually . . . we were doing something different, rather than sitting in spelling classes . . . I didn't feel like there was danger, nothing close enough'. Understanding involved drawing together previously disconnected threads. Where events had been routine and 'ordinary', they became extraordinary. Julie, in the 1950s remembered being looked after by her father, who was previously a combatant in the Far East in the Second World War:

> He was stroking my brow [when I was poorly and feverish] and he was saying that when he was really ill with this fever and thought he was going to die and how he was thinking about this cool place in Wales, and this waterfall.

Claudia remembered being told as a child that being a skilled baker saved her father's life in the Second World War. The ordinariness and necessity of bread making was juxtaposed with the brutality of war:

> When they were captured, [he] was given a choice of going with the Russians . . . or going with the English and he chose to come with the English . . . His skills as a baker, was one of the things that helped him . . . He was very fortunate, because most of the people that were with his group, that asked to go with the Russians were taken down the road and shot.

In the family, a similar process occurred as different threads of experience and memory were woven together to explain and cope with unusual, strange and frightening events connected with war. This interplay could generate humour. Cathy shared a repeated gas mask story:

> He came round, apparently, in the middle of the night and hammered on the door and, I don't know how many times I heard this tale. My Gran opened the front door and saw him standing there with his gas mask and everything and said something like 'Jesus, Joseph and Mary, they've landed!'

George recounted two stories, one linking war with the needs of a mouse and one, with an accident in the blackout which he called 'The Nose Story':

> [Mum] would go down to the munitions factory . . . She used to feed the mouse that used to come out through the grill . . . After the munitions

factory, she'd have to walk back in blackout and there was a phone box at the start of the alleyway and she walked into the phone box and broke her nose!

Everyday life and war interplayed in such stories. Cathy's story contained the interplay of gas masks, aliens from outer-space and the alien enemy. In George's stories, the mechanics of war (munitions making) was juxtaposed with an act of kindness to a mouse. The blackout, intended to prevent injury, interplayed with an accidental injury caused by the blackout, recorded forever in a bumpy nose.

Children also had to resolve the different messages contained in wider narratives of war they experienced. At school, Claudia was treated differently because of her German/Romanian heritage and the way this related to the war stories shared with English children. At home she learned something of her family's experience and position:

> If they . . . started talking German amongst themselves, you knew that you shouldn't be listening . . . I understood what they were talking about, except the complicated words . . . There were anxieties about things . . . concerns about family . . . what was happening to them . . . how they'd been treated.

Claudia had to weave these threads of memory from past times and different places and sometimes 'close her ears' to cope. A new conjoining of experience provided new insight in to how war was practiced, managed, survived and perceived, ' . . . otherwise unconnected narratives may be brought into contact, or previously connected ones may be wrenched apart' (Massey, 2005, p. 111). By weaving of threads of memory and experience from complex and overlapping temporal and spatial influences, children came to understand war and conflict from their own standpoints.

Conclusion

Children's experience of war and conflict may be direct and indirect. Memories hinge on clusters of war related events such as hiding, escaping and being bombed. Both Rehana's first-hand and Pamela's second-hand experiences of sheltering show this. Places of passage, such as bridges, and places of shelter, provide targets and crystallize events. Even when diluted with the passage of time, memories involve all the senses, noise, smells and images and many emotions, including both fear and humour. Children share familial, community and national narratives that are laden with associated emotions from past and present time and are concerned with future planning (Misztal, 2003). Enemies and allies are constructed in particular ways in these narratives and children such as James, are taught particular allegiance. War experiences may be softened and altered in different ways when they are shared with children, for example, for Martin and George there was more emphasis on camaraderie and adventure than death and dying in their fathers' war stories. This aspect of the relationship between war and childhood, may lead some young people to more easily join armies.

Children's understanding of war and conflict involves the interplay of different threads of memory and experience. This positions children in particular ways, making some, such as Claudia, more vulnerable than others. In fleeing from war and its aftermath children with different war heritage arrive in the same places. The collective narratives of war and conflict they experience may not accommodate their position.

Children understand war in relation to their everyday childhood. Experiences are counter-posed with domestic routines, schooling, household and family relations. They understand war and conflict at the level of these everyday human experiences and, like Paulina, question war in relation to the loss of these relationships. At the same time they may be caught up in war games that isolate particular 'outsider' children. They may be drawn in as combatants in particular conflicts and sometimes forced into these roles as child soldiers.

Although there may be attempts to silence these matters, children are often the first victims of war, for example, during the writing of this book, 300 Palestinian children were killed in Gaza (Amnesty International, 2009) and the Saville Inquiry (Saville et al., 2010) reported that in Northern Ireland, 6 children (under 18) were killed by British troops on 'Bloody Sunday' (30 January 1972). There is also resistance to war among children. This was the case in relation to the Vietnam War when many from Martin's generation demonstrated. In South Africa, when Richard was 15, Black children and young people rebelled in Soweto, after Government insistence that they be taught in Afrikaans (Soweto Rebellion, 2010). In response, on 16 June 1976, the police opened fire and killed over 600 people, many of whom were children.

Although children may absorb some of the rhetoric related to war and conflict, they may also be less convinced by war rationales, for example, school strikes were organized by children and young people to protest against the United Kingdom's pending role in the Iraq War (Cunningham and Lavalette, 2004). However, some children have no choice but to participate in conflict, being 'locked in' particular positions, 'Children experience the world as it is manifest, and they are part of the ideology, war and corporate greed that is exported from the boardrooms and strategic command centres of Washington, Paris and London' (Aitken, 2001, p. 6). At the roots of the conflicts that children experience and feel the effects of, there are powerful less visible forces at play related to colonization and decolonization, the carving up of empires and the furthering of the social and economic interests of particular social elites. In this respect, in particular, there are silences in relation to war and conflict in childhood that those with a commitment to children have a responsibility to uncover.

Chapter 9

Children and Consumption

There were people caught in the volcano . . . intimate relationships were actually going on . . . When we looked at the buildings . . . glasses but they looked like pot cups . . . tables and the pictures on the ceiling . . . clothes in the wardrobe, that were really solid and you could actually see the little jewels on them . . . you could see the sparkle . . . I think it was a place where they bathed, because there were seats at the side . . . you could see that the water was in there, but because of the lava, it had gone solid. It was wonderful, even the flowers in the garden were like stone.

(Lara)

Introduction

When remembering her visit to Pompeii when she was 14, Lara was drawn to the everyday intimacies, including the domestic implements, furniture, creative arts, clothes, bathing arrangements and gardens. This chapter considers children's involvement with consumption and their experiences of the changing technologies and styles related to domesticity, communications, fashion and music. These changing arrangements involved complex temporal influences and competing ideas about how everyday life should be lived (Misztal, 2003). They involved children and their families in dreams for the future, not necessarily of their own making, but with which they were deeply engaged. Consumer artefacts were created with particular groups in mind. New ways of living provided deep interest and informed everyday routines. Lara captured some of this complexity in her description of Pompeii, where it is difficult to separate the artefacts from the everyday lives of the families buried after a volcanic eruption. Robins (1996) argues that in order to understand consumption, it is important to be sensitive to, ' . . . the vertical dimensions of power and ideology and the horizontal dimensions of contexts and everyday life' (quoted in Kenway and Bullen, 2001, p. 28).

Children and their families drew on dominant culture and technology to accomplish their daily lives. This involved negotiating, 'the interplay of competing tendencies' (ibid., 2001, p. 4) as well as 'private memory and public memory' (Misztal, 2003, p. 64), 'One of the central features of consumer culture is the availability of an extensive range of commodities, goods and experiences which are to be consumed, maintained, planned and dreamt about' (Kenway and Bullen, 2001, p. 9 quoting Featherstone, 1992).

The way that consumer goods were marketed generated new forms of social segmentation (Aitken, 2001). The styles advertised, relied on and exploited social class, ethnicity and gender, creating the desire to live in particular ways, differentiating one group from another. The acquisition of particular goods fulfilled desires, generated feelings of new belonging and distanced one group from another. It also distanced families and children from the ways they had previously lived. Subtle processes of marketing meant adverts were ' . . . used in a multiplicity of seductive ways unconnected to the original product' (Kenway and Bullen, 2001, p. 14).

This chapter first considers how children's families tried to keep up with the changing times, including their sense of social advancement and the idealized versions of family life presented to them:

> The modern individual within consumer culture is made conscious that he speaks not only with his clothes, but with his home, furnishings, decoration, care and other activities which are to be read and classified in terms of the presence and absence of taste. (ibid., p. 20 quoting Featherstone, 1992)

Second, it focuses on the changing technologies at home and how these affected children, including the acquisition of domestic 'labour-saving' devices. This part includes discussion of the changing cultural expectations of women and is again linked with discussion of social class advancement:

> In twentieth century advertising the imagery of childhood became vital in the tapestry of the consuming family – as a motivation for adequate provisioning, as an indicator of family pride and virtue, and as an easily understood symbol of the long term benefits of continued economic prosperity. (ibid., p. 41 quoting Kline, 1993)

Third, the chapter considers how children engaged with and enjoyed the new discoveries and designs, including their excitement at the spectacle involved. Fourth, the largest part of the chapter considers children's 'young times' as consumers, journeying through youth cultures and markets. This final part of the chapter considers how they carved out space and time for themselves through negotiating consumer culture (Thomson et al., 2002; Russell and Tyler, 2005). It discusses their use of leisure spaces (Green et al., 1987), their developing musical allegiance (Laughey, 2006), the ways in which they drew on fashion (Konig, 2008; Rysst, 2010) and their developing awareness of their own sexuality in relation to the social expectations of the times (Foucault, 1980b; Edwards, 2004; Pini, 2004). From a social memory perspective, children's unique engagements with consumption involve their own attempts to 'immobilize time' (Misztal, 2003, p. 112) and to explore personal possibilities, 'in relation to others, to the past and to the future' (ibid., p. 78).

Families Keeping up with the Changing Times

Children and their families came to desire commodities that became relative 'necessities' in relation to the society and time in which they lived. Low income and unemployment made it much more difficult to afford things. The pleasures of acquiring new things were captured by Lara's description of getting a new car in the early 1970s:

> Mum got a Ford Anglia and it was burgundy red and it was really, really nice . . . 'See how many cars you can see that look like ours' . . . every car looked like ours . . . they were the most popular cars on the road . . . Going to [the seaside] . . . I had an orange dress on and orange shoes and white socks with orange trim on and my sister had purple dress on and purple shoes and socks with a purple trim and I had orange ribbons and she had purple ribbons . . . We went on the dodgems, sat on the sand and we had fish and chips for the first time in a restaurant . . . I remember walking back to it, really proud, 'This is our car' . . . and we were all stood having photographs like that, all smiling . . . 'Look at us in our car'.

Memories of the car were captured for the family archive. The new car provided a 'good life', a sense of belonging, pride, pleasure and highlighted the difference from the past. The new clothing, the trip to the beach, the restaurant, the car and the photos were woven together in Lara's memory. Such commodities were markers of social inclusion and that life was being lived in socially acceptable ways in relation to the new styles of the time.

Of course the society that was constructed through advertising was an incomplete story, based on ideas about how lives should be lived, not how they really were. The new goods altered everyday cultural arrangements at a very intimate level. George's family got a television in the 1960s:

> You would always have the television on when people came to visit . . . You would turn the volume down, not so that you couldn't hear but just so it was low . . . You wouldn't alter the seating necessarily. They would just join you round the telly and you'd talk a bit across them.

He explained how the celebration of consumption informed the working-class street culture of his childhood. Things could be purchased that maximized space and convenience in the small terraced houses. Getting access to these things was a shared venture. As one family acquired something, new desires were generated in others:

> You had the living room and then you had your staircase . . . They cut out part of the wall, so you opened up your staircase. This was seen to be very sophisticated . . . everyone had varnished wood and bits of bamboo, with fairy lights on and my Auntie . . . underneath the staircase, where everyone had their cupboards . . . they made like a cocktail thing there, even though they didn't ever have cocktails.

These arrangements were marketed through magazines that drew on the living styles of better off groups. In the everyday lives of children and families the distinctions between need and desire blurred. Richard remembered the purchase of a phone in the early 1970s:

> There was a very fashionable phone called a TRIM phone . . . a little square phone . . . the mouthpiece was a really thin straight piece of plastic . . . They were the thing to have . . . [Mum and dad] really wanted a red one . . . but the guy brought a green one, 'Oh have you not got a red one?', 'Oh I might have one in my bag, I'll go and have a look' . . . he came back with a red one . . . coming home from school . . . we all gathered round and stared at this red phone, and thought it was wonderful that they'd managed to persuade the guy to give them a red one . . . It made a sort of like a chirping noise . . . it was modern! It didn't ring like the old fashioned one.

The fact that the phone was red and was of a particular style made it more special in the family and a sign that they were truly entering the modern world (Kenway and Bullen, 2001). The purchase generated a new sense of social advancement and was celebrated. Yet the red phone was also more than this. It maintained vital connections to family thousands of miles away in England, where Richard's grandparents lived. It involved family continuity regardless of its style.

As well as representing a different sense of social inclusion, the acquisition of goods was a very private and intimate experience. The technologies provided new ways to live and also to 'remember' important turning points in the family. In the early 1980s, Tessa's sister qualified for some jumping championships, 'They'd videoed it and so we'd bought the tape but had nothing to play it back on. So we got the video recorder to play back my sister jumping a horse, not because it was the thing to have'. They were a means of continuing everyday life and family ties. In South Africa in the 1960s and 1970s, 'One of the key times to listen to the radio was on a Friday morning, where there was family comedy shows on, and we'd sit together as a family and listen to the radio in this room' (Richard). In northern England in the 1950s, 'I have a particularly fond memory of listening to "Polly Oliver" on a Saturday evening . . . dad had made thick toast with lots of butter and we had it round the fire when listening to the radio' (Kate).

The idea that the technologies and media in themselves threaten childhood has been challenged in research that shows that it is not technology that damages family communications but attitudes to children (Plowman et al., 2010). Where there was conflict in families the commodities and their uses would also be associated with conflict, 'My father disapproved of music being played in the house but my mother used to play music while he was out' (Pamela). Drawing on an idealized version of family life, responsibility for healthy and happy childhoods became a central element in the way commodities were marketed to families (Kenway and Bullen, 2001). But keeping up with the changing times, required money and employment. Failure to keep up resulted in exclusion (Bauman, 1998). Managing to keep up generated a sense of belonging and distance from the circumstances left behind.

Domesticity and Labour-saving Devices

Consumer marketing drew on ideas about appropriate family roles. New home based technologies were claimed to save time and energy for women. These ideas were grounded in and reinforced the real divisions of domestic labour uncovered through market research. Julie's early years as a teenage mother in the late 1960s were hampered by inadequate equipment:

We'd a cellar with an old washer and a mangle . . . all these plastic pants that went round nappies. Putting them through the mangle . . . Walking two miles with the kids in the pram to get cheaper shopping . . . the wheel'd fall off the pram.

As well as women, older girls in working-class families were more likely to be involved:

We had a coal fire, and that was one of my responsibilities, as the eldest, was to clear it out and to make it . . . I remember having to put the news-paper up, to get the draft up, so when we got the gas fire, that was abso-lutely fantastic. (Paulina)

The new advances in domestic technology reflected and allowed increasing levels of women's participation in the workforce. Increased separation and divorce and the movement for women's equality were also significant influences. The 'new woman' in marketing imagery in the West was expected to be efficient, domestic, motherly, glamorous and socially engaged and to effortlessly weave paid work, housework and child care. More collectivized forms of domesticity and child care were less visible. Changing cultural expectations of mothers meant they were prime targets of marketing. Housework became a 'performance of femininity' (Kenway and Bullen, 2001, p. 41) and the consumer culture exploited ideas about 'good mothering' (Silva, 1996).

The new domestic goods (when they could be afforded) did save domestic time and energy which was helpful to women caught up with paid work and child care. They were also signs of social class advancement. In the West in the 1950s and 1960s the White working class saw occupational advancement because of economic growth related to inward and outward migration (see Chapter 3). Resources and labour harnessed from the developing world generated more consumer goods (Kenway and Bullen, 2001). The acquisition of automatic washers, fridges, cookers and furniture, reflected social mobility and shaped the lives of particular children. Claudia's childhood reflected this. Her family eventually

Got a fridge . . . an inside toilet . . . a washing machine . . . but you still had to wring things and rinse . . . but it was electric. We had sort of a boiler which heated the water and we had two radiators . . . one was in the dining room and one was in the bathroom.

Domestic labour was still the major responsibility of women in these changing times. The technology was not that advanced and workforce participation limited the time for housework. Clearly not all families could afford these things. Through the 1970s, Apara's single mother

> couldn't afford an automatic washing machine. She [washed clothes] in the bath . . . on a Saturday . . . She'd start to get depressed about it on Friday and she'd always be in a really filthy mood . . . It was just hard work and you've got four kids.

The acquisition of domestic commodities were significant events in children's lives. They changed patterns of domestic labour, reflected changing workforce participation and affected the well-being and moods of their mothers in particular.

The Spectacle of Consumption in Childhood

The acquisition of commodities were turning points in family life, marked by excitement at the design and uses of the items, the time and leisure they were intended to buy, the related social status and sense of social inclusion:

> It's to do with people moving on isn't it . . . families moving on into better positions . . . It was changes . . . not just in things, but in . . . what was expected of you . . . peoples' ideas of what you could and couldn't do. (Claudia)

Children shared the celebration when new things were brought into the house, 'Quite important events in the family . . . We'd all be quite excited about them arriving . . . There'd be, almost a culture grown up around them . . . "This is something new and interesting"' (Richard). They examined the mechanisms in particular detail, less hampered by expectations of its intended purpose, they could imagine different uses for the technology. Here are two descriptions of similar items from the 1960s:

> Sort of dresser, that had cupboards at the bottom and a thing that came down in the middle that you could do preparation on and inside that space then would be compartments of some kind, and there were drawers in it somewhere, and the top opened, with glass doors, and it was green and cream, or something like that. (Claudia)

A fold up thing in the kitchen . . . which was a unit, which had cupboards and then you folded up the bottom and it would have legs out. So on certain occasions at weekends – for your weekend Sunday lunch, they pulled that out and we'd eat on that. (George)

Relatives, friends and neighbours enjoyed each others' acquisitions; marking these events and sharing in the peculiarity and novelty. In the 1960s, George's neighbour acquired, ' . . . a sliding door and everyone going to look at it . . . Her daughter pretending it was a lift, to us all "Going Up" and sliding across'. Children were fascinated by the real and imagined uses of items, perceiving some of them as almost magical, 'We had a very early television . . . it had doors that shut in front of the screen. I remember creeping down from bed and trying to watch through the crack in the door' (Kate).

I remember the first time I saw a microwave. Somebody made a baked potato at a friend's house. She said, 'Do you want a baked potato?' 'No, I'm hungry now!' She said, 'No, it'll be ready in five minutes!' It was like a magic trick, this baked potato coming out. (Cathy)

I remember the first time I saw colour television, very clearly . . . We were in somebody's flat somewhere and it was cricket on the television. I remember being stunned by that. (Martin)

Children developed their own imaginative understanding of how these mysterious artefacts worked and how they might shape the future. To do this they drew on other knowledge and experience, connecting threads of memory. Rehana found an explanation and made a future plan in relation to a new Bush radio that her father had sent from England to Pakistan:

Grey . . . round dial at the front and a handle . . . All the elders sitting around it . . . All these little voices coming out of it . . . I used to wonder . . . Were tiny little people sitting inside this radio? . . . 'One day this radio is going to break and these little people are going to come out, and I'm gonna make friends with them, and I'm gonna put them on my hand and talk to them' . . . I had heard so many 'Arabian Nights' stories, of all these little dwarfs and things.

Children enjoyed the different experiences and imagined new futures. Martin, already interested in science because of his parents' influence (see Chapter 5) became deeply engaged with stories from the scientific world and science fiction:

> Uri Gagarin going into space. We found out at a petrol station . . . I remember the petrol pump [man] saying something to my dad about the Russian's sending somebody into space. So the whole thing around space exploration was all a part of my teenage years . . . Eagle, Dan Dare . . . H. G. Wells . . . Animal Farm, 1984, Brave New World . . . Arthur Clarke . . . Asimov.

The new discoveries provided games and creative activities, and opened up new possibilities:

> We got a computer when I was about 17, a ZX Spectrum, and I can remember thinking, 'This is it. I'm going to be a computer programmer' . . . I could make it scroll my name in different colours and obviously I'd become an astronaut. (Apara)

Children enjoyed the spectacle of the new technologies and examined in detail the mechanisms. They developed humorous and magical explanations and began to imagine their futures differently.

Youth Cultures and Markets

At different times children and young people were identified as active consumers and a range of different goods were aimed specifically at them at different times. This generated a range of complex choices and desires (Konig, 2008). Some were more caught up than others in the dominant youth cultures of their time, but all were touched by them. Their desire and ability to join in related to their age, how close or distant they felt to the youthful styles, their social class, ethnicity, gender and where they were born.

Tessa lived in a rural village environment and felt she lacked the 'cool' associated with the new trendy life styles. At school in the early 1980s, 'We were definitely the untrendy group . . . we had the horses . . . you didn't have the spare money for the records . . . No, we were always very . . . definitely . . . un-cool . . . ' James' childhood was affected by war and strong religious beliefs. The streets where he lived were not safe places for children to freely gather. Leisure spaces were segregated by religion and political beliefs. The new youth cultures were associated with physical and moral risk and some became linked to the civil rights movement which was associated with the Nationalist struggle in Northern Ireland. For James 'The opportunities weren't there in that respect. The activities that we . . . were involved in, were much sort of safer, were more collegiate'.

Dreams for the future were kindled in many ways in childhood and the new youth styles were just one part of that equation. Several children were drawn to the 'youth' styles through their associations with younger adults in their families. These contacts felt free of some of the restrictions and surveillance of their homes. As Madhi said, ' When you went . . . all the rules of daily life didn't apply'. In the 1950s and 1960s Claudia, visited a family friend, 'She was my absolute favourite, I adored her . . . She used to let us go and buy pick n mix . . . She seemed very young to me and very with it . . . lots of books, kindness'. In the 1970s and 1980s, Apara visited a young student aunt who, ' . . . mesmerized me . . . [someone] had painted her toenails . . . it was the most glamorous thing in my entire life . . . She lived by herself . . . She had bean bags . . . she was so trendy and right on'. In the 1980s and 1990s, Madhi also visited her aunt, 'She was quite cool . . . Her house was the only house we could eat meat in . . . She'd pay for you to all go to the cinema or go to the local shop and buy loads of ice-cream'. See how over the decades their language shifted as they in turn indicated that the youth cultures were 'with it', 'trendy' and 'cool'. Children's changing desires chimed with particular commodities that were marketed to them in different decades:

> One of my friends had a plastic Beatles' wig and I really, really wanted one . . . I had a picture of John Lennon that I got with fish fingers . . . [My dad] bought me a 'Party Boy' transistor radio and that was really good. (George)

Within each generation, groups of children and young people made personal choices related to different possible styles of living, negotiating the contemporary consumer culture in their own way (Thomson et al., 2002; Russell and Tyler, 2005). Although subject to the manipulations of 'branding', they selected and modified, joined in and withdrew, and tailored things to their own needs and desires, constructing their lives out of what was available at the time (ibid.). This involved choosing to go out (or not), listening to and buying music and following fashion. Of course, all this cost money and the degree of participation was different for each child.

Going Out

Places outside each home became associated with groups of children and young people. Some of this space was carved out by them for play and leisure (see Chapter 10), and some places were designed to attract children and young people, 'At the same time that children become an integral part of the commodified package of capitalism, specialized spaces are constructed and their contents consumed' (Aitken, 2001, p. 151). Sometimes they had adult permission and sometimes not. In the 1980s, in northern England, Tessa and her friends enjoyed going to the local picture house, 'Very tiny . . . three rows from the back and we used to sit in a row up there and there'd only ever be us in . . . a gang of us . . . having a bag of sweets'. In the 1970s, Richard went to the drive-in movies with his friends in South Africa, 'There was a row at the back, like a shelter, with seats in . . . There was a shop that you could buy sweets and popcorn'. In both cases the pleasures of going out were linked with the absence of adults and the freedom to eat sweets. In the 1960s, Julie played truant and was involved in coffee bar culture, 'We played pinball . . . We made one cup of coffee last most of the day . . . playing truant from school . . . meeting people'. Martin and his friends escaped out of the window at boarding school at night and went to the, ' . . . railway station . . . There was a café that was open . . . It was sitting, chatting. It was more the fact of the escape that was something'. For both, the pleasures involved freedom from school and the associated adult surveillance.

However, young people's leisure spaces were sites for the leisure of some groups and not others (Green et al., 1987). In the 1990s, Madhi and her friends who, ' . . . could be black, could be white, could have been Irish, Asian', felt uneasy. They were on their way to a Rave (an all night dance party):

> It was this very country place and we were walking to the pub and someone pipes up, 'Oh you know what's going to happen don't you?' And we were like, 'What?' He goes, 'You know that when you walk in you're just gonna get the eyes', and we all just laughed, 'cause nobody had to explain what that meant.

Social inequalities were generated in the youth leisure market and by the attitudes of some who dominated the leisure spaces (Henderson et al.,

1996). For some children, particular leisure space was not conceptualized as time for themselves, but as time for others:

> I wasn't ever much of a joiner inner . . . I often felt excluded from those kinds of spaces, because of my experiences of racism, especially at things that weren't very well supervised . . . Very often the very children that went were the very children who'd beat me up at school. (Apara)

Freedom from adult surveillance felt dangerous in these circumstances. Each leisure space contained complex fusions of cultural memory (Gilroy, 1987/2002) and signals related to ethnicity, gender, sexuality and social class, some accentuated for market purposes, others not. Richard experienced particular representations of 'race' through the leisure market targeted at privileged White groups in South Africa:

> You could go to see traditional Zulu dancing . . . It'd be black people dressed up, in feathers and all the rest of it, who were putting on a show. So there was this, pastiche, stereotypic view . . . of Zulu culture . . . stand in line and dance.

This market ' . . . variously efface[d] and emphasize[d] racial differences' (Lury, 1996 in Kenway and Bullen, 2001, p. 20) and distanced White children further from the oppressed majority of Black people. In South Africa at this time, all public leisure space was segregated, much of it completely inaccessible to Black children. The 'traditional' dancing exoticized differences between White and Black people, concealing and legitimating the underlying inequalities and the brutalities of apartheid. Hence, experiences of leisure spaces were unequal.

A real sense of leisure and pleasure was gained where children felt free from judgment and free to roam. When asked about her leisure, Rehana discussed a range of places where she felt at ease with friends:

> I'd go to the cinema . . . to town with my friends . . . window shopping. I'd go to park with my friends . . . city library also had common rooms, and we used to hang around there a lot . . . Didn't feel repressed or restricted in any way.

Pathways through the youth culture and leisure space were more open to some than others. The youth styles provided material for children to select from or reject in relation to the other complexities of their lives.

Music

Music was a complex vehicle for participation and knowledge building. All music contained different weaves of cultural memory (Gilroy, 1987/2002):

> I got very much into blues . . . initially . . . white blues . . . John Mayall . . . Muddy Waters, who I remember seeing in York when I was probably about 16 . . . Reading about the history of the blues . . . Robert Johnson, Charlie Patton . . . steeped in stories about American Slavery . . . one of the reasons why I was very much opposed to some of the racism that was occurring in this country at the time. (Martin)

As well as providing children and young people with social memories that they might not otherwise have encountered, music involved opportunities to relate to others. Young people allied themselves to particular sounds. The choices they made related to their position, circumstances and beliefs. Choices sometimes involved adult disapproval, '[Paul] playing his Animals record, and his father doing his grumpy old man "They are bloody animals, they're all bloody animals!" and I'm thinking "Oh God"' (Claudia). Sometimes adults approved, for example, those new to a place needed to learn the new cultural arrangements:

> When we came here [from the Caribbean] we adopted the music that was here . . . a childhood of Bing Crosby . . . waking up to 'I'm Dreaming of a White Christmas'. (Paulina)
>
> The whole family used to sit and watch Top of the Pops . . . even my dad, even my mum. (Rehana)

Styles were not homogeneous, although some forms dominated. Children's musical allegiance emerged from complex spatial and temporal influences. They were very individual. In the 1950s and 1960s Sylvia liked Cliff Richard and later the Beatles, whereas Martin, a boy of similar ethnicity, age and class, ' . . . always identified more with the Stones than the Beatles . . . That's probably the rebel side of me coming through'. Born a little later, Paulina, of Caribbean heritage, began to listen to, 'Calypso music . . . it was on the underground market . . . Reggae, Soul, things like Desmond Dekker'. In the 1970s and 1980s, Lara loved all the Black popular music of the times, 'Motown, funk and soul . . . Michael Jackson, I was, yeah, head over heels. Diana Ross, I liked all them . . . George Benson I think was one that I loved. Billie Ocean'. Apara, got into Punk and then when she moved to a more middle-class school, was attracted by Goth:

Something that was punk and I just loved it . . . doing the 'Dying Fly', on the floor . . . you just basically twitch . . . The DJ put the Sex Pistols' 'God Save the Queen' on . . . the headmistress jumping onto the stage and literally ripping it off the turntable . . . The first record I did buy was Goth, it was Siouxie and the Banshees.

The music, the dancing and the social disapproval of adults were linked. Later Apara said that Goth provided her a cloak, a sense of belonging and made it easier to relate to her peers (see below). In the 1980s and 1990s new combinations of sound and explicit new cultural fusions became available. Madhi took advantage of a range of opportunities:

My sister started listening to . . . Soul, Hip Hop, R&B and also some Ska . . . when I was with them, I used to listen to that kind of music . . . When I was out with my friends . . . more Indie music . . . Then Dance music . . . You didn't listen to the commercial charts, 'cause that was very unhip, uncool and we listened to a whole array of pirate music . . . Hearing about these illegal raves . . . how the police clamped down . . . I knew that there was Ecstasy and these acid tab things going around . . . having discussions in my peer group 'Would you? Would you?' . . . 'cause we all wanted to be cool.

Music was a continuing thread in her middle and late childhood. In 1994, when she was 16, Public Order legislation was amended to enable harsher policing of Raves (Muncie, 2009). The state sought to control young people gathering in large numbers. Involvement therefore meant risk and testing the boundaries of law.

Musical allegiance in childhood was fluid and dynamic, a significant part of everyday relationships (Laughey, 2006). Choices related to social position, to complex influences from peers, family, community, and to the sounds themselves. Music informed social interaction, social understanding, and imagined futures. Even when they did not 'go out' or dress fashionably, the new music styles of each times touched their lives in important ways.

Fashion

Clothing involved a very personal presentation of self. The choice to 'go out' or not would relate to access to the desired clothes. Rysst argues that children and young people interpret clothing differently to adults, and in ways that adults find difficult to understand, for example, where adults might see something as over sexualised, a child might not view the item in this way at all (2010). What might, on the one hand, appear outrageous to an adult, might also rely on adult attitudes and conventions (e.g., ideas about gender appropriateness). Choice was also informed by the child's sense of what was appropriate for 'children' and what was more appropriate for young people (Konig, 2008).

Early childhood clothing could be remembered with pleasure. Lara's orange-spotted dress was a vivid pleasure in her memory. Paulina also remembered 'special' childhood clothing which was woven with her memories of religion, 'It was a time I got to dress up. Right posh frilly dresses and lovely hats and stuff like that. So I do remember it being a happy time'. Childhood clothing was also associated with adult imposition:

> When I was little my mother used to make a lot of my clothes . . . she made me terrible clothes . . . a crimplene hunting jacket . . . a pair of draw string trousers . . . a safari suit, made of orange toweling, to wear on the beach. (George)

It is hard to tell whether these clothes were experienced as terrible, as well as being remembered as such. These items were based on the apparel worn by another social class at an earlier time (see Rachel, Chapter 2). The youth market provided a range of new clothing opportunities, 'We all used to go shopping on a Saturday afternoon . . . to buy some new clothes, to go to the disco in the evening, so we could all show off our new clothes' (Lara). Window shopping was an important part of this process because these items were costly. The passion clothes could generate in childhood should not be underestimated. They were longed for, worked for, hidden from adults and sometimes adored:

> Buying my first pair of shoes myself . . . feeling so excited . . . I had a wardrobe . . . Lying in bed and opening the door, so I could look at my shoes . . . I was too scared to wear them, 'cause they were just so gorgeous . . . They had a heel . . . I wasn't allowed to wear heels . . . sort of square cut at the front . . . with a band across the middle, and the front of the shoe had three different colours – pink, purple and this sort of beige background. (Claudia)

Clothing involved experimentation and challenges to the status quo, but was also about being safe, being the same as their friends, avoiding judgment (Lees, 1993) and continuing to be loved in their families:

> When I was 17 I had my ear pierced, 'cause all my friends were . . . My mother refused to speak to me for a week. . . . I would creep up behind

her and then I'd get my ear, and zoom round to the front of her, and put it straight in her face. (George)

George teased his mother, which might have incited or cooled her rage. At least communications were kept open. Apara, who had experienced a lot of racist violence, said that the choice to become Goth provided safety, more reliable friends and less conflict:

> You've *got* to wear black stuff. . . . I was just mesmerized, it was just love at first sight . . . Goths are never gonna be in a fight, cause if you spend three hours to get your hair to stick up, a fight is gonna totally ruin it, plus, you might break a nail, and that goes for boys as well as girls, and that would be tragedy. I've never ever seen a fight involving Goths!

Rachel would have chosen Punk, but her other (sports) allegiances made that less possible so she chose the New Romantics:

> I really admired Punks, but I couldn't do it, 'cause I was playing too much sport . . . there's a kind of look you have to have . . . having to conform, for trials for teams . . . you couldn't have funny looking hair.

The New Romantics provided gender fluidity in clothing which enabled Rachel to feel safe as a young lesbian; to pass, if necessary, but also to interact as she chose (see Chapter 2). Hence, clothing choices varied in relation to children and young people's developing sense of who they were, who they wanted to be and how they would be accepted.

Sexuality

Fashion, music and 'going out' were part of some everyday childhood experiences but not the whole story. The styles marketed to the young also formed part of the social production of sexualities (Foucault, 1980b; Edwards, 2004). Children became aware of this, as the interactions around clothes generated expectations that did or did not relate to their own desires:

> dresses with zips up the middle. I had an orange one . . . they were like a sort of shift . . . and a collar . . . a zip with a big ring on. They got the boys all excited; you had to put a safety pin behind 'cause they'd try to pull your zip down. (Claudia)

Claudia knew the dress was associated with risk and she enjoyed this aspect, but was not sure why, or on whose terms. As George said, 'there was sexuality in clothes':

> When Glam came in and I was very aware of David Bowie, you know, being bisexual, and I remember once getting my hair cut like him . . . and wanting to go to a concert and my mother forbade me because he was a 'Nancy Man' and a bit funny.

Wider social influences provided children with frameworks through which sexual feelings and encounters could be understood. Some came from religion, which in banning certain behaviour, showed children the way, 'I leaned about sexual pleasure because my friend had a book from the nuns telling you which bits not to wash too much' (Sylvia). As a young teenager, Kate paid penance for her secret desire in the following way:

> I remember my friend blackmailing me when I was about 13/14 because I had a crush on one of the boys and to stop her from telling him I had to stand on a chair and say, 'That was Adagio by Beethoven' over and over. This was the music that had been played at assembly.

Young people's sense of their sexuality and expectations of relationships emerged through social frameworks of memory (Halbwachs, 1925/1992) including patterns of family life they had experienced and the moral discourses they had encountered. Youth cultures modified these and provided some new frameworks for understanding. Julie and Rachel remembered how they settled into particular sexual identities and relationships:

> I got into sex quite young . . . looking for love and friendship . . . If something went wrong, you didn't think it was men bullying you, or making you do anything or, no, it was you . . . had boyfriends, a lot. I thought I was quite promiscuous. (Julie)
>
> I had boyfriends, like you had to . . . doing it begrudgingly, because of the peer pressure . . . When anyone announced that they were having a party, it would be this massive frenzy of . . . 'Have you got a boyfriend?' . . . it was just excruciating . . . girls were just allowing themselves to be trashed really . . . I just thought, 'I'm not interested in this. It's not even vaguely exciting, or thrilling or enticing for me, physically, or emotionally or sexually'. (Rachel)

For Julie and Rachel, events did not feel within their control. Both referred to the dangers of girls' reputations being tarnished. Julie, remembering experiences from the 1960s, talked of her 'promiscuity' and Rachel, recalling the late 1970s, referred to girls being 'trashed'. Both experienced some coercion, in Julie's case 'men bullying' and in Rachel's, 'you had to' and a lot of peer pressure. Julie was looking for love and friendship and Rachel realized her own needs would not be met this way. Ten years apart, both drew attention to the form 'compulsory heterosexuality' took in the youth cultures of the time (Rich, 1980; Papadopoulos, 2010 citing Buckingham and Bragg, 2004).

Julie 'settled down', 'When I met my ex-husband we fell in love and decided we'd have a baby together and get married, in that order. He had to leave school . . . I'd already left'. Having linked her previous sexual experiences to her loneliness, this relationship and becoming a mother gave her a sense of security. An added bonus was she no longer had to have lots of boyfriends. Rachel 'found out' about lesbianism through the events, magazines, styles and music of the time. She cautiously began to buy *Gay Times* magazine,

> 'Rock Follies' . . . There was a woman . . . [Julie Covington] who had short hair, who could sing . . . I would just go and see whatever she was in . . . terrible teenage crush . . . A woman who was there, for exactly the same reason . . . We totally kind of connected . . . That was sort of my coming out process . . . I thought, 'That explains it! Now there's a name for it, fantastic'.

In this way Rachel found a new sense of belonging and a better place that chimed with her personal desires.

The cultures and commodities of particular times and places were part of the wider social production of sexualities. Although heterosexual pathways were generally dominant, different forms of sexuality and life style were visible. In the 1960s, the 'permitted promiscuities' related to the social movements of the time laid Julie open to some male bullying. In the 1970s, more visible gay, bisexual and lesbian cultures provided a way through for Rachel.

Conclusion

Children's experiences of consumption are part of their everyday engagement with wider social change. These are journeys they are involved with

independently and as part of their families. The social relations of consumption shape everyday childhood, informing children's needs and
desires. Children are involved with their families in enjoying the acquisition of new commodities. They celebrate these as representing social
advancement and benefiting the family. See how Lara and Richard enjoyed
the new Burgundy Ford Anglia and the red TRIM phone. Acquiring new
domestic commodities are important turning points in families. They
inform everyday domestic routines and relationships in the home. Paulina
and Claudia remembered the difficulties their mothers experienced and
the resultant impact on their moods inefficient domestic equipment and
the burden on their mothers and themselves.

Consumer marketing relies on the selective promotion of ways of life
that both reflect and distort realities on the ground and create new forms
of inclusion and exclusion that are felt by children. Children and young
people draw on contemporary consumer culture, tailoring things to their
own circumstances and desires, creating identities, developing relationships and distancing themselves as they need and are able. Many young
people remain distant from particular youth cultures. Some just cannot
afford to join in. Some (like James) associate them with risk. Other (like
Tessa and Rachel) have more pressing interests. Tessa spent her much of
her young time with horses, and Rachel, in sporting activities. Children
like Apara and Madhi can become quite expert at reading the signs of the
times and learn the associated hierarchies and values in relation to their
own safety and well-being.

Children draw on complex threads from their own experience to navigate contemporary cultural arrangements. They develop allegiance to particular sounds and select particular clothing and styles. These might give
them pleasure and allow them to blend in or gain visibility as they choose.
They may also disappoint. New consumer commodities might improve the
quality of their family life, the speed of communications, and their individual and shared pleasures. They might gain them entry to particular groups
and places but they might not. Children and young people are involved in
very careful navigation of this area and they do consider their own safety
and complex needs when making decisions but consumer markets may
create illusory expectations; the commodities and styles might not live up
to their claims (just as having labour-saving devices did not mean that
domestic labour was equally shared). The drive for profit creates new forms
of market segmentation (e.g., the pink and blue markets of childhood
toys). The desires that the consumer market generates in young men and

women may be very different and not tailored to either of their interests (Papadopoulos, 2010). At the time of writing, cuts in public expenditure on leisure and youth services may well lead to increased private provision and further reduce democratic accountability in this area (Taylor, 2010). Leisure spaces may become more exclusive and specialized, open to some and not others.

Chapter 10

Children: Play, Parties and Parades

There was this big powerhouse that used to supply electricity to the city. Even
though it said 'Danger', so many volts . . . 'Don't Cross', we still used to sneak up
there . . . somebody had broken holes in the walls . . . three pools that looked like
swimming pools . . . all the boys used to sneak in there and start swimming.

(Rehana)

Introduction

This chapter explores children's play including their participation in wider
social play (sport, parties and other social festivities). The children in this
research played on building sites, in a dry dock, near train lines, in agricultural settings and near an electricity power station. The creation of play
space involved the making of dens in bushes, coal holes, cupboards and
under furniture and buildings. Play involved toys, fantasy, role play, arts,
stories, music, media and animals. All this involved children in deep emotional, physical and mental creativity as they wove, connected and juxtaposed different threads of social memory, 'Children learn that one object
can stand in for another. A piece of swirling blue fabric can be a river, a
box can become a boat and a stick can be a crocodile' (Olusoga, 2009,
p. 43). Through play, past and present times were woven in new and memorable ways and children imagined their future times differently, 'In play
the roles and rules of the world can be experienced and explored . . . . '
(ibid., p. 47).

Play is an ambiguous concept. On the one hand, childhood may be conceptualized as integrally playful, on the other, play is only one aspect of
childhood as children may be deprived of play (Broadhead, 2003; Brown,
2003; Brock et al., 2009). Play is not the preserve of childhood as adults
continue to play, albeit in more time permitted ways and particular settings. In this chapter the focus is on those activities respondents remembered as playful, together with those wider family, community and national

times that involved space for social play (celebratory and commemorative practices). Cohen (1985) explains the role of such times in confirming and supporting the development of social identities. They mark transition in communities, through, for example, coming of age ceremonies and carnivals (Morrow, 2003).

The childhoods in this research were full of play. Even where circumstances worked against this, such as poverty, sexism and racism, children continued to play, 'Children's special capacity and creativity made them fully capable of integrating play into daily life in multiple ways' (Bai, 2005, p. 28). In addition, particular social events structured the calendars of their everyday childhood and created space for social play. Religious and state calendars generated holidays, rest days and festivities, which were also times for the collective remembering of particular events, for example, victories in war. Everyday childhood was structured in relation to such events and the commitments confirmed there. Each event involved threads of social memory connecting children to other places and times. Each event generated its own pathways to the future (Misztal, 2003; Adam, 2006). Different festivities were designed in the interests of some rather than others, cementing particular interests. Children experienced these events close up and at a distance.

This chapter concludes the data analysis, highlighting the creativity of children and their deep social involvement beyond the spaces which are traditionally associated with childhood. The children in this research were positioned differently to each other and to adults. They had their own personal forms of engagement. There were differences in their space–time location and heritage, but whatever their position, all were deeply involved in weaving the social fabric through play (Neale and Flowerdew, 2003, p. 192). The focus on personal and social play in this chapter gives attention to the complex relationship between family, community and the wider social world in their lives (Cohen, 1985, p. 54). Play is a lens to explore their experiences of personal and social transition.

This chapter is in six parts. First, children's personal play times are discussed, considering some of the commodities, experiences, feelings and activities involved (Henderson et al., 1996). Children's play may show how aspects of power and powerlessness are reversed and how indoor and outdoor places are woven (Haug, 1992; Christensen and O'Brien, 2002; Hallden, 2002; Rasmussen and Smidt; 2002). Second, outside play is considered, including children's experience of the space around them, their enjoyment of freedom from supervision and their safety. Children in outside spaces have often been viewed by adults as taking too much freedom and consequently penalized (Ward, 1978; Pearson, 1983; Ennew, 2002; Morrow, 2002).The third part of the chapter considers children's engagement with organized sport, bearing in mind the dimensions of class, gender and other divisions involved (Glyptis, 1989). It includes discussion of being a sports fan, where a pool of shared memories might connect a child to a team and other supporters (de Groot and Robinson, 2008). In the fourth part, family play times are discussed, including the affirmation of familial bonds, the loosening of rules and the humorous connections that are made. In a similar vein, in the fifth part, community festivities are discussed. These arise in the particular interests of groups and in response to major and sometimes traumatic social events, more distant in time. The festivities repeat and alter the past. Finally, national play times are considered. Particular times are structured into each calendar related to national events. Children have different degrees of closeness and distance to these events, and the associated celebrations and commemorations. Such events might relate to particular sides in national and international struggles with which their families are or are not aligned. In conclusion, wider social influences and children's engagement are both considered. Play may be conceptualized as a site of both personal, social and political change (Shaw, 2001) involving political acts that are ' . . . a means of taking control and finding meaning' (Burden, 1998, p. 10).

Play Times – Inside to Outside

The full range of experiences associated with play were hard to remember, being so embedded in the everyday. Memories revolved around the special, significant and out of the ordinary. Memories of inside play were less vivid and rich than those of outside play, ' . . . I cannot remember any . . . specific events in those rooms' (Julie). The whole of the home was a potential site of play, bearing in mind that everyday childhood may be conceptualized as continuously playful. Respondents found it easier to remember particular events, places, games and toys. Negotiating a place to play was part of the complexity of adult–child relationships in the home. Parts of the home were designated by adults as special areas where children could play, 'We had an upstairs bathroom put in. Before it became a bathroom it was empty with a plasterboard table in it and I had potatoes, carrots and parsnips with eyes, noses etc to make faces' (Kate). Parts of the home were carved out by children. Richard created a place to keep his toys safe from his siblings:

There was a corner . . . between the lounge and the dining areas and that's where I'd set out a train set . . . That's where I knew I could leave stuff down . . . There was the back of one of the chairs that was facing the lounge. That would mark the space where it would be okay.

Children's play was associated with particular toys and games. These generated desires and strong memories from childhood. They reflected wider social relations related to class and cost, gender and ethnicity. Kate had, ' . . . dolls in my bedroom and a pram that was kept under the stairs'. Martin had, ' . . . this large train set, which actually lived under the bed in my mum and dad's bedroom . . . it slid under and came out'.

Play did not necessarily equate with pleasure. Children became frustrated as they tried to resolve particular problems, 'I can remember making a dolls house with cardboard boxes . . . making my own flour and water paste . . . it just collapsing obviously and getting very cross with it' (Julie).

I can remember sitting there and doing knitting with one of those awful knitting kits . . . plastic needles and awful wool and somehow my knitting got smaller, not bigger! Trying to work out what had happened, but getting into this awful mess. (Claudia)

Children practised particular tasks and social roles, encountering barriers to overcome. They reproduced, adapted and juxtaposed different elements from the available social fabric (Neale and Flowerdew, 2003). In role play and fantasy, their dreams for the future were particularly visible:

We used to do scenes from East Enders. My sister and I would make fish and chips and things and we'd pretend we were Cathy in the cafe, and somebody would come and say 'I want chips' and you'd have a conversation . . . Then you'd pay them with the monopoly money. (Madhi)

This repeated role play drew on popular culture to set the scene (an English soap opera). It involved the pleasure of the special food treat. The children transformed the scenario. Instead of waiting for others to provide the treat, they were in control. They created the imaginary dinner. They generated the polite social atmosphere of the sale and conducted the financial transaction. In the real world this treat would be relatively rare and adults would choose the time. Through the game the children took control of the process. The game reversed their dependencies; aspects of power and powerlessness were 'reversed in the dreams' (Haug, 1992, p. 68). Sometimes the fantasy was less in the control of the child. Kate was playing, ' . . . Indians with my brother and dad . . . we had a pow wow . . . dad passed his cigarette round as the pipe of peace and I sucked in smoke and coughed . . . I definitely didn't like smoking'. Through such games, children (and families) transformed social relations, 'within the walls of the ideological' (ibid., p. 67). Here the family developed play from edited and altered accounts of 'Cowboys and Indians' (the imperial contexts removed). From children's perspectives such adventure stories referred to the world beyond home and were full of imaginative potential. Kate's garden provided an imaginary game about an alligator, a metaphor perhaps for the risks and adventures to be encountered outside:

> There was a huge puddle/pond at the top of the garden . . . my dad and brother had told me there was an alligator in it. Instead of going straight in for my dinner I splashed around in the water shouting for 'Mr Alligator' until my mum came out to see what had happened to me.

Play involved children in weaving indoor and outdoor spaces (Christenson and O'Brien, 2002).The wider social world shaped home and provided social fabric for play. Friends visited to play. Play involved attention to pets, including bringing them in, taking them out and visiting them outside in regular feeding, cleaning and grooming routines. The fluidity of indoor and outdoor in play was nowhere more apparent than in children's creation of dens. These were special 'inside' child places where adults were not expected to enter but to remain on the horizon. These were places that a child could be alone. Apara's favourite place was, ' . . . between the front door and the glass door . . . I used to take my blanket down and make a little den inside it . . loved that cocooned little feeling'. Kate liked, 'A bit of the garden had raspberry canes . . . I fought my way into the middle and sat in a hidey hole eating raspberries and hiding from everyone'. Paulina's first home was raised up above ground on stilts (to prevent flooding and the entry of creatures). This made under the house an ideal play space, 'That is definitely my main memory of the house in the Caribbean, is playing in the space under the house. It felt safe. It was the space where you ran and hid if you were being naughty'. Dens were shared with siblings:

> This space under the stairs . . . my brother and I, as a hidey hole . . . indoors with blankets and table covers . . . used the tables and the dining room chairs . . . my mother used to make us lunch and we'd take it and eat it in the den. (Pamela)

We used to climb in . . . when [the coal] was going down, so you could still reach to get out . . . it was lovely. We could hear mum saying, 'Dinner's ready' and we'd be 'Shhhh' and then suddenly it'd be daylight and she'd be, 'Come out of there. You're black already, why do you want to be blacker?'. (Lara)

Dens were created with communities of other children:

We had a big tree and there was a shed in the big tree, and we used to make lots of dens and have tarpaulin and string and lots of things . . . that was our space. It had a tyre from the tree . . . it had hay and straw. (Tessa)

Everyday routines were established. The den evolved in familiar play territory relatively cut off from adults but sometimes containing a familiar adult presence at a distance:

We used to call it, 'Our little jungle' . . . it was always overgrown . . . we used to take our private things and an old radio . . . old pieces of carpet, old deck chairs, anything, that would make it our own. We had a secret password to get in . . . we used to have a certain knock . . . and if anyone used to throw old mattresses out, we used to drag them into the den, so that we had something to sit on . . . You could still hear my mum calling us when it was dinner time. (Lara)

In these places everyday life, domestic routines and social roles were repeated and reorganized. Dependencies were reversed as children took on the powers of adults, yet adults bounded the activities, providing food, nagging about cleanliness and imposing time limits.

Children's play involved crossing boundaries between inside and outside, whether in reality or in the imagination (Christensen and O'Brien, 2002). It also involved crossing boundaries between self and others, and created distance from familiar adults:

It was that moving around space . . . between our house and the next house down, this big patch of grass . . . where a lot of us played . . . We moved into a village and the outside space was the whole village . . . outside space was more than just us . . . always part of a group. (Tessa)

Rehana described an escape from inside to outside, away from her grandma's gaze and into the sun. A warm dry climate in Pakistan created architectural fluidity between inside and outside. The dangers of the sun were not heeded by the children:

> As soon as my grandma would fall asleep and we heard the snoring, we'd all lift our heads up, look at each other, twinkle in our eyes, and off we'd sneak out, off to the roof top, in the mid-day sun . . . run around the roof top . . . You've got this sense of space around you, all the time.

At a similar time, but in England, the weather created clearer dividing lines and there were cleaning rituals associated with George's movement from inside to outside play:

> My mum used to hypo the steps in the yard and the paving stones to get rid of germs . . . The arena for play had to be disinfected . . . Then of course I'd go and play in the entry, which is full of filth.

The space between inside and outside also contained some symbolic value. In England, higher status homes had gardens separating home and community. Pamela lived in such a house but enjoyed the proximity to community afforded by her working-class grandmother's house which had a very small front yard, 'We used to sit on the front door step and watch the world go by and chat with the neighbours and the other children'. The semi-private outside space surrounding the home was remembered as a route to and from other places, providing some of the (alleged) safety of home but new connections. Home and community life overlapped in these spaces. Community beckoned Madhi and her sister and they developed games in the garden, imagining they were moving through the neighbourhood as adults:

> 'Right, we've got our money, now that we've been paid, so we'll go shopping,' . . . We used to create spaces in the garden, which were like . . . where we lived . . . There was a roundabout in our garden, an area where all the shops were, and we used to say, 'Let's go to the shops', and then get on our bikes and go round and round.

Play was continuous and expansive. It was also particular, and associated with specific artefacts, games and places. Time to 'play' and 'not play' were structured into the day, week and year in the child, family, community and national calendars. The available social fabric informed play as children juxtaposed, repeated and altered different elements. It was solitary and collaborative, could be distant from, yet bounded by familiar adults. Time and space to play was carved out by children.

Play Times – Outside

Playing in the community introduced rich new social fabric, including new games, new children to play with and complex new social relations (Ward, 1978). As with home-based play, play outside could be felt as continuous and expansive, that is, not restricted to particular activities but more associated with feelings of pleasure and freedom. Julie expressed the complexity of feelings and activities she associated with outside play:

> I used to take people's dogs for walks . . . Playing on a derelict house where there'd been a fire . . . Groups of kids playing out together, playing in the streets . . . Lots of friends and games and freedom to play out . . . Riding the horses. I remember one wonderful night, where the horse escaped and I rode bareback to get the horse back in.

In Julie's experience, being young, free to roam and choose what she wanted to do was in itself play. The freedom from parental supervision was part of play but familiar adults framed many of the memories. They were in the background, paying attention at a distance. In the dead end of the back lane behind Apara's grandparents' house, 'We used to play out for hours . . . We couldn't be seen, but we could be heard . . . No cars ever came down, so it was a safe place to be . . . It was a kid's kingdom then'. In the institutional care of a boarding school there were also places freer from adult supervision:

> There were rugby pitches in winter, cricket pitches in summer . . . playground areas around the houses, where we could play evenings, weekends . . . You could get quite a long way away from house masters and prefects . . . part of the control process.

The release from aspects of adult supervision was remembered with some pleasure, however, other adults and new sanctions related to play were encountered. Children's safety was also a concern. For George, 'There was no green space, apart from school fields . . . We used to climb over the gate, which was locked . . . We were told off loads of times, but once the headmaster confiscated our coats and the police came'. For Claudia, 'There was a barn with hay . . . dangerous places . . . wonderful places to play in. The farmer . . . would try and chase us out'.

Playing with other children also involved new rules and relations informed by wider social expectations, divisions and hierarchies. This informed and altered play relations, restricting play for some, such as Madhi, 'At primary school, we were playing Superman, and they made me be some damsel in distress that they had to rescue and I remember feeling really frustrated', and for Lara and her brother as:

> I remember mum saying, 'If you're skipping on the path, keep an eye on your brother' . . . These teenage boys surrounded him and started calling him 'Black' . . . 'You need to get a bath' . . . 'God forgot to paint you white' . . . I went absolutely berserk.

Racial abuse, sexism and other differentiation led some children to stay inside for safety. Whether the experience of outside play remained pleasurable related to these wider power relations within communities. As with all leisure (see Chapter 9) places pleasurable for some were frightening for others (Green et al., 1987). Wider community conflict diminished the possibility and heightened the risks of playing out (Leonard, 2010). In Northern Ireland in the 1970s, ' . . . a lot of people stayed in and watched television' (Lara). Particular solidarities developed and the potential for violence was high, 'Some of those feelings that keep those boys together, they're that powerful, huge powerful emotions . . . Trying to intervene, hack in that, anybody's got a real job on haven't they?' (James)

Nevertheless, the outside environment had the potential for rich and expansive play because of the complex threads of social memory and temporal influences for children to weave. Such play was remembered with nostalgia:

> There was the freedom attached to going out . . . a garden . . . a huge apple tree, which was great for climbing . . . some outbuildings . . . a bricked stove in one . . . You could pull all these cast iron bits out of this thing and hide . . . making mud pies . . . decorating them with dandelions . . . We made fishing rods out of bits of tree . . . pieces of string . . . with a safety pin on the bottom and a worm . . . go to woods . . . Coming back with armfuls of bluebells and taking them back to the old people that lived in the almshouses . . . found a dead badger once . . . Great big trees that had fallen down in some storm . . . groups of us . . . galleons, different things, castles. Clambering and scrambling around them and getting scruffed and dirty and always being in trouble for getting

dirty . . . A really bad winter . . . walking on top of snow . . . waste deep against the edges of the fields . . . There'd be a crust on the top, and you'd be light enough, and every now and then, it'd give way and you'd fall in . . . but how exciting that was.

The outdoors could provide a sense of freedom, new connections with the environment and unique play places. Claudia engaged with the changing seasons and landscape and with other children. She recreated the social life she knew on her own terms. Her play involved journeys through the garden to other places and journeys to imagined times. Her outside play crossed boundaries between known and unknown; permitted and not permitted.

The geographies of play were different in relation to the social fabric of each area, containing different degrees of safety and danger (Neale and Flowerdew, 2003; Cross, 2008). Both urban and rural landscapes afforded trepidation, excitement and different play opportunities. Children engaged playfully with the whole of the building process, from buildings going up to their falling down and dereliction:

The building sites were play grounds . . . you could go in and pile bricks up and move stuff around . . . Going into houses before the floorboards were there but the joists were down . . . walking across joists . . . up and down ladders, on scaffolding. (Martin)

Dilapidated school . . . broken windows and whatever else, so it was fairly dangerous. (Paulina)

concrete columns of an old building and an overgrown concrete swimming pool near it, so that was all very exciting. (Rachel)

Economic production provided special settings. In a city port in South Africa Richard played in a dry dock, ' . . . like a dried canal . . . a big dip down at one point into this concrete basin . . . one lad actually did manage to fall down . . . broke both his legs'. In Pakistan, Rehana played in irrigation puddles:

We used to play in the water all day . . . fields that were cultivated . . . something which was bored in the ground and they'd be pumped with a motor. They'd have this massive pipe of water coming out into different puddles and the water would be routed to different fields.

Streets, streams and railways provided different exciting play, involving building, riding, splashing and jumping. Paulina talked of the streets, ' . . . streets used to go down to the wall . . . bits of wood and old bicycle wheels . . . you make things like scooters . . . water running through . . . falling in . . . people used to dump their rubbish in it'; Apara and Claudia, the railway, ' . . . a fence . . . undergrowth, a steep bank, and at the top, was the railway . . . I only climbed up about halfway . . . [my brother] did climb up to the top'. 'Under the railway on a concrete slab . . . we'd spend hours . . . we shouldn't be there . . . being under there when trains came over was very exciting and scary'. These experiences, remembered retrospectively, were woven with feelings of nostalgia, excitement and awareness of risk. Play in such settings was illicit, dangerous, repeated and exploratory, providing different opportunities to be socially involved.

Memories of outdoor play also hinged on particular games that involved complex physical and social manoeuvres and careful counter posing of different elements. To play badly might mean humiliation and children felt a burden of responsibility to play 'well'. Games experienced in the 1950s and early 1960s included:

'Cogog' . . . A tennis ball you put on a spot, somebody kicked it like mad . . . it'd roll in any direction . . . everybody went off and hid. The person who was seeking had to go get the ball, bring it back and then do hide and seek . . . Absolutely terrifying when it was my turn to be on, but the thrill of the game. (Julie)

In the mid-1960s Paulina played many different games:

'Murder Ball' . . . when you throw the ball at each other and you've got to try and dodge it . . . 'Rounders' . . . 'Rugby against the Balls' . . . 'Two Balls', 'American skipping', 'Proper Skipping' . . . Oh I used to love it! . . . and 'Hula Hoops' . . . 'Hopscotch'.

In the 1980s, Madhi played, ' "Knock down Ginger" . . . really naughty . . . where you go running up round the street and knock on people's houses and runaway!'

Being outside added new dimensions to play. Sometimes, play could be felt as a continuous part of being out; at other times play was felt to be restricted. Outside play was informed by dominant social hierarchies and involved challenges to these. It involved the need to navigate the new adult and child priorities encountered. Outside play involved the continued weaving and juxtaposition of different threads of social memory and the carving out of space time for self.

Play Times – Sport

Physical and social dexterity were important elements of play. Children were drawn to and distanced from different organized sports. Each sport had a cultural history informed by class, gender and particular processes of social transition (Glyptis, 1989). There were particular difficulties. Rehana's grandmother identified her as a 'Tomboy' as she enthusiastically participated with her brothers, playing cricket on the roof of the house (Deem, 1995). Julie could not fully participate in tennis because of her family's financial situation and because she was never taught tennis (a more class privileged sport). Swimming was more available to her through the provision of municipal pools. For some girls, football was never an option, always associated with boys, 'The boys' playground had the football on . . . but there was a building between, you couldn't even see them' (Tessa). Madhi's and Rachel's passion for sport was informed by a growing understanding of their different position to boys. In the 1970s, Rachel was the only girl picked for the teams, ' . . . football or cricket . . . that was when I got a sense that I could do sports . . . when boys pick you above themselves . . . I got a sense of where I stood in the hierarchy' (Rachel). But the social hierarchies of the game eventually pushed her out:

> Somebody's dad showed up with a strip, with shirts and goalposts, rather than two jumpers, and I was like 'Wow, we're being a team', and the next thing, I got tapped on the shoulder and to say, 'Can you move away now, we're about to start' . . . I just got on my bike and pedalled furiously . . . didn't know what to do with that . . . so upset . . . gone home and hid my upsetness.

She continually fought for football space:

> I went to my primary school teacher, 'Can I play football with the boys?' 'Oh no, you can't do that, you're a girl' . . . put a girls' team together in primary school . . . but we were only allowed to play the boys below us, to keep it 'safe'! . . . I got to secondary school . . . 'Can I play football?' 'Yes you can' . . . but then I never got to play the games, cause the F.A. had a ruling then to say that football is not a suitable game for women and girls.

In the 1980s and early 1990s, Madhi and her friends still had to struggle for football space:

> The boys . . . used to monopolize the playground . . . Sometimes we were allowed to play but the boys were just shits to us really . . . After the 1990

World Cup . . . we wanted to play football, so we played on the left hand side, which just happened to be the female side . . . One of the male teachers gave us a ball.

The social hierarchies and relations of sport influenced self-esteem and friendships. The arrangements of sports provided particular opportunities and challenges that involved careful navigation, 'I can remember being quite pleased, because I was quite good in goal, I always used to be picked first . . . quite an esteem building thing, that you weren't one of the last ones to be picked' (Richard). Later, Richard experienced Afrikaans rugby which felt to him like organized violence, ' . . . it was compulsory . . . I got tackled by some oik, who managed to chip my tooth . . . it really hurt and I was determined I wasn't going to do it anymore'. He succeeded in being pulled out and began to play basket ball which suited his height and abilities. Children might be judged and bullied if they failed to 'come up to scratch', 'let down the side' or were perceived to be different. The awareness of this potential could create a threatening environment, 'I stopped playing . . . It was an all boys' school, so I didn't like the team games in the all boy environment' (George). Friendships could be sustained or fail in relation to involvement in sport, 'My best friend . . . fell out with me because I was playing in a different team . . . Then she thought I'd said something . . . and she was being all pally pally with somebody else' (Madhi).

The passionate nature of team support (Percy and Taylor, 1997) shaped Cathy's childhood. She, her sister and her father supported Liverpool:

Once you were encamped, that was it. You were in it, and you would be in it until you died and it would not be as nothing to you, ever. If your team was doing well or badly, it would always be a matter of concern and feeling an association.

A pool of shared memories connected children such as Cathy to her team and other supporters (de Groot and Robinson, 2008). As with religion, sporting rituals, special clothing, particular artefacts and other shared practices confirmed these feelings of belonging (Percy and Taylor, 1997):

The whole day had been mapped out for you. If Liverpool were at home . . . we would get up . . . go to town on the bus . . . come back, get off the bus . . . get our fish and chips, walk home, have them, eaten them by half past 12. Dad would come back from the pub and we'd get in the car and we'd travel to Anfield and we'd always park in Sunlight

Street . . . Walk the last mile to the ground . . . There's this swelling crowd, the nearer you'd get . . . Having to keep hold of each other . . . if you were in the Kop, walking along past about fifty blokes all lined up, weeing up against a wall . . . Very happy memories really of the matches, the screaming and ranting.

Supporting the team became deeply rooted, connecting everyday life to the team and city at sporting times (Jones, 2000). When not actually at the match, Cathy remembered:

Liverpool was just absolutely incredibly [quiet] that day . . . That was all that anyone was interested in . . . There'd be great decoration and the city would look very different . . . From about 2 o'clock the city was silent. There was just nobody outside. At key moments, there'd be screaming everywhere, across the whole city!

She belonged to something much wider than herself and her family. These events took her out of ordinary childhood into special times invested with symbolism and future hopes for her team (Percy and Taylor, 1997, p. 37). This continued through adulthood, 'Fan testimonies abound with the observation that the game induces a kind of all consuming, irrational and totally childlike happiness in adult persons' (Giulianotti and Armstrong, 1997, p. 8). It has been argued that football is one remaining source of mass collective rituals, providing continuity, social meaning and a sense of lifetime commitment for children in many countries (Hognestad, 1997).

Sport was a time when particular forms of adult and child play were socially permitted, differentiated by class, gender, ethnicity, age and ability. Sport informed the childhood calendar and created particular desires, opportunities, social and physical challenges for children. This involved children in careful navigation as they tried to carve out space and time for themselves. Acceptance in particular sports and related networks could engender a deep sense of social belonging. Being pushed out or excluded generated feelings of anger and failure. The remainder of this chapter continues to explore children's experiences of more collectivized play times.

Families Play

Parties and other family gatherings were part of the calendar, creating space for families and children to play. There were resonant memories of such parties, of grandparents behaving in silly ways, of luscious food, dressing up, music, dancing and hearing jokes and stories from the past:

> A big huge, extended family party . . . in this tiny little terraced house. . .
> All the old music hall songs . . . [Grandfather] used to play the spoons . . .
> A real knees up, which spilled out into the street and the back yard . . .
> Oh I loved it . . . Go and help yourself to food and have food pressed on
> you . . . fancy cakes and things that we never got at home . . . Sit on the
> front doorstep and eat these things. (Pamela)

Family play was marked by the loosening of rules and limits on children's behaviour and the generation of humorous and strange 'out of the ordinary' connections. In these ways, for example, a tea cosy became Grandpa's hat, 'Always did the same jokes . . . We put the tea cosy on his head, 'cause he was balding. It was supposed to keep him warm and then he would pretend to forget until he got outside the door' (Apara). Family parties also linked to particular religious calendars, whether or not beliefs were shared. James remembered the deep pleasure associated with these days, 'Christmas and Easter were big events in our lives; big family events . . . Real wonderful feelings of happiness and all the childhood things of suspense, of looking forward to and just wonderful days'. Apara, from a non-religious family, also enjoyed such days, but to a different narrative. The stories passed down to her from the past related to a pagan rather than Christian heritage, 'We all just used to love Christmas . . . it was talked about as the Mid-Winter feast . . . it was always about pagan and food, and having a good time . . . We always celebrated Christmas with absolute gusto'. In these parties, performance was important, whether this involved dressing up, telling jokes or making music. Performance gave Lara deep pleasure and confidence:

> Not only did we celebrate our birthdays, we celebrated our name days . . .
> after the saints . . . Every Sunday we used to have to do a performance. . .
> My dad used to say, 'Go in the bedroom after dinner while we're tidy-
> ing . . . think of a song you want to sing, produce a dance, get the key-
> board out or the xylophone, and do something, so when me and your
> mum sit down, you can sing or dance for us.'

As well as making music and dancing, performance involved making unusual connections, parodying and reversing particular roles and developing some distance from everyday relationships. Clearly the nature of such celebrations varied in relation to the quality of family life and individual experiences. Play spaces for children and adults were sometimes shared and sometimes quite distinct, 'The parents stayed downstairs and got drunk, but we just had our own world upstairs every New Year' (Tessa).

Losses and departures in the family were also marked by ritual and shared remembering (see Chapters 3 and 6). Boundaries between family and community; fun and sadness blurred in family parties. A party before Rehana emigrated from Pakistan involved, 'My school friends, teachers. . . kids in our street, in the neighbourhood . . . lots of little presents . . . My dad threw this party for everybody . . . they all were crying for me'.

In childhood, such gatherings marked the passing of time and provided vivid clustered multi-sensory memories that stood out from the everyday. The events remembered strengthened the children's ties to their family biographies through repeated jokes, stories and shared performance. They provided opportunities for separate and shared play. They contained the sadness related to lost kin and departures as well as the pleasures of nice food, humour and music. These were important playful gatherings, weaving threads of familial memory and cementing bonds They could also deteriorate into conflict where conflict featured in family life. The festivities provided children with further markers and guidelines to the future.

Communities Play

Similarly, the community (whether neighbourhood or community of interest) provided times for shared play. Children could be at the heart of community celebrations or at the margins, as particular interests dominated. Community festivities arose in the particular interests of groups and in response to major and sometimes traumatic social events, more distant in time, repeating and altering such events. Particular respondents, whose interests and commitments were closely entwined with those around them, remembered events vividly. The memories were again, multi-sensory, including music, colour, dressing up, performance, excess and 'out of the ordinary' behaviour where social roles and artefacts were transformed playfully and the usual power relations were temporarily reversed (Haug, 1992). In Carnival, for example, 'They revel in considering disorder, ambiguity, artificiality, the strange, the exotic and the spectacular, and the capricious mixing of codes that produces stylistic promiscuity' (Bakhtin, 1968, quoted in Kenway and Bullen, 2001, p. 25).

Carnival was significant for Paulina. Although carnival invited some spontaneity, space and time for carnival was in reality carefully negotiated and planned through the year in the communities in which she lived in

St Kitts and England. Space and time for children was negotiated as part of this planning, through, for example, the different structuring of daytime and night-time activities. Each year conflicting interests were mediated. The movement of people had to be carefully orchestrated to avoid injury. The interests and perspectives of men, women, children and adults, could be different; dangerous for children, where drunken adult men dominated. The planning of carnival involved complex negotiations between community and state, bearing in mind the precariousness of that relationship (see Chapter 7).

Each carnival contained complex influences and was practised in different ways to celebrate particular communities. Carnival contained hopes and desires for a better future in response to a difficult past and was a time to transcend everyday social relations, moral and economic demands (Kenway and Bullen, 2001). Paulina remembered the trepidation, excitement and pleasure in St Kitts when she was very young, 'They have what they call "the bull", which they try and frighten people into keeping calm, not pushing . . . obviously "Arghhh", but at the same time enjoying it'. In England, preparation built up over time, 'I remember Dad . . . taking us along to this woman in her house . . . and helping her cutting stuff out and she'd be sewing away'. Paulina's most vivid memories were of her participation in the carnival itself:

> I was Cleopatra . . . long silver trousers and then a head piece that came down . . . thinking it was the BEST THING . . . I was always biggest for my age as well, so I remember comments, some people saying, 'You should have been a Queen' . . . being involved, the colour, the fun of people dancing along . . . It will always be a part of me.

Carnival, provided her a deep sense of belonging and an experience of high social status. It was an important opportunity to transcend everyday childhood and to imagine other powerful identities, strengthening her self-esteem and confidence for the future.

Children in the research experienced a wide range of structured times when communities played, which took them out of the everyday and also informed everyday relations. Children participated in a number of festive social gatherings which involved people in similar situations to themselves and their families. There were social events that arose through the caravanning holidays that Tessa went on. Pamela attended parties where her parents worked. When Julie had to stay in hospital, there were sometimes parties organized on the wards. . Such festivities were remembered in relation to the children's other experiences. Julie disliked hospital parties because she disliked being in hospital (see Chapter 4). She delighted, however, in the 'Bonfire party', 'I thought I organized a bonfire night, got everybody together . . . fire outside . . . the whole street coming together . . . sitting on settees . . . crackerjacks, worrying that they'd land in the settee and burn you'. Her sense of belonging and pleasure was bound up with an important feeling of being in control of events.

The social calendar of childhood contained a range of opportunities unique to neighbourhood and community of interests. In relation to these there could be shared and separate times for children, families and wider communities to make playful connections. Through community play, previous community relations were remembered and altered and communities moved on, taking children with them or not, depending on how the children were positioned. Where there was conflict within and between communities, this had to be managed as it could escalate. When communities played, they wove, connected and altered threads of community memory, reversing what were believed to be dependencies. Particular guidelines for the future were transmitted to children.

Nations Play

The times for child, family, community and national play blurred in childhood. Particular times in the calendar were set aside in relation to national events that children had different degrees of closeness and distance to. Such events might relate to victories in battle or the wedding of royalty, 'Festive elements and the sharing in adult amusements also contribute to some forms of children's play, indicating a conjunction between the world of children and that of adults' (Bai, 2005, pp. 27–28).

In Northern Ireland, the 12th of July celebrations confirmed the beliefs of the Loyalist community and reflected the shared hopes of James' family and community who pressed the British Government to quell the Nationalist movement (see Chapter 8):

12th of July . . . very laden with emotions . . . very powerful and very exciting but fraught, fraught times, with danger and violence and feelings of anti . . . a real cocktail of times and very potent . . . but wonderful to take part as well. A sense of self and identity, just unknown to me now, absolutely unknown. Nothing I've seen even touches on that.

The affirmation of common bonds was felt deeply by children locked into conflicted communities and caught up in war. Nationalist communities feared and opposed these days where they felt threatened and were sometimes attacked.

There was distance in Richard's account of a similar victory celebration in South Africa. His everyday childhood was structured in relation to a Boer national calendar. Although White, he was learning to hate apartheid, and this memory contained both his adult and child understanding. One official bank holiday celebrated

> white victory over the Zulus . . . The Battle of Blood River . . . They killed so many Zulus it turned the river to blood . . . Talked about at school . . . 'These brave Boers', who'd shot these people with their guns who only had spears . . . 'Marvellous victory' and 'Isn't it wonderful ' . . . Before we broke up, 'Don'tforget the reasons why'.

Richard's parents gave him an alternative critical account to understand these celebrations. Nevertheless he enjoyed the holiday from school. He explained how deeply the Boer memories, rehearsed in such events, influenced his childhood in ways he was less conscious of at the time:

> I imbibed some of this . . . there was a strong culture of self sacrifice . . . We were taught very powerful stories of individuals who had sacrificed their own lives . . . to protect or save other people . . . Rachel De Beer was this little girl . . . She found herself with a younger brother . . . out in the middle of nowhere . . . This is supposed to be a true story . . . it was freezing cold, and to protect her little brother, she shed most of her clothes, wrapped him up and then put her own body over him . . . of course she perished, but he lived and that was the thing about self sacrifice.

Of course this culture of self-sacrifice, the related 'character building' of White children under apartheid and the way that 'martyrdom' was celebrated continued a thread of Boer memories related to the oppression of the Black majority in South Africa and the struggle with the English over the colonial spoils. These 'national' festivities and stories distorted the past selectively. Some children would be drawn in more than others, depending on their position and the counter narratives that informed their childhood. Some children (in this case Black children) would be completely pushed out. Richard recognized that the feeling that he ought to sublimate his personal needs to those of others was deeply learned at this time. The pressure to sublimate self was a strong feature of the 'moral' education of other children (see Chapters 2 and 6). National play times contained important messages about who and what was important in the social order.

The royal celebrations in the early 1980s were experienced at some critical distance by Madhi (see Chapter 2). She didn't attend the parties. The celebrations were constructed around an imaginary past of loyalty and deference to the Crown (Hobsbawm, 1983) which her family were distant from because of their past experiences of British colonialism. These events nevertheless perpetuated formative stories and could generate a sense of being part of something at a very young age. In the 1950s when Kate was 3, ' . . . there were coronation events. I was dressed up in red white and blue crepe paper and went to an event in a hall'. Children had to navigate competing versions of such events from family and community. The difficulties in this were evident in Apara's account of the Silver Jubilee celebrations (1977):

> My family were not happy at the idea of me learning the national anthem . . . There were lots of parties . . . They'd spent their entire life never standing up for the national anthem . . . The thing that annoyed me was the fact that people looked at me and assumed I was [not standing] because I was black, and it's nothing to do with that. It was to do with the working class, communist part of my family . . . I wasn't going to let my family down.

Apara worked out that it was fine to attend the parties but not fine to bow the knee. She shared her (White) grandparents' and mother's critical stance, but was positioned differently. Her different behaviour would be perceived through her colour; her colour would be blamed for her failure to praise royalty. This was a real fear grounded in her growing experience of racism.

From a child's perspective, where there was no immediate threat in their lives, or particular felt national connection, national play times celebrated fossils from the past (Halbwachs, 1925/1992). They were felt of no real significance other than providing play opportunities. The drip, drip of social messages contained in these events might have shaped their future expectations but what was more memorable were the opportunities for a holiday from school, a party and other peculiar links. Claudia was aware of the funeral of Winston Churchill but her attention was elsewhere. The funeral festivities were an opportunity for play:

> I can remember thinking, ' What is all the fuss about?' . . . I used to have a friend . . . who was posh . . . she lived in a big Georgian manor . . . going

there to watch . . . Her Grandma was there and . . . never got out of bed all day and I remember thinking, 'That must be what posh people do.' She had a television in the room . . . We were in there playing and watching at the same time and she farted. I remember thinking, 'Posh people shouldn't do things like that, it's very rude'. (Claudia)

Children, their families and communities were aligned differently in relation to these national play times and commemorations. Where there was conflict, such events could perpetuate it and some communities needed to keep a critical distance. Nevertheless, these national play times provided opportunities to play at a number of levels, creating holidays from school, parties and parades. They affirmed particular commitments and belonging. Children navigated these events to carve out space and time for themselves. Even where these times were remembered as without great significance, they provided opportunities and furniture for play and transmitted particular morals and values which children 'imbibed'.

Conclusion

Play is a continuous and expansive part of childhood, yet children are also restricted in relation to play. Times for play are structured into the childhood calendar. The wider social fabric provides unique play material, including particular artefacts, games and sporting relations which children must navigate. In indoor and outdoor play, children weave this social fabric, counter posing different elements, reversing perceived dependencies and challenging perceived inequalities. See how Madhi and her sister took pleasure and control by developing a game from a soap opera they watched on the television. All the children carved out their own personal and shared play spaces, through, for example, den making. Their dens were formed from the social relations and artefacts of the times and their play spaces reflected the wider domestic, industrial and agricultural landscapes.

Children faced restrictions and social hierarchies. In Apara's case, it was not the dangers of the physical environment that kept her indoors, but the social attitudes and abuse she faced. When children began to engage with organized sports, they also engaged with new fields of social memory. This might lead to their exclusion, for example, Madhi and Rachel struggled to be included in football. This might lead to their withdrawal and lead them to choose particular games over others, for example, Richard avoided the male team violence of rugby and chose a sport that suited his height. Shared social memories of the particular team she supported provided Cathy with a deep sense of social belonging.

Families, communities and countries have their designated play times and children participate in different social festivities. Pamela, Apara and Lara enjoyed shared family celebrations which were full of play, including performance, music and humour. Tessa enjoyed the separate children's space during these events. Rehana remembered the significance of the parties that marked her leaving Pakistan. Through shared play, particular familial and other bonds may be affirmed. In her community, carnival provided a deep sense of belonging and pride for Paulina, as did the Orange parades for James, in his. Other children might feel fear at such events, for example, if they are less well managed and dominated by adult drinking or are associated with conflict. Children from Catholic communities in Northern Ireland, still fear and resist Orange Day events (Leonard, 2010). Children have to navigate the complex social relations of such events. Apara's refusal to stand up for the national anthem was viewed as related to her colour rather than her politics. Nevertheless, she enjoyed the feasting during the Silver Jubilee celebrations. Sometimes such events just mean a day off school, nevertheless, particular social memories are inevitably shared with children and there are social silences. This is how Richard 'learned' about a White child's martyrdom under a regime that persecuted Black children, 'The grand rituals of life are often depicted as "moments of truth" when the real status of the child is revealed' (Ericsson. and Simonsen, 2008, p. 400).

Wider society provides templates for appropriate play, for example, requiring children to sublimate 'childish' and playful desires (Bai, 2005) and requiring gender appropriate play. The significance of play may be absorbed into political or schooling agendas (Kenway and Bullen, 2001). However, play is significant at many social levels. Collaborative play is an important way in which social change is marked by children, families, communities and countries. Play is a site of personal, social and political transition (Shaw, 2001). This is demonstrated in the ways in which children and adults, use play to reverse everyday social roles, routines and relationships and imagine these differently, with themselves in more control. Carnival, for example, is part of a process of community transformation and involves the temporary command of space and some distance from everyday social and economic hardship. National festivities and holidays also reflect particular interests and power relations; with which children may be more or less comfortable.

Children play alone and in exploratory collaboration with others (Green, 1988). They play at a distance from familiar adults, resisting scrutiny (Wimbush, 1988) but their childhood is also structured in relation to shared play with adults, where, for example, threads of family memory are shared. The risks to children may change over time as the wider social and physical environment changes, but children's opportunities to fully participate would be enhanced if it were accepted that children and adults share social worlds. Shared playtimes develop and structure those worlds and enable different levels of control by both children and adults.

Chapter 11

Conclusion

Introduction

The research in this book has considered children's involvement in wider social change, focusing on aspects of their everyday experience that have been less considered in general childhood research (see Chapter 1). This concluding chapter, first, revisits the key research concepts and questions (Chapters 1 and 2) considering how memory, space and time shape children's wider social engagement. Second, it reflects on the methodology, considering how layers of memory informed the research through the selectivity of memory at a number of levels. Third, it considers the implications of the research in relation to the present and future times of children.

Memory, Space, Time and Social Change

Children and adults share the same social worlds but not on the same terms, nor with the same interpretation. The children in this research navigated complex overlapping influences from the past and present. Through the complex interplay of familial, community and wider social memory, they engaged with different social expectations and frameworks for action (Halbwachs, 1925/1992; Misztal, 2003). Threads of social memory suggested their social position, how they should behave, what they should believe and the significance of particular institutions and artefacts. As they moved through space and time from home to community and through changing environments, they made new connections, crossed boundaries and developed particular understanding, beliefs and allegiances of their own (Lefebvre, 1991; Massey, 2005). The children counter posed different elements of the social fabric and developed associated hopes for the future. They engaged with wider social events through weaving complex temporal and spatial influences (Davies, 1990; Adam, 1995; Neale and Flowerdew, 2003). Their everyday experience was part of, not separate from, wider social relations. These aspects are now considered in more detail.

Family Archives and Everyday Childhood

The children in this research shared selective stories from their family archives. Rehana's mother died when she was 4, however, she and her family sustained her mother's memory, and this process was formative throughout her childhood (Chapter 6). The importance of appropriate values and behaviour was transmitted through the family archives. Apara's childhood was shaped by a continuous family narrative about the importance of working-class struggle. She was repeatedly told about the experiences of particular kin, for example, her grandmother, who stole meat to feed the family during the depression (Chapter 2). There is no doubt that both Apara and Lara drew strength from the family archives to manage their experiences of racism as children. The family archives marked different aspects of family and social transition. For example, in addition to the direct experiences of migration of Apara, Paulina, Rehana and Richard, previous family migrations continued to shape children's lives. This occurred through stories, communications and visits to kin. Lara spent formative times of her childhood in Italy, Claudia in Germany and Madhi in India. Children, such as Rachel and Pamela, learned of other places and times through stories of family migration to Canada in the past (Chapter 3). The family archives also transmitted messages and a position in relation to war. In addition to the direct war and conflict experiences of James, Richard and Rehana, children's lives were informed by family war memories; stories and relics from the family archives (Chapter 8). In these ways children became aligned with their family biographies in particular ways. Particular threads from a familial past continued to inform their every day experience (Halbwachs, 1925/1992; Misztal, 2003). There were also silences and distortions in the family memory (see below).

Community Archives and Everyday Childhood

Children also shared selective community memories. Paulina learned that the police could be a threat to her community, through news of events in her local community, including the death of David Oluwale in 1969 and 'Bonfire Night 1975' (Chapter 7). Her involvement in local carnival gave her a deep sense of pride and belonging (Chapter 10). James, growing up in Northern Ireland, also learned that community involved danger and was a source of deep belonging (see Chapters 6 and 8). Rehana remembered how the Indian 'enemy' was constructed in relation to the Indo-Pakistani wars she experienced (Chapter 8). Tessa remembered struggles related to fox hunting, fearing that the animal rights groups would hurt her neighbours (Chapter 7).

War and conflict could lock some children into particular community positions, while others were able to move more freely. Children's changing sense of belonging involved their engagement with the different community, religious and secular arrangements of the time. For Paulina, Rehana and Kate, religion was a deep source of social identity and hopes for the future (Chapter 6). Cathy and Julie moved with more distance between different religious arrangements. Through her father, Cathy developed a deep sense of belonging to one of her city football teams. In later childhood, children engaged deeply with different community interests. Apara chose to be a Goth; Rachel, a New Romantic. Rachel turned to feminism and Madhi became aware of the relevance of Black struggles for social change (Chapters 7 and 9). In these ways children became aligned with particular community narratives and pools of shared memory that continued to influence their everyday childhood in particular ways (ibid.). These were particular fusions of memory that they felt some connection with. These also involved silences and distortions in relation to the past.

National Archives and Everyday Childhood

Children experienced the power of the social order through the authorities delegated to adults in their lives. National memories were constructed in particular interests and in relation to internal and external country influences. Children learned that the state, through particular institutions (such as schools) and particular functionaries (teachers and the police), might be disciplinary, supportive and neglectful in relation to different facets of their childhood. Ideas about 'race', nationality and a child's legitimate social place were involved. Apara, for example, encountered different, racist and cruel treatment at school. Richard was also on the receiving end of school brutality. In his case, the institution was (ostensibly) concerned with the advancement of White children and he was taught how to shoot to kill Black people as part of his education (Chapter 8). Migration as a young child gave economic benefits to Richard's family, whereas Apara experienced it as a step down. The well-being of immigrant children related to the nature of the welcome in the destination country (Chapter 3).

Children and their families were more or less aligned to particular national narratives. The Orange parades related to King James 'victory' in Ireland were celebrated by James and his Protestant family (Chapter 8). The celebrations relating to the 'victory' of the Boers over the Zulus in South Africa were kept at some critical distance by Richard and his English family. Nevertheless, Richard 'imbibed' concepts of martyrdom and sublimation of self from Boer culture (Chapter 10).

Particular international struggles continued to shape childhood after events had long passed. Pamela and George 'remembered' vivid images from the Second World War, which ended before they were born (see Chapter 8). Madhi 'remembered' the impact of colonialism on her parents and grandparents (see Chapter 2). Claudia, as a young German/ Romanian girl in England in the 1960s, had to navigate competing threads of war memory from family and peers. These were long, strong social memories that deeply influenced childhood, being laden with associated emotions from the past. In these ways enemies and allies were constructed in particular ways and children were taught particular allegiances and isolation. Experiences from the national past could be softened and exaggerated, for example, there was an emphasis on resilience, camaraderie and adventure, rather than death and dying in the stories of war that were shared with some children. See how George, Julie and Martin 'remembered' that their fathers had 'good' wars (Chapter 8).

Social Silences and Everyday Childhood

The selectivity of memories (Hobsbawm, 1983; Haug, 1992) also generated silences that had particular implications for children. Dominant collective memories were shaped by the 'public' interests of nation, ethnicity, class and gender. Much responsibility in relation to children was located in the private realm of 'home' (Chapter 4). Memories of being hurt by or bullied by parents, or of witnessing domestic violence were hard to articulate and understand as children (and adults). Some communities did respond to such events in a collective fashion (see the response to domestic violence in Lara's community, Chapter 7) but the social frameworks available to children to understand such experiences were limited.

Ideas about sexuality were mainly constructed around privacy and heterosexuality (Chapter 7). The social dominance of heterosexual and patriarchal relations was such that the sexual harassment of children was internalized as a personal responsibility (see Julie's experiences of being 'flashed at' in Chapter 2). Some experience was hard to articulate and understand within the available social frameworks. Within religious memory, homosexuality was (mostly) constructed as sinful; within the medical lexicon; as illness (Foucault, 1980b). Growing up gay, lesbian and bisexual, young people such as George and Rachel turned to the growing lesbian and gay movement and popular culture which contained less oppressive, more liberating and broader representations of potential sexualities.

There were clichés and fossils in the social memory related to childhood. Julie and Rachel experienced the pressure to be heterosexual and sexually active (see Chapter 9). Paulina, Sylvia and Pamela experienced some harsh authority from their fathers (see Chapters 4 and 7). In relation to the routines of home some parents were more visible than others and there were uncertainties when particular parents were unable to meet social expectations, for example, when unemployment struck (see Pamela, Chapter 5) or when parents were ill and injured. There were shadowy times in the memory related to the well-being of mothers, including hints of their depression. Their attempts to 'maintain hygiene' were sometimes experienced by children as restricting play; fathers might be viewed as more special because of more limited contact with children and their subsequent greater playfulness (Chapter 4).

Children Navigate Social Landscapes

The meanings and uses of particular places such as home, work, school, community and religion, appear more fixed to adults. In childhood these places are less distinct. Play and work, play and domesticity, play and faith overlapped and blurred in children's experience. Cathy played in her father's lorry while he combined caring for her, with his work (Chapter 5). Kate became religious for a time and this framed her desires for the future, to run an orphanage and her desires in the present; the boy in the church choir (Chapter 6). Places were imbued with particular expectations of children, informed by a hierarchy of values, for example, 'learning' was expected to take precedence over 'play' at Lara's school. Lara circumvented such expectations as she 'played' with her teachers, making them the butt of her jokes (Chapter 7).

Moral narratives were woven through all the spheres of childhood. The public spheres of work and consumption were the main places of financial transaction (earning, buying and selling). Tessa's grandfather told her that to want payment for family based work was wrong (Chapter 6). Religion was (allegedly) more associated with giving than taking. Madhi's father required her to sublimate her personal desires by participating in religious giving (Chapter 2). It was Cathy's and her sister's moral duty to clean the home while their mother cleaned elsewhere to earn money for the family (Chapter 4). These distinctions related to places for spending, earning, giving and taking, were neither natural or straightforward for children; they had to be learned. The games Madhi and her sister played (Chapter 10) involved their control of money.

Supposedly distinct social spheres blurred in childhood. Rehana's desire to belong and be like the older children, involved desires to fast, to be blessed and to wear particular clothes (Chapter 6). Rachel desired the gender fluidity of the New Romantics because it allowed her to blend in and come out as she chose (Chapter 2). Children circumvented social barriers and boundaries (Ardener, 1993, p. 12) climbing over physical and metaphorical 'walls and fences' to play and explore (Chapter 10). In navigating these social landscapes, children encountered other ways of living which they counter posed with their own, practicing the differences of social class, gender, ethnicity and religion (see George and Claudia, Chapter 4). Particular journeys, places of passage and hiding, crystallized their memories of childhood. Although the landscape prescribed particular routes, they deviated from expected pathways, for example, Richard jumped the separating barrier on the apartheid bridge (Chapter 2) and Martin began to align himself with the political left, while his mother voted Conservative and his father Liberal (Chapter 7).

Children Weave Multiple Times

Wider social and environmental influences informed childhood through the complex relations of time. On the one hand, children had limited control of time as their time was colonized through the connected clocks of home, school and work and their futures were imagined for them (Adam, 2002). On the other hand, they controlled time through weaving multiple temporal influences and connecting past, present and their imagined future time. Their play involved the continuous counter posing of different elements from the social fabric, for example, Madhi and her sister drew on popular culture and their experience of the city, reversing adult child dependencies in their games (Chapter 10). Richard and Rachel worked for a personalized and more human response from their teachers in the highly regulated and regimented space of school (Chapter 7). George tailored music and clothing to his own circumstances and sense of himself in relation to others, the past and the future (Chapter 9). Acquiring new commodities, music and clothing provided important turning points. These could signal particular social acceptance and more social control (Chapter 9).

Times for play were ambiguous. Play was in one sense a continuous and expansive part of childhood, but it was also restricted and structured into the calendar (Chapter 10). Children, families, communities and nations had their own play times, where they marked social transition and asserted power in particular ways. Children participated in all these levels of play and the social fabric provided unique play material. Play at all these levels provided the opportunity to exercise control.

The work of Halbwachs (1925/1992) and Misztal (2003) highlight the importance of understanding connections between personal, familial and collective memory in order to understand children's everyday experience. The work of Lefebvre (1991) and Massey (2005) illuminate children's navigation of and engagement with social landscapes. Adam (1995) and Neale and Flowerdew (2003) draw attention to the ways that children are involved with social change, weaving different temporal influences and carving out space and time for themselves.

How Layers of Memory Informed the Research

Aitken asks, 'What biographical baggage do we as researchers and adults, bring to the study of children and youths?' (2001, p. 8). The research in this book is best understood as constructed through layers of memory. This is both its strength and limitation. In Chapter 2, I discussed the complexities of a methodology that draws on adult reminiscence to elicit children's experience. This is complicated further by adopting concepts of memory that involve both personal and collective elements. It is important to acknowledge that the accounts of childhood discussed in this research have been filtered in different ways. First, there is no doubt that the respondents selected memories from childhood that were filtered through their subsequent experiences and ideas about childhood. Second, the events respondents remembered were grounded in collective memories from further past. Third, academic debates about childhood informed the way the researcher constructed research questions and the methodology. Fourth, the researcher's memories of her own childhood were a significant filter. These aspects are now discussed in turn, in relation to the limitations and strengths of the research.

Respondent Memories of Childhood

When asked to recall the important events from childhood, respondents selected memories with retrospective knowledge and understanding. The experiences they described were framed in their present experiences including their own commitment to children's futures (see Chapter 2). Tessa talked a lot about play, not only because of her playful childhood, but because of her professional commitment to children's right to play. Richard selected memories of apartheid, not only because it was powerful in his childhood, but also, so that it should never happen again. There must also have been many silences; memories respondents chose not to share.

Respondents personal memories involved reconstructions of the past. Some aspects of childhood were remembered and other aspects were not. Their memories coalesced and they found it hard to distinguish personal experiences from memories based on family stories they had been told. Family, community and national memories were shared with them throughout childhood and beyond. It was impossible to say how far into adulthood some of these stories continued. It was therefore very difficult to link specific social influences to the specific times of childhood. Respondents were unsure and may have remembered the past inaccurately.

Despite this, it is clear that the childhoods they recalled were grounded in real social events, real relationships and real feelings. Whether memories were based on first- or second-hand experiences, they were laden with associated emotion. Through these reconstructions, details of different childhoods emerged in relation to the wider society, including powerful formative experiences related to migration, social movements, religion, policing and war. The experiences respondents remembered involved threads of social memory from further past that shaped the landscapes they moved through as children. In this way, Claudia and Sylvia experienced the aftermath of a war they had not directly experienced. The consideration of memory as both personal and shared draws deeper attention to the wider social relations of everyday childhood including the power and dependencies involved.

Researcher Memories of Childhood

At the time of this research and its writing up, I work in the academic area of 'Childhood Studies' which draws on different ideas, to explore particular spheres of childhood and particular interventions in children's lives. The area is informed by different values, for example, it is associated with social justice, equality and children's rights and attempts to position children as full and equal human participants in the social world. The breadth of this research has necessarily involved wide academic reading and ideas from other academic spheres are readily drawn on in different chapters. My academic position and biography have influenced the direction of this research and shaped progress in conscious and less conscious ways.

In addition, my personal memories of childhood have informed the direction of the research. While interviewing the respondents I decided to answer the research questions myself (I am 'Sylvia' in the research). I did this for two reasons. First, I knew that my experiences as a child were significant and might be needed to fill in gaps. I was, for example, the only respondent of recent Jewish heritage and had particular experiences related to war, migration, religion and home (see the relevant chapters). In addition, it was important to see how my childhood informed the overall shape of the research, providing another lens through which it was constructed. In my own childhood, I learned early the significance of war even though I did not experience it. My father was a refugee from Nazi Germany and I learned the horrors of the Second World War, repeatedly watching films/documentaries when they were shown on television. He had very dark moods and I later learned (from other family members) of his separation from his family, the loss of an uncle in Auschwitz, and his terrible experiences at the Battle of Dunkirk (June 1940). There was conflict between my parents and religious difference was a continued theme. When they split up I quickly learned about poverty and different aspects of the state, beyond school including the courts, social welfare and health services (when my mother was ill). I became increasingly aware, as an adult, of the significance of past social events related to war, migration and religion, in my own childhood. These experiences consciously and less consciously informed what I looked for in other childhoods, where and how I probed as I carried out the research. The attention to the wider influences of war and migration, for example, reflected my childhood experiences and consequent priorities and the ways these were discussed (see e.g., Chapter 8). Personal biographies channel our research perspectives and focus our gaze in particular directions. This research clearly includes an attempt to understand my own, as well as other childhoods, in relation to wider society.

This research involves the complex interplay of memories of childhood. These come from respondent, researcher and other academic scholars. It is not intended to make any historical claims, but is concerned to widen the lens and consider the complex ways in which children engage with social change beyond the spheres traditionally associated with their lives, 'Rather than insisting on an opposition between memory and history, any attempt at a general interpretation of the past has to accept the interrelations of history and memory and has to rely on both their methods of inquiry' (Misztal, 2003, p. 107). Childhood here is filtered and altered through different layers of memory. The research therefore must be accepted as involving partial, selective and constructed accounts of children's experience. However, the research is not based on fabrication. It is grounded in real events from the past, related to children's experience of social change. These are real childhoods that require much more attention.

The Implications of the Research

Huyssen argues, 'The 21st century looms like a repetition: one of bloody nationalisms and tribalism, of religious fundamentalism and intolerance that we thought had been left behind in some darker past' (1995, p. 8). Although concerned with past childhoods, this research is also concerned with childhood in the present and future. Both the participants and the researcher entered into this project with a concern to deepen understanding of children's lives, the effects of social change, inequalities and social power. Different issues emerge from each chapter that have current significance.

At the time of writing there is much intolerance faced by children and families who move to the United Kingdom as immigrants, whether as refugees or seeking work. It has only recently been announced that such children will no longer be detained if their family's immigration status is unclear. Nevertheless, they may be separated from their parents and they may face deportation to their country of origin (Travis, 2010). Chapter 3 argues that there is a need for all children to know their migration heritage, whether this has involved family moving for work, marriage, to flee persecution or war. It is important that all understand such heritage and that their 'ordinary' visits and communications with kin in other places are consequent on migration. It is important to reposition our understanding of migration as central rather than marginal to all children's experiences in order to increase the acceptance of others and recognize the benefits of new arrivals (Hayter, 2000).

Chapter 4 emphasizes the importance of understanding home as an outcome of movement and change. Those who work with and for children should avoid conceptualising home as separate from the wider society. The social relations of home are deeply informed by wider social practices and inequalities. Children's 'home' life has been blamed for the 'failures' of particular children in wider society, where wide social class inequalities are highly significant (Jones, 2002; Wilkinson and Pickett, 2009). It is easy to pass social responsibility back to the family rather than addressing the failures of the state, market and social relations of employment. Chapter 5 argues there is a need to reconsider the complex and multi-faceted significance of work in relation to children's everyday lives. There is a need to be very aware of how reduced employment (Elliot, 2010) involves more than the loss of important material resources, but also involves children's everyday lives, their care, their long term emotional security and their ability to gather their own tools for future employment such as education, social networks, material resources and self-esteem.

Our understanding of religion and childhood also needs some repositioning. Religious practices may be seen as relevant to some children (who may be identified as belonging to particular faith communities) and not others. Chapter 6 revisits the place of religion in children's lives, not in any theological way, but by recognizing the complex ways that threads of religious memory inform the fabric of social life that all children engage with, whether they 'belong' to a faith or not. Distinctions between secularism and religion conceal many of the meaningful experiences of childhood. Respect for faith and an understanding of belonging should not serve to further conceal the abuse of children (Butt and Asthana, 2009). The complex ways religion informs childhood, need further unravelling.

In Chapter 7, children's complex and multifaceted engagements with the state and civil society are considered. Children's experiences lead them to align themselves in different ways (or to remain unaligned). The form that their political engagement and learning takes may be less visible if the focus is solely on the politics of their formal representation. This has a relatively small place in relation to the very wide canvas of past and present social events that they experience (that are filtered through family, community and national memory).

Chapter 8 considers memories of war and the ways that war directly and indirectly shapes childhood in powerful ways. The influences of war come through shared memories passed down the generations as well as everyday conflicts. Selective remembering may conceal some of the brutalities of war (the good wars of fathers) and also lock children into partisan or vulnerable places. The children who are victims of war may slide from attention in the propagandas of opposing sides (Saville Inquiry, 2010). Rehana's memories of being shelled over 40 years ago convey an experience that is not time bound and is shared by all children who experience shelling in present time.

The discussion in Chapter 9 shows how carefully children navigate consumer society. General household consumption is very important to them, as well as the markets that are tailored particularly for them. Some children distance themselves from the youth consumer markets more than others for a variety of overlapping reasons, for example, their interests may lie elsewhere or they may not feel safe. There is a real anxiety that more and new forms of gender and sexual objectification will inform marketing strategies (Papdopoulos, 2010). Children are astute and select carefully in relation to their complex needs and desires, engaging in multifaceted an complex ways, but they are also presented with raised hopes and dangerous cul-de-sacs.

Chapter 10 shows how deeply children share adult worlds and, through play, are involved in marking social transition and exerting power and creativity, despite the, ' . . . unwanted patches . . . set aside to contain children and their activities' (Ward, 1978, p. 204). The social fabric and landscape provide material for play, where dependencies may be reversed and other futures imagined. This process happens individually, among children, jointly in families, in communities and is structured into the national calendar. Times for play may be colonized by competing interests (through, for example, special days for saints, royalty and victories in war (Adam, 2003)). A broad conceptualization of play gives visibility to children's deep engagement in wider social life, their potential and the complex social navigation they must engage in.

Bibliography

Adam, B. (1990), *Time and Social Theory*. Cambridge: Polity Press.
—. (1995), *Timewatch, the Social Analysis of Time*. Cambridge: Polity Press.
—. (1998), *Timescapes of Modernity. The Environment and Invisible Hazards*. London: Routledge.
—. (2002), 'The gendered time politics of globalization: Of shadowlands and elusive justice', *Feminist Review*, 70, 3–29.
—. (2003), 'Reflexive modernization temporalized', *Theory Culture and Society*, 20 (2) 59–78.
—. (2006), 'Time', *Theory Culture and Society*, 23 (2–3) 119–38.
Adichie, C. N. (2007), *Half of a Yellow Sun*. London: Harper Perennial.
Aitken, S. (2001), *Geographies of Young People: The Morally Contested Spaces of Identity*. London: Routledge.
Aldridge, A. (2006), 'Religion', in G. Payne (ed.) *Social Divisions*. Houndmills: Palgrave Macmillan, pp. 133–54.
Amnesty International. (2009), 'Operation Cast Lead: 22 Days of Death and Destruction', http://news.bbc.co.uk/1/shared/bsp/hi/pdfs/02_07_09_gaza_report.pdf, (accessed 6 May 2010).
Ardener, S, (ed.) (1993), *Women and Space. Ground Rules and Social Maps*. Oxford: Berg.
Aspden, K. (2008), *The Hounding of David Oluwale*. London: Vintage Books.
Atwood, M. (2005), *Curious Pursuits – Occasional Writing 1970–2005*. London: Virago.
Bai, L. (2005), 'Children at play. A childhood beyond the Confucian shadow', *Childhood*, 12 (1) 9–32.
Barry, M. (2006), *Youth Offending in Transition*. London: Routledge.
Bauman, Z. (1998), *Work, Consumerism and the New Poor*. Buckingham: Oxford University Press.
Blanden, J., Gregg, P. and Machin, S. (2005), 'Intergenerational Mobility in Europe and North America. A Report by the Sutton Trust Centre for Economic Performance LSE', http://cep.lse.ac.uk/about/news/IntergenerationalMobility.pdf, (accessed 12 May 2005).
Blankemeyer, M., Walker, K. and Svitak, E. (2009), 'The 2003 war in Iraq, an ecological analysis of American and Northern Irish children's perceptions', *Childhood*, 16 (3) 229–46.
Bornat, J. and Johnson, J. (1997), *Community Care: A Reader*. Basingstoke: Macmillan.

Bourdieu, P. (1986), 'The forms of capital', in J. Richardson (ed.) *Handbook of Theory and Research for the Sociology of Education*. New York: Greenwood Press, pp. 241–58.

Bourdieu, P., Chambordon, J-C. and Passeron, J-C. (1968/1991), *The Craft of Sociology. Epistemological Preliminaries*. New York: Walter de Gruyter.

Bowyer Bell, J. (1997), *The Secret Army: The I.R.A.* New Jersey: Transaction Publishers.

Brannen, J. (2004), 'Childhoods across the generations storied from women in four-generation English families', *Childhood*, 11 (4) 409–28.

Bridges, L. J. and Moore, K. A. (2002), *Religion and Spirituality in Childhood and Adolescence*. Washington: Child Trends.

Broadhead, P. (2003), *Early Years, Play and Learning. Developing Social Skills and Co-operation*. London: Routledge.

Brock, A., Dodds, S., Jarvis, P. and Olusoga, Y. (eds) (2009), *Perspectives on Play. Learning for Life*. Harlow: Pearson Longman.

Brown, F. (ed.) (2003), *Playwork: Theory and Practice*. Buckingham: Open University Press.

Brownmiller, S. (1975), *Against Our Will: Men Women and Rape*. New York: Ballantine.

Burden, J. (July 1998), 'Leisure, change and social capital. Making the personal political.' Paper presented at Leisure Studies Association International Conference 'The Big Ghetto' at Leeds Metropolitan University.

Butt, R. and Asthana, A. (29 September 2009), 'Sex abuse rife in other religions says Vatican' in *Guardian* online, (accessed 7 August 2010).

Candappa, M. and Egharevba, I. (2002), 'Negotiating boundaries: Tensions within home and school life for refugee children', in R. Edwards (ed.) *Children Home and School Regulation Autonomy or Connection*. London: Routledge Falmer, pp. 155–71.

Castles, S. and Kosack, G. (1973), *Immigrant Workers and the Class Structure of Western Europe*. London: Oxford University press.

Christensen, P. and O'Brien, M. (2002), 'Children in the city: Introducing new perspectives', in P. Christenson and M. O'Brien (eds) *Children in the City: Home Neighbourhood and Community*. London: Routledge Falmer, pp 1–12.

Cohen, A. (1985), *The Symbolic Construction of Community*. London: Routledge.

Coleman, R., Sim, J., Tombs, S. and Whyte, D. (2009), 'Introduction: State, power, crime', in R. Coleman, J. Sim, S. Tombs and D. Whyte (eds) *State, Power, Crime*. London: Sage, pp. 1–19.

Cousins, C. (1987), *Controlling Social Welfare. A Sociology of State Welfare Work and Organisation*. Sussex: Wheatsheaf Books.

Cross, R. (2008), 'Provision for child health', in P. Jones, D. Moss, P. Tomlinson and S. Welch (eds) *Childhood: Services and Provision for Children*. Harlow: Pearson Education, pp. 109–23.

Cunningham, S. and Lavalette, M. (2004), ' "Active citizens" or "Irresponsible" truants? School student strikes against the war', *Critical Social Policy* 24 (2) 255–69.

Cunningham, S. and Tomlinson, J. (2005), ' "Starve them out": Does every child really matter? A commentary on section 9 of the Asylum and Immigration (Treatment of Claimants, etc.) Act 2004', *Critical Social Policy* 25 (2) 253–75.

Dalley, G. (1996), *Ideologies of Caring*. London: Macmillan.

Davidoff, L. and Hall, C. (1995), ' "My own fireside": The creation of the middle-class home', in S. Jackson and S. Moores (eds) *The Politics of Domestic Consumption. Critical Readings.* Hemel Hempstead: Prentice Hall/Harvester Wheatsheaf, pp. 277–89.

Davies, K. (1990), *Women and Time. The Weaving of the Strands of Everyday Life.* Aldershot: Avebury.

Davis, J. (2004), 'Disability and childhood: Deconstructing the stereotypes', in J. Swain, S. French, C. Barnes, C. and C. Thomas (eds) *Disabling Barriers – Enabling Environments.* London: Sage, pp. 142–48.

de Groot, M. and Robinson, T. (2008), 'Sport fan attachment and the psychological continuum model: A case study of an Australian football league fan', *Leisure/Loisir: Journal of the Canadian Association for Leisure*, 32 (1) 117–22.

Deem, R. (1995), 'Feminism and leisure studies', in C. Critcher, P. Bramham and A. Tomlinson (eds) *Sociology of Leisure. A Reader.* London: E. and F. N. Spon, pp. 256–69.

Delphy, C. (1995), 'Sharing the same table: Consumption and the family', in S. Jackson and S. Moores (eds) *The Politics of Domestic Consumption. Critical Readings.* Hemel Hempstead: Prentice Hall/Harvester Wheatsheaf, pp. 25–36.

Dinham, B. with Sarangi, S. (2002), 'The Bhopal gas tragedy 1984 to ? The evasion of corporate responsibility'. *Environment and Urbanisation*, 14 (1) 89–99.

Drakeford, M., Scourfield, J., Holland, S. and Davies, A. (2009), 'Welsh children's views on government and participation', *Childhood*, 16 (2) 247–64.

Driver, Tom (1991), *The Magic of Ritual: Our Need for Liberating Rites that Transform our Lives and our Communities.* New York: HarperCollins.

Dummett, M. and Dummett, A. (1982), 'The role of government in Britain's racial crisis', in C. Husband (ed.) *Race in Britain: Continuity and Change.* London: Hutchinson & Co., pp. 97–127.

Edwards, R. (ed.) (2002), *Children Home and School Regulation Autonomy or Connection.* London: Routledge Falmer.

Edwards, R. and Duncan, S. (1997), 'Supporting the family: Lone mothers, paid work and the underclass debate', *Critical Social Policy*, 53 (17) 29–49.

Edwards, T. (2004), 'Sexuality', in J. Roche, S. Tucker, R. Thomson and R. Flynn (eds) *Youth in Society.* London: Sage in Association with the Open University, pp. 168–76.

Elliot, L. (2010) 'Budget will cost 1.3 million jobs', *Guardian* June 29 www.guardian.co.uk/uk/2010/jun/29/budget-job-losses-unemployment-austerity, (accessed 28 July 2010).

Ennew, J. (2002), 'Outside childhood, street children's rights', in B. Franklin (ed.) *The New Handbook of Children's Rights: Comparative Policy and Practice.* London: Routledge, pp. 388–403.

Equality Commission for Northern Ireland. (2010), 'Anti-discrimination law in N Ireland-a brief chronology', www.equalityni.org/sections/default.asp?secid=5, (accessed 16 February 2010).

Ericsson, K. and Simonsen, E. (2008), 'On the border, the contested children of the Second World War', *Childhood*, 15 (3) 397–414.

Foucault, M. (1980a), 'Truth and power', in C. Gordon (ed.) *Power/Knowledge. Selected Interviews and Other Writings 1972 – 1977 by Michel Foucault.* New York: Panthean Books, pp. 109–133.

—. (1980b), *The History of Sexuality Vol. 1.* Translated by Robert Hurley. New York: Vintage.

Fox-Harding, L. (1996), *Family, State and Social Policy.* Houndmills: Macmillan.

Gallagher, M. (2006), 'Spaces of participation and inclusion?', in K. M. Tisdall, J. M. Davis, M. Hill and A. Prout, (eds) *Children, Young People and Social Inclusion.* Bristol: Policy Press, pp. 159–78.

Gamarnikow, E. Morgan, D. Purvis, J. and Taylorson, D. (eds) (1983), *The Public and the Private.* England: Gower.

Giddens, A. (1991), 'Structuration theory: Past, present and future', in C. Bryant and D. Jary (eds) *Gidden's Theory of Structuration. A Critical Appreciation.* London: Routledge, pp. 201–21.

Gilroy, P. (1987/2002), *There Ain't No Black in the Union Jack.* London: Routledge.

Giulianotti, R. and Armstrong, G. (1997), 'Introduction: Reclaiming the game – an introduction to the anthropology of football', in G. Armstrong and R. Giulianotti (eds) *Entering the Field. New Perspectives on World Football.* Oxford: Berg, pp. 1–31.

Glyptis, S. (1989), *Leisure and Unemployment.* Milton Keynes: Open University Press.

Goffman, E. (1961), *Asylums. Essays on the Social Situation of Mental Patients and Other Inmates.* London: Penguin.

Goldsmith, Lord QC (5 October 2007), 'Citizenship: Our Common Bond', www.justice.gov.uk/reviews/docs/citizenship-report-full.pdf, (accessed 3 December 2009).

Goldson, B. and Muncie, J. (eds) (2006), *Youth, Crime and Justice.* London: Sage.

Green, E. (1988), 'Women doing friendship: An analysis of women's leisure as a site of identity construction, empowerment and resistance', *Leisure Studies*, 17, 171–85.

Green, E., Hebron, S. and Woodward, D. (1987), 'Women, leisure and social control', in J. Hanmer and M. Maynard (eds) *Women, Violence and Social Control.* London: Macmillan, pp. 75–92.

Gregson, N. and Lowe, M. (1994), *Servicing the Middle Classes: Class, Gender and Waged Domestic Labour.* London: Routledge.

Grewal, S., Kay, J., Landor, L., Lewis, G. and Parmar, P. (1988), *Charting the Journey. Writings by Black and Third World Women.* London: Sheba Feminist Publishers.

Habashi, J. (2008), 'Palestinian children crafting national identity', *Childhood*, 15 (1) 12–29.

Habermas, J. (1981/1987), *Lifeworld and System: The Theory of Communicative Action. The Critique of Functionalist Reason, Volume Two.* Cambridge: Polity Press.

Halbwachs, M. (1925/1992), *On Collective Memory.* Introduced by L. Coser (ed.) Chicago: University of Chicago Press.

Hall, S., Critcher, C., Jefferson, T., Clarke, J. and Roberts, B. (1978), *Policing the Crisis: Mugging, the State and Law and Order.* Basingstoke: Macmillan.

Hallden, G. (2002), 'Children's views of family, house and home', in P. Christenson and M. O'Brien (eds) *Children in the City: Home Neighbourhood and Community.* London: Routledge Falmer, pp. 29–45.

Hammerton, J. (1992), *Cruelty and Companionship. Conflict in Nineteenth Century Married Life.* London: Routledge.

Hansard, (1977), *Mr Liddle Towers.* HC 12 Deb, 941 cc 232–44, http://hansard.millbanksystems.com/commons/1977/dec/12/mr-liddle-towers, (accessed 8 August 2010).

—. (1979), Mr Airey Neave: Tributes HL Deb 2nd April, 399, cc 1693–7. Debhttp://hansard.millbanksystems.com/lords/1979/apr/02/mr-airey-neave-tributes, (accessed 8 August 2010).

Harris, N. (2000), 'Should Europe end immigration controls?' *The European Journal of Development Research*, 12 (1) 80 – 106.

Haug, F. (1992), *Beyond Female Masochism. Memory – Work and Politics*. London: Verso.

Hayter, T. (2000), *Open Borders. The Case Against Immigration Controls*. London: Pluto.

Henderson, S., Holland, J., McGrellis, S., Sharpe, S. and Thomson, R. (eds) (2007), *Inventing Adulthoods a Biographical Approach to Youth Transitions*. London: Sage.

Henderson, K. A., Bialeschki, D., Shaw, S. M. and Freyysinger, V. J. (1996), *Both Gains and Gaps. Feminist Perspectives on Women's Leisure*. State College Pennsylvania: Venture Publishing.

Hill, M. and Tisdall, K. (1997), *Children and Society*. London, Longman.

Hirschon, R. (1993), 'Essential objects and the sacred: Interior and exterior space in an urban Greek locality', in S. Ardener (ed.) *Women and Space. Ground Rules and Social Maps*. Oxford: Berg, pp. 70–86.

Hobsbawm, E. (1983), 'Introduction: Inventing traditions', in E. Hobsbawm and T. Ranger (eds) *The Invention of Tradition*. Cambridge: Cambridge University Press, pp. 1–14.

Hognestad, H. K. (1997), 'The Jambo experience: An anthropological study of hearts fans', in G. Armstrong and R. Giulianotti (eds) *Entering the Field. New Perspectives on World Football*. Oxford: Berg, pp. 193–211.

Holloway, S. L. & Valentine, G. (2000), 'Children's Geographies, and the new social studies of childhood' in Holloway, S.L. & Valentine, G. (Eds) Children's Geographies: Playing, Living, Learning (Routledge, London), pp. 1–26.

Hunt, P. (1995), 'Gender and the construction of home life', in S. Jackson and S. Moores (eds) *The Politics of Domestic Consumption. Critical Readings*. Hemel Hempstead: Prentice Hall/Harvester Wheatsheaf, pp. 301–13.

Huyssen, A. (1995), *Twilight Memories. Marking Time in a Culture of Amnesia*. London: Routledge.

Illich, I. (1973), *Deschooling Society*. London: Penguin Education.

Jaques, E. (1982/1990), 'The enigma of time', in J. Hassard (ed.) *The Sociology of Time*. London: Macmillan, pp. 21–34.

James, A. and James, A. L. (2004), *Constructing Childhood. Theory, Policy and Social Practice*. London: Palgrave.

Joly, D. (1996), *Haven or Hell: Asylum Policies and Refugees in Europe*. Oxford: Macmillan.

Jones, C. (2002), 'Children, class and the threatening state', in B. Goldson, M. Lavalette, and J. McKechnie (eds) *Children, Welfare and the State*. London: Sage.

Jones, C. and Novak, T. (1999), *Poverty, Welfare and the Disciplinary State*. London: Routledge.

Jones, I. (2000), 'A model of serious leisure identification: The case of football fandom', *Leisure Studies*, 19, 283–98.

Jones, P. (2009), *Rethinking Childhood: Attitudes in Contemporary Childhood*. London: Continuum.

Jordan, B. (1998), *The New Politics of Welfare*. London: Sage.

Kellett, M. (2005), *How to Develop Children as Researchers: A Step by Step Guide to the Research Process*. London: Sage.

Kenway, J. and Bullen, E. (2001), *Consuming Children: Education-entertainment-advertising.* Maidenhead: Open University Press.

Kirkpatrick, L. A. and Shaver, P. (1990), 'Attachment theory and religion: Childhood attachments, religious beliefs and conversions', *Journal for the Scientific Study of Religion*, 29, 314–35.

Konig, A. (2008), ' "Which clothes suit me?" The presentation of the juvenile self', *Childhood*, 15 (2) 225–37.

Kristeva, J., Jardine, A. and Blake, H. (1981), 'Women's Time', *Signs* 7 (1) 13–35.

Land, H. (1991), 'Time to care', in M. MacClean and D. Groves (eds) *Women's Issues in Social Policy.* London: Routledge, pp. 7–19.

Laughey, D. (2006), *Music and Youth Culture.* Edinburgh: Edinburgh University Press.

Layder, D. (1993), *New Strategies in Social Research.* Cambridge: Polity Press.

Lees, S. (1993), *Sugar and Spice. Sexuality and Adolescent Girls.* Harmondsworth: Penguin.

—. (2002), *Carnal Knowledge. Rape on Trial.* London: Penguin.

Lefebvre, H. (1991), *The Production of Space.* Oxford: Blackwell.

Leonard, M. (2010), 'What's recreational about "recreational rioting"? Children on the streets in Belfast', *Children and Society*, 24 (1) 39–49.

Massey, D. (2005), *For Space.* London: Sage.

Matthews, M. H. (2003), 'Inaugural editorial: Coming of age for children's geographies', *Children's Geographies*, 1 (1) 3–5.

Mayall, B. (2006), 'Child-adult relations in social space', in K. M. Tisdall, J. M. Davis, M. Hill, and A. Prout, (eds) *Children, Young People and Social Inclusion.* Bristol: Policy Press, pp. 199–216.

McCarthy, J. R. (2007) ' "They all look as if they're coping, but I'm not": The relational power/lessness of "Youth" in responding to experiences of bereavement', *Journal of Youth Studies*, 10 (3) 285–303.

McDowell, L. (1997), *Capital Culture. Gender at Work in the City.* Oxford: Blackwell.

Mills, R. W. (2000), 'Perspectives of childhood', in R. W. Mills, and J. Mills (eds) *Childhood Studies: A Reader in Perspectives on Childhood.* London: Routledge, pp. 7–38.

Misztal, B. A. (2003), *Theories of Social Remembering.* Maidenhead: Open University Press.

Moinian, F. (2009), ' "I'm just me!" Children talking beyond ethnic and religious identities', *Childhood*, 16 (1) 31–48.

Montgomery, H., Burr, R. and Woodhead, M. (2003), *Changing Childhoods. Local and Global.* Chichester: Wiley and Sons, and The Open University.

Moran, J. (2001), 'Childhood sexuality and education: The case of Section 28', *Sexualities*, 4 (1) 73–89.

Morris, J. (1991), *Pride Against Prejudice: Transforming Attitudes to Disability.* London: Women's Press.

Morrow, V. (2002), 'Children's rights to public space: Environment and curfews', in B. Franklin (ed.) *The New Handbook of Children's Rights. Comparative Policy and Practice.* London: Routledge, pp. 168–82.

—. (2003), 'Moving out of childhood', in J. Maybin and M. Woodhead (eds) *Childhood in Contexts.* Chichester: Wiley and Sons and Open University, pp. 267–301.

Moss, D. (2006a), 'Pathways through Childhood', Research Proposal, Leeds Metropolitan University, unpublished.

—. (2006b), *Gender, Space and Time: Women and Higher Education*. Washington: Lexington, Rowman and Littlefield.

—. (2008), 'The social divisions of childhood and access to services and provision', in P. Jones, D. Moss, P. Tomlinson and S. Welch (eds) *Childhood: Services and Provision for Children*. Harlow: Pearson Education, pp. 39–52.

Moss, D. and Richter, I. (2011), 'Changing times of feminism and higher education: From community to employability', *Gender and Education*, 23 (2) 137–51.

Moss, P. (2006), 'From children's services to children's spaces', in K. M. Tisdall, J. M. Davis, M. Hill, and A. Prout, (eds) *Children, Young People and Social Inclusion*. Bristol: Policy Press, pp. 179–98.

Mullender, A., Hague, G. and Imam, U. (2002), *Children's Perspectives on Domestic Violence*. London: Sage.

Muncie, J. (2009), *Youth and Crime, 3rd Edition*. London: Sage.

Murcott, A. (1995), ' "It's a pleasure to cook for him": Food, mealtimes and gender in some South Wales households', in S. Jackson and S. Moores (eds) *The Politics of Domestic Consumption. Critical Readings*. Hemel Hempstead: Prentice Hall/ Harvester Wheatsheaf, pp. 89–99.

Mzamane, M. V. (1987), *The Children of Soweto*. London: Longman.

Neale, B. and Flowerdew, J. (2003), 'Time, texture and childhood: The contours of longitudinal qualitative research', *International Journal of Social Research Methodology*, 6 (3) 189–99.

Neale, B. A., Irwin, S. and Mellor, D. (2007–2012), 'Young Lives and Times Research', E.S.R.C. University of Leeds, www.timescapes.leeds.ac.uk/research/ projects/young-lives-times.php, (accessed 6 August 2010).

Novak, T. (2002), 'Rich children, poor children', in B. Goldson, M. Lavalette and J, McKechnie (eds) *Children Welfare and the State*. London: Sage, pp. 59–72.

Olusoga, Y. (2009), ' "We don't play like that here": Social cultural and gender perspectives on play', in A. Brock, S. Dodds, P. Jarvis, and Y. Olusoga (eds) *Perspectives on Play. Learning for Life*. Harlow: Pearson Longman, pp. 40–64.

Overlien, C. and Hyden, M. (2009), 'Children's actions when experiencing domestic violence', *Childhood*, 16 (4) 479–96.

Pahl, J. (1995), 'Household spending, personal spending and the control of money in marriage', in S. Jackson and S. Moores (eds) *The Politics of Domestic Consumption. Critical Readings*. Hemel Hempstead: Prentice Hall/Harvester Wheatsheaf, pp. 53–66.

Papadopoulos, L. (2010), *Review. Sexualisation of Young People*. Home Office. The Stationary Office.

Pearson, G. (1983), *Hooligan. History of Respectable Fears*. London: Macmillan.

Percy, M. and Taylor, R. (1997), ' "Something for the weekend, sir?" Leisure, ecstasy and identity in football and contemporary religion', *Leisure Studies*, 16, 37–49.

Pini, M. (2004), 'Technologies of the self', in J. Roche, S. Tucker, R. Thomson and R. Flynn (eds) *Youth in Society*. London: Sage in association with the Open University, pp. 160–67.

Plowman, L., McPake, J. and Stephen, C. (2010), 'The technologisation of childhood? Young children and technology in the home', *Children and Society*, 24 (1) 63–74.

226 *Bibliography*

Radford, J., Hanmer, J. and Stanko, E. A. (eds) (1988), *Women Policing and Male Violence*. London: Routledge.
Rasmussen, K. and Smidt, S. (2002), 'Children in the neighbourhood: The neighbourhood in children', in P. Christenson and M. O'Brien (eds) *Children in the City: Home Neighbourhood and Community*. London: Routledge Falmer, pp. 82–100.
Refugee Council. (2010), 'Report states detention unnecessary for children at Yarl's Wood', www.refugeecouncil.org.uk/news/archive/news/2010/March/240310_newsyarlswoodowersreport, (accessed 6 May 2010).
Rich, A. (1980), 'Compulsory heterosexuality and lesbian existence', *Signs*, 5, 4.
Rose, G. (1993), *Feminism and Geography. The Limits of Geographical Knowledge*. Cambridge: Polity Press.
Russell, R. and Tyler, M. (2005), 'Branding and bricolage, gender, consumption and transition', *Childhood*, 12 (2) 221–37.
Rysst, M. (2010), ' "I am only ten years old": Femininities, clothing-fashion codes and the intergenerational gap of interpretation of young women's clothes', *Childhood*, 17 (1) 76–93.
Saadawi, N. El (2007), *A Daughter of Isis. The Autobiography of Nawal El Saadawi*. London: Zed.
Saraswathi, T. S. (1994), 'Women in poverty contexts', in R. Borooah, K. Cloud, S. Seshadri, T. S. Saraswathi, J. T. Peterson and A. Verma (eds) *Capturing Complexity. An Interdisciplinary Look at Women, Households and Development*. London: Sage, pp. 162–78.
Saville, Lord Hoyt, W. and Toohey, J. (2010), 'Report of the Bloody Sunday Inquiry'. London: The Stationary Office. http://report.bloody-sunday-inquiry.org/, (accessed 3 August 2010).
Sayer, A. (1992), *Method in Social Science. A Realist Approach*. London: Routledge.
Shaw, S. (2001), 'Conceptualising resistance: Women's leisure as political practice', *Journal of Leisure Research*, 33 (2) 186–201, 198.
Silva, E. B. (ed.) (1996), *Good Enough Mothering? Feminist Perspectives on Lone Motherhood*. London: Routledge.
Sivanandan, A. (1990), *Communities of Resistance. Writings on Black Struggles for Socialism*. London: Verso.
—. (2001), *Three Faces of British Racism*. London: Institute of Race Relations.
Smith, D. (1987), *The Everyday World as Problematic. A Feminist Sociology*. Milton Keynes: Open University Press.
Solomos, J., Findlay, B., Jones, S. and Gilroy, P. (1982), 'The organic crisis of British capitalism and race: The experience of the seventies', in Centre for Contemporary Cultural Studies (eds) *The Empire Strikes Back. Race and Racism in 70s Britain*. London: Hutchinson, pp. 9–46.
Soweto Rebellion. (2010), in *Encyclopaedia Britannica* from Encyclopaedia Britannica online www.britannica.com/EBchecked/topic/557167/Soweto-Rebellion, (accessed 3 August 2010).
Taylor, A. (2010), 'Salami slicing will not work society', *Guardian* 10th March www.guardian.co.uk/society/2010/mar/10/prevent-cuts-in-childrens-services, (accessed 6 May 2010).
Thomas, K. (1990), *Gender and Subject in Higher Education*. Buckingham: The Society for Research into Higher Education and Open University Press.

Thomson, R., Bell, R., Holland, J., Henderson, S., McGrellis, S. and Sharpe, S. (eds) (2002), 'Critical moments: Choice, chance and opportunity in young people's narratives of transition', *Sociology*, 36 (2), 335–54.

Travis, A. (2010), 'Children in immigration centres face deportation within weeks', *Guardian* online, 5 August, www.guardian.co.uk/uk/2010/aug/05/children-immigration-centres-deportation-scheme/print, (accessed 10 August 2010).

Twigg, J. (2000), *Bathing. The Body and Community Care*. London: Routledge.

United Nations Climate Change Conference. (2009), Copenhagen www.denmark.dk/en/menu/Climate-Energy/COP15-Copenhagen-2009/cop15.htm, (accessed 6 August 2010).

Urry, J. (1991), 'Time and space in Gidden's social theory', in C. Bryant and D. Jary (eds) *Gidden's Theory of Structuration. A Critical Appreciation*. London: Routledge, pp. 160–75.

—. (1996) 'Sociology of time and space', in B. S. Turner (ed.) *The Blackwell Companion to Social Theory*. Oxford: Blackwell, pp. 369–95.

Ward, C. (1978), *Children in the City*. London: The Architectural Press.

Weber, M. (1948/1991a), 'The social psychology of world religions', in H. H. Gerth and C. Wright Mills (eds) From Max Weber: Essays in Sociology (Routledge Classics in Sociology). Abingdon: Routledge, pp. 267–301.

—. (1948/1991b), 'Religious rejections of the world and their direction', in H. H. Gerth and C. Wright Mills (eds) From Max Weber: Essays in Sociology (Routledge Classics in Sociology). Abingdon: Routledge, pp. 323–59.

Weeks, J. (1977), *Coming Out. Homosexual Politics in Britain from the Nineteenth Century to the Present*. London: Quartet Books.

—. (1999), *Making Sexual History*. London: Polity Press.

Welch, S. (2008a), 'Children's rights and realities', in P. Jones, D. Moss, P. Tomlinson, and S. Welch (eds) *Childhood: Services and Provision for Children*. Harlow: Pearson Education, pp. 7–21.

—. (2008b), 'Education: Service or system?' in P. Jones, D. Moss, P. Tomlinson, and S. Welch (eds) *Childhood: Services and Provision for Children*. Harlow: Pearson Education, pp. 75–95.

Whannel, G. (1998), 'Electronic manipulation of time and space in television sport', in S., Scraton (ed.) *Leisure, Time and Space: Meaning and Values in People's Lives*. Eastbourne: Leisure Studies Publications, Vol. 57.

Wilkinson, R. and Pickett, K. (2009), *The Spirit Level: Why More Equal Societies Almost Always Do Better*. London: Allen Lane.

Williams, F. (1989), *Social Policy: A Critical Introduction*. Cambridge: Polity Press.

Williams, P. (1987), 'Constituting class and gender. A social history of the home 1700–1901', in N. Thrift and P. Williams (eds) *Class and Space. The Making of Urban Society*. London: Routledge and Keegan Paul, pp. 154–204.

Wilson, A. (1978), *Finding a Voice. Asian Women in Britain*. London: Virago.

Wimbush, E. (1988), 'Mothers meeting', in E. Wimbush and M. Talbot (eds) *Relative Freedoms. Women and Leisure*. Milton Keynes: Oxford University Press, pp. 60–74.

Index

Lightning Source UK Ltd.
Milton Keynes UK
UKHW02f2347220118
316653UK00004B/214/P